MW01039569

SCAN ARTIST
SCAN ARTIST
SCAN ARTIST
SCAN ARTIST
SCAN ARTIST
SCAN ARTIST
SCAN ARTIST
SCAN ARTIST

SCAN
How Evelyn Wood Convinced the World
That Speed-Reading Worked
ARTIST

MARCIA BIEDERMAN

CHICAGO
REVIEW
PRESS

Published by Chicago Review Press Incorporated
814 North Franklin Street
Chicago, Illinois 60610
ISBN 978-1-64160-162-7

Library of Congress Cataloging-in-Publication Data

Names: Biederman, Marcia, 1949– author.
Title: Scan artist : how Evelyn Wood convinced the world that speed-reading
    worked / Marcia Biederman.
Description: Chicago, Illinois : Chicago Review Press, 2019. | Includes
    bibliographical references and index.
Identifiers: LCCN 2019001289 (print) | LCCN 2019003575 (ebook) | ISBN
    9781641601634 (adobe pdf) | ISBN 9781641601658 (epub) | ISBN 9781641601641
    (kindle) | ISBN 9781641601627 (cloth)
Subjects: LCSH: Wood, Evelyn Nielsen, 1909–1995. | Speed-reading. | Women
    educators—United States—Biography. | Businesswomen—United
    States—Biography.
Classification: LCC LA2317.W656 (ebook) | LCC LA2317.W656 B54 2019 (print) |
    DDC 428.4/3—dc23
LC record available at https://lccn.loc.gov/2019001289

Typesetting: Nord Compo

Printed in the United States of America
5 4 3 2 1

To the memory of my parents,
who gave me their hard-earned money
for an Evelyn Wood course

Contents

Prologue   ix

1   Charm School   1
2   Third-Reich Interlude   17
3   Habits of Highly Effective Readers   35
4   We Have Liftoff   53
5   The Kid Farm   69
6   Bunk and Debunkers   87
7   Civil War   101
8   Consulting the Oracle   113
9   Times Are A-Changin'   129
10   Snake in the Grass   147
11   White Knight   161
12   Rehab   177
13   Carved in Stone   191
Epilogue   205

Acknowledgments   211
Notes   213
Selected Bibliography   237
Index   239

Prologue

THE BIG STORIES OF THE 1961 National Education Association convention were supposed to be about federal aid to education and school desegregation, but a middle-aged teacher from Utah and her pubescent student grabbed the headlines instead.

It was June 26, the first real working day of the weeklong event, following its official Sunday opening with the read-aloud of a message from President John F. Kennedy. At this point, the press area of the Atlantic City Convention Hall had produced plenty of soiled coffee cups but few typewritten pages. JFK in absentia did not make good copy. Today's advance transcripts of the evening speech by Jonas Salk seemed equally inauspicious. The legendary medical researcher had no new discoveries to report.

However, the newshounds soon found a suitable equivalent. Hard-nosed as they liked to seem, most journalists present were pushovers for a new brand of snake oil. The information explosion was in full swing, and millions of words were gushing out. Reporters and other professionals of the era were gripped with self-doubt. How could they keep up?

The Atlantic City convention promised a seaside cure. Listed in the program as simply "Wood Dynamic Reading Process—Evelyn N. Wood, assistant professor of reading, University of Delaware, Newark, Delaware," it was one of dozens of presentations offered to the ten thousand delegates in the cavernous convention hall. But Evelyn turned it into the main event.

Short, middle-aged, and invariably described as a "schoolteacher" with all the dullness that implied, Evelyn played the part of emcee before an audience of 150. The stars were two Wilmington, Delaware, high school students trained by Evelyn in what she called her "revolutionary" reading method. Audience members were invited to choose a book from a stack of volumes never before seen by the youths. Each student in turn would have three minutes to tear through a section and report on the contents.

A stopwatch ticked, and the audience gaped as seventeen-year-old Robert Darling ripped through 120 pages, running his fingers down each before turning to the next. He closed the book to deliver a detailed summary that drew exclamations from his dazzled listeners. He spoke for fifteen minutes, five times as long as he'd spent reading.

Science has since shown that such "free recall" testing is subject to fabrication. No course or technology has produced outsized gains in reading speed without sacrificing comprehension. Readers who skip or scan might try to fill in missing pieces through inference. But this is skimming, and decades of experimentation have shown its abysmal effects on grasping an author's intended meaning. Speed-reading marketers still flourish on the internet, but federal regulators have stopped some from making extraordinary promises.

In 1961, however, Evelyn had a nervous world in her palm. She opened the floor to questions and let the young man explain her method. Reading down the page rather than across it allowed him to absorb "concepts and thoughts" rather than individual words, he said. He credited her for his prowess, eliminating any need for her to blow her own horn.

"Tell him how many books you've finished in this past year, Bob," prompted another youth in the Wood entourage.

"Seven thousand," Darling reportedly replied (although he'd later protest that he'd been misquoted and that a more accurate figure was *several* thousand), prompting sharp inhalations of breath and much scribbling in reporters' notebooks.

Louise Mahru, also seventeen, got her own turn to demonstrate. She nearly matched Bob's rate and did it in French, a language she'd studied for only one year in high school, the audience was told. But by then, the newspeople were mentally composing lead paragraphs. Racing back to the typewriters, phones, and coffee urns provided by the NEA to facilitate coverage of more consequential issues, they filed breathless reports on the Wood method.

"One Hundred Twenty Pages in Three Minutes," read the headline of an Associated Press wire piece run in dozens of papers, sometimes under other titles, like "Bookworm Turns—Page a Second" and "NEA Agog at Boy's Skill." The "revolutionary reading method . . . raised gasps of astonishment," wrote the Chicago News Service, while a Eureka, California, paper quoted a local educator who called it the "high spot" of the convention.

And yet "the 'dynamic' reading method offered little more than what had been taught in reading development courses around the country," wrote George Gerbner, the dean of the University of Pennsylvania's Annenberg School for Communication and the author of a 1967 study of the event. But, he continued, "the name of Mrs. Wood was likely to ring bells in the mind of an alert reporter." Her first "publicity coup," Gerbner wrote, was to inspire four US senators to demonstrate and endorse her methods on national television. Placing young Bob Darling on display was, he said, "her second master stroke."

In fact, these were only a few of her genius moves. If Bob Darling was the "reading wizard," as the U of Penn paper dubbed him, Evelyn was the half-hidden woman behind the curtain, pulling the strings but not demanding we pay no attention to her. All her life, she'd sought the limelight—as a prize-winning orator in junior college and a champion university debater; as the wife of the president of an overseas Mormon mission; and as director, playwright, and lyricist of an elaborate pageant, staged with special effects and a cast of one thousand in Salt Lake City's Mormon Tabernacle.

"Slim, earnest" Evelyn, as *Time* magazine described her, had an enviably spare silhouette at age fifty-two, probably owed to a hyperthyroid condition for which she'd eventually have surgery. She cultivated the schoolteacher title, but it was inaccurate. A Utah school district had allowed her to pilot her method on its students, but as dean of girls, she normally worked outside the classroom.

The section of her résumé most relevant to her current enterprise was unknown to the media. Years of directing young people, on stage and on radio, had guided her choice of Bob Darling as her demonstrator. He not only had excelled in his class at his hometown's Evelyn Wood Reading Dynamics institute, one of twenty-two in the country, but also was an accomplished student pianist who'd soloed with the Wilmington Symphony Orchestra. He could read books, and he could read audiences.

Most importantly, he was unshakably loyal to Evelyn, who had been his teacher but was now his employer, paying for his appearances according to terms negotiated by his father, an executive at DuPont, Wilmington's dominant employer, and his mother, a member of the symphony's auxiliary. Interviewed recently, Bob said he regarded Evelyn as a second mother, albeit one who didn't drop her guard. "Everything she said was in complete sentences, with a capital at the beginning and a period at the end," he recalled. She got along well with his mother and sister, shopping with them at upscale consignment shops run by clubwomen. Soft-spoken and customarily attired in sweater sets, she struck Bob as a "Mount Holyoke or Wellesley lady," like his mother's friends. There was, however, the occasional jarring note that revealed her origins in the intermountain West, a world away from the quiet restraint of the Seven Sisters colleges, as when Evelyn gave Bob a copy of the Book of Mormon. Despite his prodigious reading speed, he never bothered to read it through.

Otherwise, Evelyn kept her piety under wraps. She never discussed religion with Bob's Protestant mother, who enjoyed lunching and shopping with her, or his Catholic father, who viewed Mormonism as cultish and demanded that she not try to convert his son. The father needn't have worried. Evelyn was on a different mission now. In young Bob— bright, personable, and six foot three—she knew she had her perfect leading man. He got star treatment, first-class lodging with fine meals, and compensation exceeding the market rate.

Even better, his family didn't need the money. Educated in excellent schools and Ivy-bound, Bob exuded the prep-school aura so coveted in the Kennedy era, and he knew it. "One thing I was paid for was a little showmanship," he said.

Another of Evelyn's master strokes was to cloak her for-profit business ($150 for thirty class hours) in an academic gown. While other educational-product merchants peddled wares in the basement—"like soap, cigarettes, and toothpaste," an AP report sneered—Evelyn's University of Delaware affiliation earned her a spot on the main floor. Even a detractor described her enterprise as only "quasi-commercial." In a nation panicked by the Cold War, the atomic bomb, and a dizzying array of rapid new developments, speed-reading was viewed as a public good.

Most inspired of all was Evelyn's reverence for the human hand, the only equipment required by her reading method. At a convention bristling with educational gadgets, another of the press's favorite themes was Teacher vs. Machine. Even educational television took on Orwellian overtones in an article deploring the conference's focus on instruction by "shadows on the silver screen, lights flashing and bells ringing to proclaim 'tilt' on academic pinball machines, and ghostly voices whispering persuasively over headphones."

As noted in the paper about media coverage, Evelyn was scarcely the first to offer a speed-reading course. Classes had been around since the 1930s, accelerating in popularity during the 1950s, as new photocopy machines and offset presses buried America in print. Many courses tried to spur reading rates with mechanical prods, like the Shadowscope, Rate-O-Meter, or the exotically named Mahal Pacer. But Evelyn knew that a skilled street-corner missionary required no fancy gear to spark conversions. At her demonstrations, hands served as pacers, hearts embraced the young people, and minds willingly suspended disbelief.

Witness the reaction of a Catholic educator who'd attended an earlier Bob Darling demonstration, six months before the NEA convention. In a letter to his mentor at the University of Ottawa, Rev. Stephen Breen wrote:

> When you see this (which you must) you will feel like Keats upon first looking into Chapman's Homer, or like we all felt when we

first heard of Hiroshima, Pearl Harbor and Sputnik. . . . Other
people taking this Evelyn Wood course . . . are now reading at
revolutionary rates. . . . Don't tell me it's impossible—I know
that, and I also know that it is being done. It's just as impossible
as the steamboat, the airplane, the internal combustion engine,
Lourdes and Fatima (almost) and extra-sensory perception. And
who knows where it will all end?

At the demo Breen attended, Bob was said to have read a few hundred
books a year. Now, only months later, the figure was seven thousand. Or
maybe it was five thousand, as Evelyn had written recently in a paper
presented to the College Reading Association.

But why cavil about such details, when, like Lourdes and Fatima,
another female name was becoming known throughout the world?

1

Charm School

On a spring day in 1923, the Statue of Liberty turned her back on the United States. Young Evelyn Nielsen was set to fix that. Arguing that this country was foremost among all nations, the fourteen-year-old would convince Liberty to embrace America again.

Evelyn was playing an American Ideal in a Central Junior High School pageant. The real Statue of Liberty in New York Harbor was a long way from Ogden, Utah, a city of thirty thousand, where Mormonism was a major cultural force. Still, many in the audience had seen the statue on their way to an overseas mission or, as in the case of Evelyn's father, while immigrating from Scandinavia under the auspices of the Mormon church.

For all their restrictive doctrines, Mormons weren't hicks. Mormons studied languages, traveled, got around. They didn't smoke or drink, but they danced, sang, played basketball, organized socials and Boy Scout troops, and went to the theater. They sent their kids to public schools that released them a few hours a week for religious instruction, and they supported theatricals like this one. As Evelyn mounted the stage of the baroque Alhambra movie palace, which seated two thousand, her devout parents were probably clapping and prompting her younger brother to do the same.

Evelyn's role was a minor one, billed on the program below History and Congress. That would change. The adult Evelyn would star

in a real-life episode of history with Congress playing the supporting role.

For now, the stagestruck adolescent was content with middle-class
life in Ogden, where her father supervised production at a knitting mill
and her mother taught etiquette at Sunday School. Here, the Church of
Jesus Christ of Latter-Day Saints happily, if sometimes incongruously,
coexisted with American pop culture. On the Alhambra's schedule, the
Ogden Tabernacle Choir rotated with silent films, vaudeville acts, and
boxing matches. After watching Rudolph Valentino flicker across the
movie screen in provocative Egyptian clothing, Evelyn dubbed a handsome church elder "our sheik." Even more thrilling than Valentino, however, was her own turn on the stage in this elaborate school pageant,
in which dramatic poses were occasionally interrupted by dance, music,
and dialogue.

Though Evelyn seldom landed leading roles, she'd been an enthusiastic supporting player since elementary school. Pageantry relied on
anatomy, and this all-female show was a production of the girls' physical
education department. Barely five feet and destined not to grow much
taller, Evelyn was insufficiently statuesque to play the statue. At least
she'd been better cast than the girls representing all forty-eight states.
In historical order, each asked to join the union—a deadly bore until
Kentucky's 1792 admission cued the chorus to belt out a Derby-themed
number.

There'd be a long wait before the girl playing Utah stepped forward, as those in the theater knew. Utah's statehood was still somewhat
of a novelty, in effect for little more than a quarter-century. Evelyn's
mother, Rosina Stirland Nielsen, called Rose, had been born to a pioneer
family in the theocratic Utah Territory. Evelyn's father, Elias Nielsen,
had come to the territory from Denmark in 1887, just before the US
Congress disbanded the church's ambitious immigration program. Of
course, the juvenile pageant made no mention of that attack on the
growth of the Latter-Day Saints Church, nor of the concessions forced
on church leaders to win statehood. Those notably included the renun-
ciation of polygamy, possibly practiced by some grandparents watching
the school play.

As mandated by the LDS Church hierarchy, the Mormon parents in the crowd had lived through an era of Americanization, seeking respectability and forging civic bonds with gentiles, as they called non-Mormons. Born on January 8, 1909, thirteen years almost to the day after Utah's statehood, Evelyn Rosina Nielsen was expected to go even further. Although male-controlled, her church encouraged higher education for both genders. In an area of the country still emerging from its frontier past, another church-approved pursuit was so-called cultural refinement.

Undoubtedly encouraged by her etiquette-instructing mother, Evelyn seized opportunities for such refinement. Two weeks after the pageant, she appeared in *A Midsummer Night's Dream* as one of Titania's servant fairies. She was playing a smaller house this time, the Central Junior High auditorium. For Evelyn, who thought of herself as literary and adored Shakespeare, this was a treasured opportunity to speak five of the Bard's lines. The set, too, must have met her romantic expectations. It was decorated with wildflowers and sagebrush plucked from the hillsides of Ogden. The city itself could have served as a stage set. The rugged peaks of the Wasatch Mountain Range towered above its brick commercial buildings, railroad yards, and residential avenues, providing a picture-perfect backdrop for nearly every urban view.

Between the whirl of school productions, Evelyn rehearsed for spring festivals and pageants mounted by the Young Ladies' Mutual Improvement Association of her church ward. The MIA, which included a male counterpart, published a magazine called the *Improvement Era*. The Mormon passion for self-improvement, admired by other Americans, would later lead Evelyn to identify a need she could fill with a product. In her youth, it kept her buzzing, as in the beehive so admired by Mormons that it became the Utah state emblem.

After graduation from junior high, Evelyn entered Ogden High School. She was never absent or tardy during her first semester, but that didn't necessarily mean she enjoyed the experience. The city's sole high school was bursting at the seams, awaiting the construction of a new building to accommodate a growing juvenile population. Evelyn had only one sibling, her brother Ariel, but other Mormon families tended to be large, and prosperous Ogden was attracting many newcomers. Manufacturing and banking had overtaken agriculture in importance to the city. Situated just twenty-five miles from the place where the first transcontinental railroad was completed in 1869 with a golden spike, the northern Utah city still drew its lifeblood from the railroads. It occupied a key position along north-south and east-west freight lines. Railroading had also brought the town a measure of diversity. Legendary jazz musicians sometimes stopped by Ogden after a Salt Lake City gig, playing the Porters and Waiters Club, founded by Pullman Company employees on notorious Twenty-Fifth Street, where bootlegging and gambling flourished. The club was on Ogden's south side, an area populated by African Americans, who were restricted from living elsewhere. Whites increasingly spread toward the east. There was only one high school, however. Everyone went to OHS.

Evelyn's high school years weren't her most noteworthy. Her theatrical career seemed to have gone on hiatus. Overlooked for leading roles in junior high, she might have found even stiffer competition at OHS. However, the *Standard-Examiner* did take notice of her fourth-place ranking in an essay contest. The essay topic was not specified, but the prize money—one dollar—was. Evelyn was then in tenth grade, competing against older students who took the top awards. Soon after that, she left OHS. By the end of eleventh grade, she'd earned enough high school credits to be admitted the following fall to Weber College.

At Weber she reawakened, excelling in oratory and debate, editing the yearbook, and dating the student-body president, Donnell Stewart. A few months into her first year, she and Don reigned over the annual prom, which Evelyn had helped plan. Hair stylishly bobbed, she wore a calf-length, scoop-necked lace evening dress as she led a line of girls over the polished wood floors of Ogden's Berthana ballroom to a queue of tuxedoed boys, headed by her date. A live orchestra played amid live ferns, and the campus paper pronounced the event a great success.

Evelyn was particularly fond of Weber. It survives today as Weber State University, a four-year institution on a verdant campus in the town's southeast corner. In Evelyn's day, the school was a two-year college housed in a Greek revival building in downtown Ogden, owned and operated by the LDS Church. This was Evelyn's first time attending a school where academics and religion were intertwined. As a younger student, in addition to attending Sunday School, she'd been released from public school for just a few periods a week of religious instruction, first at one of the LDS Primary Association schools for younger children, then at the seminary adjacent to OHS. The practice of letting students out of school for religious instruction was not uncommon in early twentieth-century America. Churches and synagogues in other parts of the nation also provided classes, as well as transportation to their facilities. Since Evelyn's school days, the practice has withstood a constitutional challenge and must still be allowed, although mainstream religions rarely promote it nowadays.

At Weber, religion permeated even the extracurricular activities. It was not that students shuffled head down through the halls, quoting scripture and singing hymns; they'd more likely be cheering at basketball and softball games or attending socials. Nor was the student body exclusively Mormon. One of Evelyn's classmates, Wilma Rubenstein, had been confirmed at a Reform Jewish temple in Salt Lake City. Still, Weber made little attempt to keep church and state separate. Soon after arriving on campus, Evelyn entered an oratory contest. The task was to argue that the church was a divine and indispensable institution, sincere in all its aspects. Quite sincerely believing this, Evelyn won one of the top three spots in a round that eliminated twenty other students. Even at the epicenter of the Mormon Culture Region—a term coined by a geographer to describe Utah and several nearby states—Evelyn stood out for her faith. Asked for adjectives to describe her, Verla Nielsen (no relation, but someone who knew Evelyn well in adulthood) immediately supplied "religious."

The only female chosen to advance to the oratory finals, she had one week to craft an oration on "Why Study the Scriptures." Confident and always overprepared, Evelyn rose before the assembled student body to give a ten-minute speech. She knew the topic well. Her life was rooted in Ogden's Fifth Ward—some two hundred people overseen by a bishop, who, despite the lofty title, had responsibilities similar to those of a Catholic parish priest—and the Weber Stake—encompassing a dozen

other wards, like a diocese. Nearly everyone she knew obeyed the scriptures, studying the Book of Mormon in eighth grade, the Old and New
Testaments in ninth and tenth, church history and doctrine in eleventh.
Any questions she had could be answered at home on Family Night,
the weekly evening reserved for parent-child bonding, as prescribed by
the church. On these nights, generally a Monday, parents played games
or practiced hobbies alongside their offspring.

Rose Nielsen was well equipped to address her children's queries.
In addition to cultural refinement, she taught spiritual living at Sunday
School. But she would likely have deferred to her husband. Elias Nielsen
had spent two suffering years as a missionary in the American West
and Midwest, ridiculed and threatened by those who had no use for
Mormons. Like many other men returning from missions, he'd been
made a member of a local quorum of the seventy, a respected role in
the church.

Judged this time by the audience, Evelyn's speech took second place.
She was probably disappointed to miss the first prize, a book signed by
Heber J. Grant, then president of the LDS Church, a position whose
occupant was sometimes called the "Mormon Pope." Still, second place
was a kind of victory. A freshman girl had stood before a crowd of
students and swayed many to vote for her.

A month after her triumph, Evelyn was invited to judge a high
school oratory contest, not at her less-than-beloved alma mater, OHS,
but at a suburban school north of Ogden. At seventeen, Evelyn was
the same age as many of the contestants and the only college student
to serve as a judge. Her colleagues on the panel were county education
officials, high school teachers, and a Weber professor.

It was an honor she never forgot. Later in life, but before she could
comfortably afford it, she donated to the high school's oratory program,
stipulating that the money be used as a prize. That was very much in the
Mormon tradition. Evelyn's family observed Fasting Sundays, skipping
two meals and donating the saved money to a relief fund for the less
fortunate. But recipients were expected to prove themselves worthy of the
gift. As an adult, Evelyn would have a young grandson sign a "residence
contract" before staying at her home, agreeing, among other things, to

clear away his own dishes. Similarly, Evelyn's support for high school oratory was for winners only.

Finding such success in public speaking, Evelyn added debating to her quiver. As a Weber sophomore, she formed half of a two-woman debate team pitted against Colorado State Teachers College. The motion proposed a constitutional amendment giving Congress power to pass uniform marriage and divorce laws. Ironically, the affirmative position was assigned to Weber, run by a church that had suffered harassment and persecution over the issue of polygamy. The secular Colorado college argued against the motion. Evelyn and her teammate scored especially high in the rebuttal phase, and the decision went to Weber.

If Evelyn's father had found an opportunity to sharpen his own rebuttals, handling the insults he suffered during his youthful mission may have been easier. Evelyn was close to both her parents but often worried about her father, a foreman at the knitting mill. He had married late—unusual for a devout Mormon. Evelyn's birth had made Elias a first-time father at age thirty-nine. Evelyn often thanked her parents for teaching her to be a "lady." Her mother, Rose, was well equipped for the task. She was one of many children born to Thomas Stirland, a successful produce broker in small-town Logan, Utah, where Evelyn's parents had met. Elias, on the other hand, was practically a blue-collar worker—a machinist who'd brought the first power equipment to Logan's Union Knitting Mills.

Elias had built a lovely cottage, the envy of his neighbors, to attract his young bride. Evelyn was born in the cottage. She was delivered at home by a midwife, as was her brother, Ariel, two years later. But soon after, Elias left the home he'd built for Ogden. He continued to work in knitwear, but his résumé grew spottier as he moved from one church-owned mill to another, filling a series of positions that weren't necessarily promotions.

Evelyn sometimes worried that her father, almost elderly in her eyes, seemed somewhat precariously employed. For now, however, her parents were prepared to send her to the University of Utah in Salt Lake City, where she could finish college and earn a bachelor's degree, while her brother entered a pre-med program. Mormons were supposed to save toward a college education for both sons and daughters. With the church as well as the mainstream culture discouraging women from careers, many daughters might never use their degrees. Still, Mormons believed that any knowledge gained on earth would be helpful in the afterlife.

Evelyn and her family bought into this wholeheartedly. Their pragmatism, thrift, and industriousness were matched by their spiritualism. Like other orthodox Mormons, Evelyn firmly believed that she and all other people had existed as God's spirit children before entering the earthly world through birth and acquiring human bodies. Imagining that she'd somehow been able to write, draw, hear, and even bake in the spirit world before inhabiting a body, Evelyn wrote this to her parents about her birth:

> I think it was one cold January night that I came. Trust me to come at night. I just couldn't find time to get away before. There were some little songs that I had to write, and some pictures to draw and a nice cake to make for one of the ladies, and a little girl's story to hear before I could break away, and that['s] what made me late. Then you noticed, that I came only half prepared. I left all my old clothes there and came to crawl into nice warm wooly ones that you had made. . . . You were all so nice to me. You may have corrected me and helped me see better, but I knew it was for the best.

Regardless of the accuracy of the theology, Evelyn's faith in church teachings is evident. Yet faith alone would not assure her a place in heaven. Mormons believe that one's works paved the path to celestial glory. With that in mind, Evelyn bade farewell to family and friends in Ogden and journeyed forty miles south to the "U" in Salt Lake City. Her motto, to be engraved one day on company letterhead, was, "Knowledge Through Reading."

Other female Weber classmates made the same short trip. Many men also enrolled but dropped their studies if called to missions. Mormon women of the era could volunteer but not until age twenty-one, when most were married or starting a career. A typical Mormon boy of the time became a deacon at twelve, assisting teachers and collecting fast money for about three years until becoming a teacher himself. About two years after that, if hardworking and churchgoing, the boy would likely be ordained as a priest. (Despite years of public criticism, the LDS Church withheld ordination from males of black ancestry until 1978.) Advancement to a higher level of priesthood and the rank of elder was required for missionaries.

Hence, a call to missionary work was eagerly awaited and enthusiastically celebrated. Within a month, Evelyn was back in Ogden at a church send-off for Wayne B. Thomas, a handsome recent Weber grad who was headed for the German-Austrian mission. She played two piano pieces at the event, singing with one, which may have produced a few giggles among listeners. Evelyn was a music lover, but she could not carry a tune.

Nor was she classically beautiful, apart from her eyes, which one admirer described as "aquamarine" and "sparkling with warmth and intelligence." Her chin receded a bit, and her nose was slightly prominent. Nevertheless, Evelyn had no trouble attracting men. As a Weber freshman dating the leader of the student government, she'd been, in effect, queen of the prom. At the U, too, she was soon dating the big man on campus: Myron Douglas Wood, the newly elected student-body president. Good-looking, with brilliantined hair and sideburns inspired by Valentino, Doug worked the same magic on Evelyn that the celluloid sheik had. By the end of the school year they were engaged.

An energetic blend of piety and college-boy frivolity, Doug had spent his first two college years at the U before leaving, like Evelyn's Ogden friend, for a German mission. As a sophomore he'd been Yell Master, or pep-rally organizer, planning outdoor line dances and pajama parties to cheer the school's teams on. Now he was back, ready to pick up where he'd left off. He won a three-way contest to become president of the student government. The position catapulted him into the public consciousness. He was a newsmaker in the Salt Lake City papers. Flashbulbs popped as he welcomed female freshmen to student orientation, notebooks captured his quotes as he probed charges of ballot-stuffing in a subsequent campus election, and interviewers sought his reflections at his graduation.

Nearly six years older than Evelyn, he'd studied business for two years at a church-run academy before enrolling as a university freshman. Business was in his blood. Every Salt Lake City resident knew William Wood & Sons, the chain of grocery stores founded by Doug's grandfather and expanded by his father. Now an older brother, Alan, was running the business. The youngest of five sons—a sister had died in childhood—Doug would have to start his own enterprise. He applauded Alan's forward-thinking decision to carry frozen food. Doug was looking toward the future too. He was interested in selling modern home appliances. Or maybe he'd stick with something traditional, like jewelry. He also had ambitions to rise in the Mormon hierarchy. Above all, he liked selling the gospel.

Telling their families about the engagement, but not announcing it publicly, the couple reluctantly parted in the summer between their junior and senior years. With a friend, Doug planned a sales trip through Wyoming and Montana, hoping to enter married life with some extra money. Evelyn kept his letters, which reveal his deep feeling and sometimes violent yearning for her. A model Mormon, Doug might have been a twenty-five-year-old virgin.

Writing Evelyn several times a week, he praised her looks and her cooking and described his misery when, for several days, no letter arrived from her. Because the song "Girl of My Dreams" reminded him of Evelyn, he badgered workers at a rural Wyoming restaurant to play it on the Victrola until he had transcribed all the lyrics for her.

In occasional digressions from the theme of love, Doug reported making some sales. However, he seemed prouder of the deals he'd made to preach in churches along the way. Even when describing feelings almost sexually, he invoked religion, writing:

> We were told once by one of our Church Authorities that when we were truly in love, we would always crave being in the company of our sweetheart. Have you ever had that feeling, Evelyn? Perhaps you might think I am asking a terribly big question, but—oh, boy!—if you only knew how I feel tonight. Gee, isn't love grand and glorious? But tough to be separated from her when you feel like I do.

Approving preparations for the wedding one year hence, Doug reassured Evelyn that she was "certainly a dandy little planner." Her side of the correspondence was not preserved, but apparently her family was pressuring her to choose a less-than-modish dress. Quoting an exaggeration of the situation from one of her letters, Doug told her she'd look fine "even in a 'gingham gown' and sunbonnet." When Evelyn suggested she might let her hair grow, Doug egged her on, telling her he liked "a full head of curls" and disparaging the shingled look, then popular, that left the back shorter than the front. Even strong views like these were phrased diplomatically. Although older and better traveled than Evelyn, and with higher church status than any woman could attain, Doug did not tell her what to do.

She was truly a dream girl for this ardent yet pious young man, who wrote, "I don't know whether I ever told you but I always longed for a girl whom I would like to take to church, and who I knew would enjoy it. Now aren't we glad we met?"

Even in these loving missives, there were hints of the insecurities common to all young adults about to face life on their own. As his sales trip neared its end, with business slow, Doug spoke of having the same "uneasy" feeling he'd experienced when released from his European mission. At times the separated sweethearts tested their love by provoking jealousy. Evelyn mentioned receiving a bouquet from a male friend, to which Doug responded. "Of course, when it comes to big new cars, I can't compete with him." His own near-infidelity topped that. Visiting an old missionary chum in Wyoming, he had asked the friend's sister to a dance, hoping to meet potential customers. Like Evelyn's etiquette-minded mother, Doug was intensely class-conscious. He told all to Evelyn, justifying his actions with middle-class snobbery: "I don't like to go to a dance stagg [sic], as you know it's hard to become acquainted with the best girls and to dance with that class, because they are not the ones who usually pick up with the strangers. It's usually those with whom I have no desire to associate. I hope you see my point, dear."

Apparently, she did. One year later, Evelyn smiled beneath a photo caption in her hometown newspaper announcing that the wedding would soon take place in the Salt Lake City temple. A Salt Lake City paper also carried the announcement, omitting the photo but mentioning Doug's student-body presidency and noting that the bride was "prominent in debate work." Evelyn and her debating teammates had just trounced Brigham Young University.

They honeymooned in the Canadian Rockies and along the Pacific Coast. Doug fished, as both he and Evelyn loved the outdoors, preferring weekends in a cabin to stays in a hotel. Evelyn's surname, spelled "Nielson" in the Weber and U yearbooks but "Nielsen" in the wedding announcements, was no longer an issue. Now she was Evelyn Wood, rhythmic and easy to spell.

Socially, she was Mrs. Douglas Wood. Married at twenty, she abandoned debating and orating to give parties for other new brides, arrange fall table settings for receptions, and attend bridge suppers. All of this was duly noted on the society pages of the Salt Lake City papers.

The Depression had hit hard in Salt Lake City, as elsewhere, but Evelyn and Doug appeared relatively unscathed. Renting a pleasant bungalow-style house on 1214 Fenway Street in the leafy southeastern part of the city, they told the 1930 census taker that neither of them had jobs nor income. That was untrue but perhaps preferable to acknowledging that Doug, the former student-body president, was a grocery store clerk employed by his father. Depression or not, people still bought food, and William Wood & Sons had opened a fourth location at the corner of L Street and Sixth Avenue, perhaps to create a job for the youngest of his sons until something else came up. The elder Wood apparently insisted that his scion rise up the ranks. For two years the city directory listed Doug's occupation as grocery clerk. With a roof that needed repair, the L Street store was apparently an afterthought in the William Wood & Sons enterprise, close to the other branches but in a different class than the flagship on 1260 East 400 South, which regularly won prizes for window displays. Still, while Doug humbled himself by stocking shelves and ringing up orders, others suffered more.

In Ogden, Evelyn's mother was patrolling her neighborhood to enforce the National Recovery Administration regulations, part of Franklin D. Roosevelt's efforts to lift the nation out of the economic doldrums. Businesses displaying the NRA logo promised to uphold the code's strict hiring and pricing regulations. Violations were not unheard of, however, so "Major" Rose Nielsen enlisted for the cause under the command of a leading figure in Mormon society, "Lt. General" Maude Dee Porter. They combed their residential neighborhoods, asking people to pledge that they would shop only at stores displaying the blue NRA eagle and report any rule-breakers.

Rose and Elias needed relief themselves. As Evelyn had feared, her father was still changing jobs. Before the stock market crash, he'd left the factory floor at Ogden Knitting Mills, where the dust and dirt would have challenged even a younger man without respiratory ailments. He'd cleaned his hands and sold knitwear to retailers. But things had gone awry. Soon after Evelyn's wedding, her father placed an ad in the Lost and Found section in the paper, offering a reward for a valise left on an Ogden street. The aging ex-machinist was searching for his sample case of dresses and church-sanctioned underwear, which, in these modern times, had shrunk from union suit to nearly risqué proportions.

The Depression did Elias a favor. His knitting mill was one of several in Ogden, and as the economy improved, the manufacturers needed more women to operate the machines. Knowledgeable about all phases of garment-making, and experienced in teaching Mormon doctrine at Sunday School, Elias began teaching vocational skills at a local public school. Appointed to the selection panel that chose the first group of trainees from a large pool of eager aspirants, he was soon training second and third groups. He taught daytime classes, suggesting he'd abandoned knitwear sales for this new pursuit, perhaps not voluntarily. At some point, he seems to have invested in Ogden property, more likely low-rent apartments than luxury housing. Recommending his father-in-law to someone in need of a handyman, Doug noted that Elias, then in his sixties, had papered "his apartment houses" himself.

In the meantime, a daughter was born to Evelyn and Doug on May 12, 1932. They named her Carolyn (soon shortened to Carol) and doted on her. She was the best and brightest girl in the world, or so they informed everyone they knew. Perhaps to mark the occasion, the patriarch of the Wood family turned the store over to Doug, ending his apprenticeship. In the year of Carol's birth, the city directory began listing his occupation as manager. Applying for a building permit a few years later, he signed himself as owner. The Woods moved closer to his food market, perhaps feeling more firmly connected to it. But, still renters, they'd move from house to house over the next few years, never settling into the storekeeping life.

The Woods kept their commercial activities quiet while informing local newspapers of Doug's rise in the ranks of religious educators. Shortly after their marriage, he began teaching religion at the seminaries attached to the city's South and East High School, rising to seminary assistant by the time of Carol's birth. Doug was now on track to become a principal. The Mormon church, which did not believe in a professional clergy, probably paid Doug little or nothing for what was essentially a part-time job. In Salt Lake City, unlike elsewhere in Utah, Mormon seminaries offered classes only before school, when relatively few students attended. Fearing church dominance of public education, the predominantly non-Mormon school board prohibited released-time, which the Supreme Court had not yet upheld.

Nonetheless, the position burnished Doug's spiritual résumé. An exemplary Mormon who now held a high priesthood, Doug was advancing toward ever higher levels of celestial glory. His wife and daughter could accompany him there, even if females could not hold priesthoods themselves. He was also aiming to become a bishop, as his father had been. That would come with a living allowance.

In the meantime, Evelyn craved more glory from this world than motherhood and entertaining could offer. She found an outlet on the Mormon "road show" circuit. The youth group of each ward was expected to produce an original entertainment for tour throughout the stake. The season concluded with an Oscar-style award presentation. Evelyn's *House of MIA* easily took the playwrighting honors. It had an encore performance in Ogden at the Berthana ballroom, where Evelyn had once glided past potted ferns on the arm of the Weber College student-body president.

Even while raising a toddler, Evelyn became a frequent visitor to Salt Lake City's historic Lion House, a gathering place for women. Here, a local personality named Katie C. Jensen was causing a stir, offering wildly popular charm school courses and publishing articles such as "The Challenge of Charm: The Art of Being a Woman." Delivering a traditional message—that women should subordinate themselves to men—in a self-promoting style that essentially undercut it, Jensen became Evelyn's entrepreneurial role model.

Jensen's frank talk about adolescent petting and wifely infidelity (curable, she said, by a husband's spanking) earned her lecture bookings throughout northern Utah and attention from both the Mormon and mainstream press. Katie C. Jensen, known socially as Mrs. William Jensen, shared Evelyn's interest in church life and contributed fees paid for her "Captivating Smartness" course to an LDS youth project. In return, the church-funded *Improvement Era* published Jensen's pieces, in which she warned married women not to forego primping, bathing, and powdering if they wished to hold on to a husband. "He did not marry a vacuum cleaner," she warned.

Setting an example for Evelyn, Jensen brashly dismissed her detractors. The church magazine printed letters from female readers questioning her promotion of cosmetics and objecting to her use of the word "spinster." Jensen replied, holding her ground. An admiring Evelyn presented her own Jensen-style talk at the Lion House as one of many participants in an "Afternoon of Charm," and promoted Jensen's classes to potential enrollees. Proud of this association with her idol, however vague, Evelyn would later exaggerate its depth.

An early expert at branding, Jensen always used her given name, celebrating marital life while rejecting the "Mrs." label for herself. While Evelyn soaked up this wisdom, an important call came for Doug. He'd been named bishop of the Wasatch ward.

No longer reliant on the Lion House for status and socializing, Evelyn now coreigned over the ward's activities in the chapel and recreation hall. Doug shouldered responsibilities for the worldly needs of scores of families residing in a southeastern slice of the city. He would officiate marriages, collect tithes, and check on the health and financial needs of his charges, also monitoring their religious devotion. Evelyn would help with Sunday School classes, which enrolled adults as well as children, and the women's Relief Society. A crowded schedule of activities bound the community to the church, including Boy Scout meetings and basketball games.

A bishop's living allowance was not enough to support even a small family. Like most other bishops, Doug continued in business while devoting forty hours or more to religious duties, which interested him and Evelyn more than food retailing. A bishop and his wife were respected figures in their ward. Their grocery was just a minor branch of the Wood family business.

A clownish error by the highest-ranking member of the church hierarchy ultimately freed the Woods from the grocery store. Word reached Doug that prophet, seer, and revelator Heber J. Grant, while traveling through Europe, named an elderly Idaho man to head the East German mission, based in Berlin. Grant did this unaware that the job had already been promised to an ambitious Salt Lake City businessman. The two would-be mission presidents waged a turf war in Berlin until Grant's choice was sent away to lead the West German mission, headquartered in Frankfurt. But the older man didn't want his consolation prize.

Doug, however, did. The Woods eagerly awaited his official appointment to a mission presidency in Germany, where the LDS Church had accommodated Nazi demands and was flourishing. Heading the Frankfurt-based mission would require travel around the entire western section of the country. For Evelyn, this would mean a vast new audience to charm.

But with Carol only five years old, the Woods would need household help. After all, Doug had not married a vacuum cleaner.

2

Third-Reich Interlude

PREPARING FOR THE MOVE to Germany would take months. Evelyn learned that the church would provide a housekeeper in Frankfurt, but that still left the question of childcare. The Woods needed a responsible English-speaking babysitter, available at all hours. Yet they couldn't pay much for this service.

Utah's child-protection agency provided the solution, placing fourteen-year-old Anna Marie Pearson in the Woods' home. By law, Anna was their foster child. In fact, she was expected to mind little Carol and perform household tasks.

Born to Mormon parents in Idaho, Anna had spent most of her life in Ogden, Evelyn's hometown. Her father died when she was young, leaving her mother overwhelmed by the care of Anna, in addition to two older children and younger twins. A year after the father's death, an older suitor took the widowed Mrs. Pearson and her brood on a winter drive through the Ogden Canyon. The car flipped off an icy road into a reservoir. Heroic motorists passing by rescued Mrs. Pearson and all five children from the submerged vehicle. However, the elderly suitor died, taking with him all hope of the family's financial rehabilitation.

Shortly before Anna's thirteenth birthday, the state of Utah declared her a neglected child and took her into custody. Too young to join her older siblings in the workforce, Anna entered the foster care system, with her mother given a year to contest the placement. No appeal was made during that period, and Anna, now available for adoption, was placed with the Woods.

In a letter to her mother, Evelyn described Anna as a kind of valued domestic servant, a "real joy," who took "such good care of Carol" and anticipated Evelyn's needs, including washing and ironing clothes. Such compliance was expected. Anna was repaying the Woods for "everything we have done for her," Evelyn added.

Now the bishop and his wife were ready to do Anna one more favor, as they saw it. In the midst of closing down their business, selling their car, and preparing their house for rental, they petitioned to adopt Anna, changing her family name to theirs and signing a decree that stated:

> Anna Marie Wood shall henceforth be regarded and treated in all respects as the child of M. Douglas Wood and Evelyn Nielsen Wood, husband and wife, and said minor and said adopting parents shall henceforth sustain each toward the other the relation of parent and child, with all the rights and subject to all the duties of such relationship.

At twenty-nine, Evelyn became the legal mother of a fourteen-year-old. The Woods, who seldom acknowledged Anna as a daughter, signed the adoption decree dishonestly. Letters to relatives suggest that Doug might have felt vaguely parental toward her, at least for a while, but with none of the intense love he felt for Carol. Evelyn clearly never saw herself as Anna's mother. The adoption was simply expedient. Anna Marie Wood could get a passport and move with them to Germany. Anna Pearson, a ward of the state, could not.

The move would take Anna thousands of miles from her biological relatives, with whom she maintained contact, to what she later described as a "tense" place. Viewed from Salt Lake City, Nazi Germany was either heaven or hell, depending on whether you read the Mormon or mainstream press. The secular *Salt Lake Tribune* ran wire stories and syndicated columns describing Hitler's "anti-Semitic drive" as "in many ways more ruthless than the Spanish Inquisiton" and raising alarms about Germany's billion-dollar rearmament. Meanwhile, the *Improvement Era* discovered a new form of feminine charm in "The German

Girl of Today," the title of a two-page tribute to these sensible, self-sacrificing maidens, praising their volunteer work on farms and in other Nazi projects "to build a superior race."

The author of that piece was Elizabeth H. Welker, wife of the president of the Swiss-German mission, which was about to be closed in the restructuring that preceded Doug's presidency. Welker's article included some gems of wisdom from Gertrud Scholtz-Klink, leader of the Nazi Women's League or, as Welker admiringly identified her, "the German woman's *Führer*." Welker, who directed church activities for girls and women in Germany and Austria, had offered her youth-education expertise to Nazi officials. In response, Scholtz-Klink offered her a ride in Hitler's limo to a Nazi youth rally.

Welker's magazine piece apparently raised no hackles in Salt Lake City. German-speaking Europeans comprised the largest population of Latter-Day Saints outside the United States, and the church hierarchy was determined to see Mormonism survive the Third Reich. These were extraordinary times in Germany, but ecclesiastical leaders could point to the twelfth Article of Faith, which requires Mormons to subject themselves to "kings, presidents, rulers, and magistrates" and obey local laws. Elizabeth Welker wasn't the only American to do so with absolute relish.

In late spring of 1938, shortly after Hitler's annexation of Austria, the Woods vacated the hip-roofed bungalow they owned at 1445 Roosevelt Street. Planning to be gone for three years, they arranged for Doug's brother Alan to remodel and rent it out. In return, Alan took ownership of Doug's beloved car, a powerful and stylish Terraplane, made by Detroit's Hudson Motor Car Company. The former grocery store clerk had come up in the world and wanted the world to know it.

A small difference of opinion between the brothers underscored Doug's business shortcoming, something that would eventually affect his future and Evelyn's. As the proud new owner of the Terraplane, Alan could sell his ancient jalopy, but he rejected an initial bid of $75 for it. Doug chided his older brother for holding out, but Alan, a partner in their father's prosperous business, bided his time and got his price. Business had been Doug's college major, but it wasn't necessarily his strong point.

Another bishop replaced Doug in the Wasatch ward. He organized a farewell testimonial to send the Woods off with string selections, remarks from ecclesiastical leaders, and a male vocal quartet. A photo on the program cover, captioned "Bishop M. Douglas Wood and Family," shows Carol seated on Evelyn's lap. Behind them stand Doug and Anna. Of the four, Anna appears the most relaxed. Her smile is impishly childish.

In the ward, it would have been difficult to hide Anna's existence. Elsewhere, the Woods didn't seem eager to publicize it. A church announcement of Doug's appointment said he would leave for the West German mission with "his wife and daughter." Similarly, an Ogden paper reported on an open house hosted by Evelyn's parents to say goodbye, at which the Woods "were accompanied by their daughter Caroline [sic]." Rose and Elias Nielsen, undoubtedly the source for this social item, made no mention of their new granddaughter.

In New York, the Woods boarded the SS *Manhattan* as a family of four. Accompanying them were five missionaries—young but holding the church rank of elder. They kept Doug's hands full. He found two of them on deck "basking in the moonlight, with girls," while a third cavorted in the ship pool with a young woman straddling his back. Another spent a night conversing with a Catholic priest about religious matters, then asked to return home. "It took us a whole day to reconvert him," Doug reported.

If Doug actually gave the elders "quite a stiff talking to," as he wrote, he was far more indulgent with Carol. Professing exasperation, he described discovering her in a shipboard lounge, where she was singing, dancing, and otherwise charming onlookers. "I'm afraid she's going to be spoiled," wrote her doting father.

Evelyn spent much of the trip in a tedious memorization task. She'd written a speech in English to introduce herself to the Frankfurt congregants. Doug provided a translation, which she was learning phonetically. Devoting two hours a day to this work, Evelyn slept little during the eight-day voyage. Sharing Evelyn's sleeplessness, Doug blamed the time changes. However, even before their departure, Evelyn had started taking medication for a racing pulse. This could have been produced by her overactive thyroid, which would eventually require an operation. Regardless, Evelyn was determined to make a big splash in Frankfurt.

The ship's final destination was Hamburg. Planning to go from there to Frankfurt, the Woods were instead called to a special meeting of European mission heads in Berlin. Presiding over this conclave was J. Reuben Clark Jr., the second-highest-ranking member of the LDS Church. A former US under secretary of state and ambassador to Mexico, Clark was in Germany to talk to high German officials about debt owed to American investors. Evidently, Clark had also negotiated assurances of safety for his American church brethren. The topic of this meeting was how to evacuate the mission in case of war.

If the meeting unsettled Doug and Evelyn, they made no mention of it in correspondence. Rather, Clark's presence and connections reassured them that no harm was likely to come to American Mormons in Germany.

Finally arriving in Frankfurt in early July, the Woods began their European adventure. This would involve spates of hard work and punishing travel—well rewarded by comfortable accommodations, servants, shopping, and, from time to time, pleasure outings. Someone back home had ribbed Doug about his upcoming "three-year vacation." The joke irked Doug, who may have sensed some truth in it.

Evelyn, however, started off exhausted. During the two days of train travel required by the Berlin detour, she'd nearly abandoned her speech but instead practiced it twenty hours more. Whisked from the train depot to the West German mission, housed in an elegant mansion on the Main River, she faced an expectant audience of German church members and American missionaries, almost losing her nerve. But "the people were absolutely thrilled," she wrote to her parents, describing the subsequent embraces and cries of *"Wunderbar!"*

Evelyn couldn't resist a dig at the wife of Philemon M. Kelly, the mission president handing the reins to Doug because he couldn't have Berlin. After three years in a German-speaking mission, Sister Kelly needed an interpreter for her speech, Evelyn noted, while "[I] said my own."

One missionary was, indeed, floored, but not by her language skills. In his diary, George R. Blake described Evelyn's "short" and "memorized" speech as a nice token but noted that "she knew no German." Overall, however, Blake wrote, "The president, and especially his wife, were pleasing beyond all expectations." He praised Doug's good looks, fluent German, "hearty laugh," and ability to remember names. Evelyn, he said, was charming and brilliant with a beautiful voice and "an unlimited knowledge of Scripture."

Continuing the charm offensive, Evelyn soon set three gooseberry pies before Doug's ten-person staff. Other than as a public-relations move, such exertions weren't necessary. The four-story mission came with a maid named Ilse. Describing her as "a very sweet black haired, black-eyed girl who speaks a very good English," Evelyn said Ilse "helped" in the kitchen, but Blake indicated she did more than that, describing Ilse in his journal as the "bestest [sic] cook." In addition, a cleaning woman came to scrub twice a week.

Doug and Evelyn had a private bath with shower next to their bedroom, while Anna and Carol slept on twin beds in another. Six missionaries shared attic sleeping quarters and a water closet, using the public baths when necessary. Meals were communal, in a dining room that could seat two dozen.

When not minding Carol, Anna washed and ironed Evelyn's clothes. Doug arranged lessons for the two girls in the home of a tutor, but Carolyn's antics were more than this man could handle, and the plan was scrapped. In mid-August, Anna was enrolled in a private school. In a short time, she placed into the class she wanted, wrote Evelyn, providing no details. In addition to her other responsibilities, Anna worked in the mission office and probably had little time to study.

The Woods took far more interest in their younger daughter's progress. They arranged to send her to a German public school, accompanied at first by their English-speaking maid to help her with translation. In a letter to her parents, a delighted Evelyn described Carol's first day at the Frankfurt school. The German girls had crowded curiously around their new American classmate until the teacher arranged an orderly greeting with, as Evelyn wrote, "the national salute." She didn't say whether she and her young child responded with a *Heil Hitler*, but that is likely. Another American-grown religious sect, the Jehovah's Witnesses, was banned by the Third Reich and suffered persecution because of its resistance to Nazism.

Asking her parents to save the letters as a substitute for a diary, Evelyn typed many pages of single-spaced chatter about indigestion and shopping, as well as missionary work. Despite the candid tone, the Woods knew that postal censors read all mail sent in and out of Germany. Excursions to the other European missions allowed them to drop their guard. In a letter posted from the Netherlands, Doug cautioned his parents, "Don't ever use the name of Hitler or Goebbels" when writing him; nor should they mention politics, including "the Jewish situation," which he discussed at some length in the same letter. Evelyn, too, warned her parents not to write about politics, but in her surviving letters from Europe, including those mailed outside Germany, there's no mention of Jews at all.

Nonetheless, Evelyn was undoubtedly involved in the "Jewish situation," as Doug put it. Both of the Woods would later say that Evelyn spent long days rewriting Sunday School and priesthood lessons. Admitting to accommodating the Nazis, Doug said, "She wrote the priesthood lessons. We never told the brethren over there, because they would have quit the church. We couldn't use too many lessons from [Salt Lake City] headquarters . . . because nearly every one was flavored with democracy and freedom and here we were under a totalitarian government. We had to delete all that, so we practically had to rewrite all the lessons."

Mormonism is known for its authoritarian character, not for frequent mentions of "democracy" and "freedom." It is far more likely that Evelyn was deleting words like "Israel" and "Zion." A 1936 Mormon manual advised "that any subject even remotely connected with the Jewish race would be better unexpressed in Germany today." The manual was published by a Relief Society, indicating that sanitizing Mormonism of Jewish references was considered women's work.

In this and her other duties, Evelyn got help from a staff, comfortably accommodated in the mission's three offices. There were some tears of loneliness at the beginning, but Evelyn soon told her parents, "This is the life." She was enraptured by Frankfurt, where on Wednesday and Saturday nights all the buildings were illuminated and "you can see the whole of the city in the water." In the middle of the river was a bathing resort and roller rink, where Doug took her skating. A photo captured slim Evelyn in a chiffon dress, gliding cautiously under her dapper husband's guidance. She was dubbed "mission sweetheart" by elders who thought her too young for the traditional title of "mission mother."

Frankfurt's Jewish community was not partaking of the gaiety. A former European mission president, Roy A. Welker (husband of Elizabeth, author of the paean to German girls), had told the church-owned *Deseret News* that Jews were safer in Germany than nearly anywhere else in the world. But Doug immediately saw that this wasn't true. In one of his first letters mailed from the Netherlands, he described the window signs marking Jewish-owned business for boycott, adding, "So far as the Jew is concerned it will only be a matter of time until he is finally pushed right out of business and will have to leave the country."

Doug's sympathy was limited. "Of course, this means a rather cruel or cold procedure to us from the outside," he wrote, "but the Germans have their reasons." While allowing that Europe had "some rather fine Jews" in medicine and "higher types of business," Doug wrote that Jews had "taken over businesses" from unwitting Germans "and have almost skinned them alive on profits."

He went on to recount a "ticklish" situation that had arisen in one of the districts he oversaw. The Ruhr district president, a German, had asked if Doug could help one of his congregants, a Mormon of Jewish ancestry. The man was a tailor, impoverished by the boycott to the point of starvation, but unable to obtain a passport or buy a ticket out of the country. "As much as we should like to help him, because of his faithfulness to the church, our hands are absolutely tied," wrote Doug, "and we wouldn't dare think of getting mixed up in any controversy with the government."

J. Reuben Clark, who had called the Berlin meeting, was probably responsible for the hand-tying. Clark personally rejected at least two pleas for aid from Mormon converts and might have instructed other

Americans to do the same, undoubtedly with enthusiasm. The Mormons' No. 2 leader was an unapologetic anti-Semite who handed out copies of the *Protocols of the Elders of Zion*, a fabricated work accusing Jews of conspiring for world domination. After World War II, Clark would help German non-Jewish Mormons emigrate to the United States, referring to them as "Aryans."

Doug found the situation regrettable, or that's how he presented it to his parents. Nevertheless, he lacked the bravery of the German district president, whose willingness to help a Mormon of Jewish background carried grave risks. Possibly to assuage his own conscience, Doug added that the man might "try to sneak over" the French border and join the Foreign Legion. The likely outcomes of this scheme—getting caught or shot—were obvious. His letter continued with his account of an incident on a German train. A German salesman sharing a compartment with Doug and his assistant heard the two Americans speaking English. Knowing the language, he asked the Americans if they were from New York. "I told him no, I didn't care to live in New York because there were too many Jews there," wrote Doug, who'd picked the wrong audience for this remark: the man revealed that he was Jewish. "Imagine how red my face was," said Doug, adding, "I immediately became interested, for I wanted to get his viewpoint." The man said that his family had been in Germany for generations, had helped the country fight two wars, always considering themselves German, "and they certainly thought it was terrible that they should be cast out at this time."

Doug characterized the Jew's views as one of "various opinions and viewpoints of the present regime of a dictator," that he planned to collect while being "very cautious to express any of my opinions." In a country full of citizen informers, the Jewish man had potentially risked his life to confide in the American Mormons, possibly hoping they'd carry his message to someone in power. If so, he was to be sadly disappointed. Doug found the German Jew no more convincing than an Austrian couple with whom, on the same journey, he discussed the Anschluss. Their chief complaint about Hitler's takeover of their country was an upcoming switch from left-hand to right-hand traffic direction, which they feared would result in automobile accidents. The couple added that Hitler would be absolutely justified in invading Czechoslovakia, as he was threatening. Their views were based on false and sensationalized reports, then rampant in the Nazi-controlled media, about the mistreatment of German nationals residing in that country. Doug, afforded access to the free press by his unrestricted travels, listened with interest.

None of these "viewpoints" dampened Doug's flat-out admiration for the führer's home building and highway construction projects. "He has certainly done a lot for the common people and the people practically worship Hitler," Doug wrote in the same letter, which was mailed from Switzerland. He was practically a fellow worshiper. "It has not been our pleasure to see Hitler yet, so we are planning a big trip over to Nürnberg in September where the Reich Partier week, or big celebration, will be held," he told his parents.

As for war, "It is the fartherest [sic] thing from their minds in Germany," Doug said.

But in September, tanks and heavy artillery rolled for days past mission headquarters in Frankfurt, and lights no longer twinkled over the Main. Hitler was arraying hundreds of thousands of troops along the border of Czechoslovakia and threatening invasion. Through connections in the German government, J. Reuben Clark received early warnings that war was possible, and the church ordered the evacuation of both the West and East German missions. The Woods initially kept this secret from their German congregants, ordering all missionaries back to Frankfurt under the guise of personnel transfers. Soon after, they announced their departure. For the first time since 1914, when American missionaries had withdrawn at the outbreak of war, German Mormons would need to handle their own religious matters.

In a letter begun in Germany but postmarked from the Netherlands, to which the Woods fled, Evelyn described the tense situation inside the mission as "a continuous line of soldiers" marched by day and night. The blackout hindered her last-minute redaction of lesson plans. "Poor Carolyn! She does not know what it is all about," Evelyn lamented without out a word for Anna.

"This is the most heart breaking [sic] thing to happen to me," Evelyn wrote. Both she and Doug enjoyed recounting tearful scenes to their correspondents. For Doug, these were spiritual moments, as when Saints in a remote corner of Germany wept at meeting him, an emissary from the American Zion. For Evelyn, one of these dramas unfolded as she bequeathed a sheaf of original plays to the mission translator, who was to assume her role as leader of the auxiliaries. "She threw her arms around me and cried, 'It has been your enthusiasm, your interest and your love for us . . . that is going to make it possible for us to carry on alone,'" wrote Evelyn.

But how would Evelyn and Doug carry on? "We have no store, no car and no job. It is quite a thing to give up for three months in Europe," she wrote, alternately assuring her parents that they need not worry and indulging in bouts of despair. "The people here do not want war," she said, but added, "However, I do not know what will happen." She said one German friend had stopped by to bid them *auf Wiedersehen*—"until we meet again . . . on the battlefield."

"Keep your chin up," Evelyn advised her parents before describing a grisly dream she'd had: wounded by an arrow, she'd crawled in pain for hours behind rows of marching soldiers before reaching safety.

But it all turned out to be a false alarm—"a fire drill," as the church called it. Britain and France signed the Munich Agreement, allowing Hitler to annex portions of Czechoslovakia where German speakers predominated. A few days after the annexation, Evelyn mailed a letter from the Dutch mission in The Hague, notifying her parents that her family and the mission staff would soon be returning to Germany.

The rambling missive began in Evelyn's typical breezy style (her customary salutation was "Dear Folks," while Doug began his letters, "Dear Mother and Father"), with world politics and office politics discussed with equal gravity. Regarding the Munich Agreement, she wrote, "Hitler . . . thought it wise to compromise and be a good egg." She chattered about a sightseeing excursion she and her daughters had taken in the Netherlands, the things she'd bought in Dutch shops, and the morning gospel classes she'd taught the missionaries before they went out proselytizing in Rotterdam. Always eager for attention, she'd turned a beach outing on the North Sea into a spectacle: her impromptu dissection of a jellyfish had drawn a crowd, she reported.

Reflecting her own ambivalence about the return to Germany, Evelyn mixed reassurances about her safety with messages bound to upset
her parents. "Now Mother and Dad, please do not worry about us over
there. We feel perfectly safe and that is our mission to go to these people
and I know the Lord will take care of us," she wrote.

On the final page, Evelyn advised her parents to send their next letter to her Frankfurt address and to avoid mentioning that she'd written
them from the Netherlands. Mail was being monitored more closely than
ever in Germany, she said, adding in a rare burst of empathy:

> You people over there just do not know what Freedom means. . . .
> When you see a friend of one of the members of the Church,
> one that came out to our meetings all the time taken and put
> in a concentration camp just because he bought a Radio and
> in fooling around with it to see how much he could get on it
> got Moscow Russia. One of the neighbors reported him and
> they came and got him and took the radio and put him in the
> Concentration camp. This has happened with one of the men
> that the boys all know. It is a crime to listen to Russia as she is
> Communistic and forces the people!

Many in Britain were applauding Prime Minister Neville Chamberlain for ensuring what he called "peace for our time" through the
Munich Agreement. Evelyn was wiser. Clearly referring to Hitler,
but not typing his name, she wrote, "We cannot imagine that out
of the goodness of his heart he is forming this alliance. . . . We all
are watching to see what he means by it, and what purpose of his
it will serve."

In her nightly prayers, Carol had been asking God to let her stay
in the Netherlands or go back to America rather than Germany. Evelyn
succeeded in convincing the little girl that she missed the Main River.
To overcome her own dread, she approached the return as an acting
role: "When we go back and hear how great Hitler is, we will have to
bite our tongues and bear it and not say a single thing about it. This
would be hard if we were discussing politics but thank Goodness we
have the Gospel to teach and do not have time to even mention the

politics. . . . It is a good training to be able to see things and then have to keep your mouth shut."

Remaining silent allowed the Woods to continue to spread the gospel in Germany. It also kept Doug employed and his family housed. Apparently worried that the Frankfurt mission could cope without him, he rushed back for a week even before his staff was allowed to follow him.

All was in disarray, at least according to Evelyn. The kitchen maid had decided to substitute for Evelyn at conferences, billing the mission for expenses until Doug put a stop to it. "It seems that these people cannot govern themselves," said Evelyn, unimpressed by the alleged master race.

As the rumblings of war quieted, the Woods resumed their usual routine. This involved extensive travel around Germany. The West German mission oversaw seventy far-flung branches, each with a meeting house, in fourteen districts. Missionaries scattered throughout the field eagerly awaited the Woods' visits. "I enjoy talking with them if I could only do it without traveling so much. We almost wear the train seats out from crossing the country so often," wrote Evelyn, complaining that she had little time to rest.

But she had no more complaints about Hitler. In November 1938, the Woods witnessed the Nazi pogrom against Jews that came to be known as *Kristallnacht*, or the Night of Broken Glass. Decades later, the Woods told a historian that they'd watched the vandalism of Jewish-owned property, seeing furniture and mattresses thrown from smashed windows. One of the missionaries in Frankfurt, Frederick Babbel, devoted pages of his journal to descriptions of his revulsion at this "inhumane" attack, which, he wrote, had occurred "under orders" throughout the country and not spontaneously, as Nazi propaganda insisted. "I had a strange feeling of . . . events being transacted which may change the course of world history," Babbel wrote. Blake also described the destruction in his diary. But in their surviving letters, including those mailed outside Nazi-controlled territory, neither Doug nor Evelyn mentioned these events.

A month later, Evelyn took her first trip to Austria. Now that the dictator was no longer threatening the Woods' livelihood, she wrote,

"Really Hitler has done a great deal for these people. They were literally starving to death." She approved of measures taken against the Catholic Church, which, she said, had squashed other sects in its iron grip. "The new government is uprooting all of those antique and crazy ideas and rating all churches the same," she said, continuing, "I wouldn't be surprised if in a few years we have a real Latter-Day Saint community there."

By Christmas, Evelyn was as enchanted with Germany as she'd been at the beginning. She still struggled with the language, painstakingly memorizing half-hour-long conference speeches. Carol was making quick strides, loving school even if not understanding all the lessons, and playing with German girls after class.

As for Anna, who laundered and mended Evelyn's clothes and the sweet little dresses that Carol flung on the floor, "She takes care of Carol so well and makes herself useful in every way that she can," wrote Evelyn. Doug customarily signed letters to his parents, "Doug, Evelyn, Carol, Anna." But, although Anna learned German and collected pleasant memories of the country's people, culture, and food, she had less pleasant memories of the Woods, who, as Evelyn's remark made clear, never considered her one of the family.

Doug's egalitarian treatment of her in the letter signatures may have been an attempt to delude himself—or others. Without the other side of the correspondence, it's impossible to know if Doug's parents ever asked after Anna, but someone in the Wood household apparently thought they were expecting Anna to write. A letter sent to Doug's parents from Germany begins "Dear Grandma and Grandpa" and is purportedly signed by Anna and Carol. However, according to one of Anna's sons, the handwriting, which changes at several points, doesn't match samples that Anna left in high school notebooks. Possibly written by a nonnative speaker of English and conveying more news about Carol than Anna, the letter's contents indicate that it was written in the Woods' absence. It might have been crafted by a household employee or mission staff member.

Evelyn enjoyed Christmas and New Year's in Frankfurt. But 1939 brought more traveling, interrupted briefly when Doug required appendix surgery. Despite her busy schedule that year, Evelyn experienced periods of loneliness. Above all, she wrote to her parents, she missed having a friend. "It is really a queer situation to not have any woman to talk to—I could never do it with these German people here even though I like them so much because they insist on looking up to me." She wistfully recalled her old habit of lying on the floor, dressed carelessly (or perhaps scantily), to read the newspapers. "All here is too public and so many men around always that I must dress up every day and all day. This is a job for me as you know how I like to do these things."

Speaking of her husband, Evelyn Wood—the woman fated to represent the stereotypical sexless schoolmarm—continued, "That is why we lay up in the bedroom with our legs up in the air and half undressed just to show a freedom that we cannot express when we are around others."

She threw herself into the rewriting of an original play she'd brought with her. It cost Evelyn some effort to trim a nativity scene and develop new material about the resurrection and Pentecost. As Doug explained to his parents, although Pentecost was not observed by Mormons in the United States, it was a big deal to Germans. The West German mission was planning a conference that would bring hundreds of church members to Frankfurt during the national *Pfingsten*, or Pentecost, holiday. Evelyn's play would be featured in this event, so she was adjusting the life of Christ to suit.

She was also gleaning ideas from the Frankfurt Opera. She sent home glowing reviews of the company's productions of *Rigoletto* and *The Merry Widow*. When new missionaries arrived near curtain time for *Carmen*, she whisked them from the train station directly to the opera. Unpacking could wait. She even begged off trips to out-of-town religious conferences when they conflicted with the opera schedule. She clearly enjoyed opera-going, although she approached it with a certain lack of sophistication. "I surely get a thump out of these German girls trying to get up and down on the stage," Evelyn wrote to her parents. "They look like miniature cows."

What fascinated her most of all was the German stagecraft. She wangled permission to spend hours pushing buttons backstage, investigating the lights and scenery, and hatching plans for her own productions. She found a willing partner for this scheme in Arnold Hildebrandt, a newly arrived missionary who was "a real artist on the violin," according to Doug. Inspired by the young man, and possibly jealous of Evelyn's attention to him, Doug asked his parents to send him his own violin, slipping into the vernacular to say, "If I practice real hard, maybe I can play second fiddle to him sometimes."

As the *Pfingsten* conference weekend approached, with people arriving by train, bus, truck, and bicycle—some from hundreds of miles away—Doug reported that Brother Hildebrandt also had "dramatic flair" and "has carried out Evelyn's ideas in a very fine way," borrowing stage lights and renting scenery from the city's professional theaters for the grand production of her revised play.

Carol had a song in the trimmed scene about Jesus's birth. Besides Evelyn's plays, there would be musical selections, including a choral number sung by the youth groups for older teenagers, the M-Men and Gleaner Girls. Anna would take part in that, Doug wrote his parents, so "for the whole conference, I think our family is pretty well represented."

In that sentence, at least, Doug acknowledged Anna at his daughter. However, while he and Evelyn frequently thanked their parents for clothes, dolls, and peanut butter sent to Carol—for Christmas, her birthday, or no special occasion—it seems nothing arrived for Anna. Evelyn answered an inquiry from her mother about how Anna was "working out" as if rating the performance of a domestic helper.

Anna chose not to discuss these years with her own children. However, according to a writer who interviewed many of the missionaries while they were living, at least one, Hildebrandt, felt sorry for Anna because of her neglect by her adoptive parents. In Utah, she would have been in high school, making friends and able to visit the biological siblings with whom she maintained lifelong contact. Now that conference season was in full swing, Doug and Evelyn went away every weekend, leaving her on childcare duty. In her precious spare time, Anna was left to arrange her own recreation in, as Evelyn noted, a nearly all-male environment.

On weekdays the missionaries were generally free after supper. Using the slang of the time for *BS*, Blake wrote in his diary that "Anna usually wants to 'quatch' (throw the bull) or wants someone to take her to the movies, but is otherwise O.K." A staff photo, in which Hildebrandt looks moodily Byronic, shows Anna crouching in the front row, her hand grasped by the kitchen maid, Ilse Kramer. This was the maid who'd annoyed Evelyn by substituting for her at conferences during the "fire drill" evacuation to the Netherlands. She may have been Anna's only female friend.

If Anna had to bear Evelyn's rejection, she wasn't the only one. In his diary, Blake professed deep admiration for Sister Wood, whom he likened to Emma Smith, first wife of church founder Joseph Smith. Yet Evelyn also had "great faults," which Blake described: "Sometimes she acts bored to the point of disgust, and tells people where they are at fault; she is intolerant toward others' faults and inconsiderate of others' wishes and desires. She has favorites and shows it *very* plainly and admits it. But she has a super-charged personality and is a grand woman."

Evelyn's boredom evaporated in the glow of the Frankfurt conference. Her lavishly staged play, *Jesus of Nazareth*, drew twelve hundred spectators. The three-day event closed at a point west of the city, where a pleasure boat took seven hundred church members down the Rhine. The Woods had made 1939 a "veritable golden age" for the West German mission, in the words of a church historian.

In July, Evelyn and Doug traveled by land and sea through Eastern Europe to the Holy Land, with stops in Vienna, Budapest, Bucharest, Athens, Damascus, Jerusalem, and Alexandria. The girls had been sent to the Netherlands, presumably invited by the president of the Dutch mission and his wife, who'd known the Woods in Utah and were now their close friends. Sailing back on the Adriatic, Doug wrote to his parents in longhand, filling sixteen pages with descriptions of Romanian poverty, Egyptian camel rides, and a cruise down the Nile. Noting that the Prague mission was now barely able to function, he admitted that, "politically, things look pretty shaky," but "we have to look at the optimistic side with our missionaries." At any sign of nervousness from Evelyn and Doug, the younger people would have refused to work, he said.

At any rate, Doug added, "We had such a good fire drill last year, that we could do it in a much easier way this time."

He soon had his chance to test that theory. Three weeks later, a telegram arrived from the church's First Presidency in Utah, instructing all missions in central Europe to evacuate to Denmark or the Netherlands. The American consulate also sent a message that "it might be best" for Americans to leave Germany. Hoping to return in a few weeks, as they had almost exactly one year before, Doug wired his missionaries and told them to leave.

But this was not a drill. On September 1, a week after the evacuation, Germany invaded Poland. The Woods were in Copenhagen when Britain and France declared war. Doug was briefly assigned to the presidency of the Swedish mission, but then the church called all Americans home from Europe.

In Germany, the pressure to look composed and impeccable meant, "I have to be a different self," Evelyn had complained. Now she was headed back to Utah—but not to be her old self. She had moved far beyond that.

3

Habits of Highly Effective Readers

GEORGE BLAKE, THE YOUNG DIARY-KEEPING MISSIONARY, understood the Woods' marriage. After his first meeting with Evelyn, he wrote in his diary, "She is her man's helper rather than his boss. . . . It may be possible that she could run the mission better than any man, but she realizes her position and is willing to take left-hand place in the partnership."

Now there was nothing to run. The Woods were home and not even in their own home. The four of them were staying with Doug's parents—still renting out their old place, perhaps because their tenant had expected them back later—until they found another home to buy and a livelihood. Their old store was in new hands, renamed McCullough's. No longer President Wood or Bishop Wood, Doug had to find something to do—as did the easily bored ex–Mission Sweetheart.

The final evacuation of the West German mission hadn't gone as smoothly as the previous year's fire drill. Doug and several of his missionaries would later present their difficulties as a Hollywood-style escape caper, complete with bumbling brownshirts and daredevil train stunts. But letters and journal entries tell a different story: all they wanted was to go back to Germany.

"We were brokenhearted because we had a good thing going with the church there," Doug told a church historian many years later. He also said that even after the outbreak of war, as the Woods spent two weeks helping to close the Swedish mission, he'd hoped he could get back to Germany.

The war was a résumé wrecker. Waiting in Copenhagen for a ship to take the German missionaries back to America, Blake described a communal letdown. He'd expected to return "in glory," he wrote in his journal. Instead, "all this ended with a thud, careers and achievements were left unfinished; Europe was past tense for us."

Not quite yet. Unwilling to retreat from the spotlight, the Woods milked their European experience for all it was worth. From his parents' home, Doug gave the *Salt Lake Telegram* a preview of a talk he'd prepared for a Salt Lake City business group. "The German press has fired a continuous barrage upon the British, blaming them for starting the war in Europe," he told the paper. Germans, he said, had heard "only the German side of the issues which involved Europe in the war."

Absent from these comments was Doug's own unwillingness to disobey church instructions by offering Germans some enlightenment. The talk was the first of a series that would take Doug and Evelyn, separately and together, to church and secular groups around northern Utah. Evelyn later told a reporter they'd given 660 lectures in a year and a half. Surely she exaggerated that figure, but the newspaper printed it. Newspapers liked big numbers, and throughout the rest of her life, Evelyn would always be eager to provide them.

Showing slides and home movies to rapt spectators, the two seemed to have settled back in their element. The girls were in school, Anna at East High, where her older biological sister was also enrolled. But home was a comedown from the high of directing a mission. There were signs of restlessness. The Woods moved into 1304 Westminster, a one-story bungalow in the same eastern part of the city as their previous home. Doug was moving from one sales job to another. Both Evelyn and Doug also taught seminary, but none of this was quite enough.

Evelyn's parents had moved from Ogden to Salt Lake City. She'd urged them to do so, though they initially resisted. When her father had been rehired at the Ogden mill, relocation had seemed unnecessary, but the job lasted less than a year. In the end the Nielsens had heeded their daughter's advice to appeal to church officials. Elias Nielsen was now a machinist for the Salt Lake Regional Welfare Center, which distributed food and other goods to the needy. His employment there indicated that he was in need himself.

For Evelyn, there was only the lecture tour. Their changing presentation themes offered a preview of techniques they'd later use in marketing. As Americans grew increasingly sympathetic to the Allied powers, the Woods tailored their approach accordingly. Anything for an audience.

In early talks, Doug appealed for tolerance toward German Americans, surely a welcome message in Utah, where thousands of Germans had settled with help from the same church program that had brought Elias Nielsen from Denmark. He painted a positive portrait of Germans, characterizing them as "the most progressive" group in Europe and saying they hadn't wanted war. For a meeting of the Lion's Club, of which he was a member, he offered the Germans' justifications for supporting Hitler's expansion plans.

The couple sometimes spoke together. Presenting on her own, Evelyn initially chose less controversial topics, like "Conditions in Germany." But things changed in 1940. Still keeping a journal as he finished his mission service in North Dakota, Blake observed that the people he met were increasingly sympathetic to Britain. "We are choosing sides and getting ready to go!" wrote Blake, a staunch isolationist. He attributed the shift to "pro-British propagandists."

Whatever Evelyn's private thoughts, she publicly made some adjustments. In January, she joined two other wives of former European mission presidents for a talk at a church conference. Evelyn brought some items she'd bought in Germany, approaching the event as a show-and-tell. Her friend from the mission in the Netherlands was to sing some Dutch songs. But dark clouds gathered over this picnic as their former Prague counterpart described how the Nazi takeover of Czechoslovakia had prohibited the Mormons from holding public meetings or preaching in the field. A wire service picked up the story, which ran in papers outside Salt Lake City.

Evelyn was quoted briefly. She said she'd never forget the cries of the German girls who begged the missionaries not to leave them. Aside from this theatrical contribution, the wire story focused on Martha Toronto, wife of the president of the Czechoslovakian mission, who said it had been useless to preach to people who saw their country crumbling around them.

Evelyn's cheery talks on life in Germany had never gotten that kind of publicity. Taking a new tack, she titled a talk "As the Door Slammed on Democracy." It worked. The *Salt Lake Tribune* gave her coverage, not just a listing. A reporter came to the Salt Lake Business and Professional Women's Club, eagerly recording Evelyn's quotes, including her comment on women's place in Europe: "I never could find it." Evelyn was done with dolls, souvenirs, and travelogues. She addressed another group with a talk on women in the Nazi government.

Around the same time, Doug was pictured in a front-page news photo. He, too, had found a way to grab attention. Invited to address one of Salt Lake City's massive general conferences, during which Temple Square could be mistaken for Times Square, Doug told fascinated listeners about the final evacuation of the West German mission, weaving a tale of miracles and derring-do.

To be sure, there had been snags. Doug's original plan was to send all the missionaries to Rotterdam. However, the Dutch border unexpectedly closed to travelers lacking a ticket to a further destination. Trying to redirect everyone to Denmark but frustrated by jammed telecommunications lines, Doug sent out an emissary with what he called "A Message for Garcia," the title of a 1936 film about the Spanish-American War. The cinematic reference, immediately recognizable to Doug's audience, set the tone for what would follow.

Embroidering facts and depicting inconvenience as peril, Doug painted a distorted picture of Mormons under the Third Reich. Ignoring the favored status earned by the church's compliance with the Nazis, Doug suggested that his missionaries had been running for their lives. In one particularly inventive flourish, he described a scene in which his messenger had openly defied the orders of a German border official, escaping the man's wrath (and, one assumes, bullets) by fleeing as a commotion fortuitously erupted nearby.

"We had seen the treatment of the Jews and we felt that we must do all in our power to see that those missionaries were safe," Doug told his church audience. The man who'd distanced himself from Jews in Germany was allying himself with their plight, now that it helped up the stakes in his story. The seeds had been sown for a myth that was soon to be widely believed: that the Mormons had been persecuted by the Nazis.

Doug's speech was printed in the *Deseret News*. In years to come, it would spawn a magazine article, a book chapter, a portion of a master's thesis, and an entire book about the evacuation of the West German mission. In one of these, a former missionary would make a particularly outlandish claim, saying that American Mormon missionaries had taken over the controls of an abandoned German train, guiding themselves by rail to safety.

As Roger P. Minert, a professor of church history at Brigham Young University, wrote, "The missionaries were in a hurry to leave at the time but were not in any danger." Indeed, Doug and some of his missionaries, including George Blake, had hoped to return to Germany even after the exchange of declarations of war. The evacuation mythmaking falls into the genre of faith-promoting literature—Doug called it a "faith-stirring story"—in which truth and imagination blend, presumably in the service of a greater good. Doug was, above all, a salesman, and he and Evelyn would spend much of their lives minimizing the importance of facts.

These days, he was selling wedding bands and school rings for the O. C. Tanner Jewelry Company, a local manufacturer with two retail locations in Salt Lake City. Doug was made manager of one of them. Meanwhile, Evelyn was preparing her own star turn at a general church conference. Utah had to brace itself. Evelyn was bringing the Frankfurt Opera's stage magic to Salt Lake City.

For three nights in October 1941, a spectacle titled "Prepare Ye the Way" played to packed houses in the seven-thousand-seat Tabernacle, with many others turned away for lack of space. Book, lyrics, and direction were by Evelyn, with music composed by N. Lorenzo Mitchell, a field secretary for the LDS Church's music committee. The *Salt Lake*

Tribune raved about the show's "superb scenery and scenic effects of a variety never before seen in Salt Lake City." The cast of 1,100, including a choir of 450, filled most of the tabernacle's floor as well as the stage.

The play was related to the Aaronic Priesthood, widely held by adolescent males—in those days, only white ones—who'd advanced through the religious ranks. Most of the performers were young. Now thirty-two, Evelyn had spent much of her life working with young people, a point she made when recruiting for Mutual Improvement Association outings, like the Mothers and Daughters week that she hosted in the Big Cottonwood Canyon, just outside the city.

But her relationship with one of her own daughters was disintegrating. While a student at East High School, Anna had taken a part-time job at the Salt Lake City's main post office. She continued working there after graduation because the Woods were charging her room and board. The relationship, "never warm and fuzzy," according to Anna's oldest child, had deteriorated further.

Soon after the United States entered the war, Doug registered for the draft, listing Sunray Heating as his employer. Thirty-nine years old, he wasn't called up. His job at the jewelry store didn't last long, although the store stayed open through wartime under another manager. Doug moved on to a civilian job at nearby Hill Air Force Base, just south of Ogden, while the jewelry store trained women to make and polish jewelry. The "Help Wanted—Female" sections of the Salt Lake papers abounded with new opportunities.

Not one to drive rivets, Evelyn went back to school. She took a full load of graduate courses at the U while simultaneously teaching at the LDS seminary attached to South High School. A woman balancing work and domestic chores was hardly a novelty during the war years—many did so in the absence of their husbands—but the *Salt Lake Telegram*, already familiar with Evelyn, singled her out for a profile, writing, "The first woman ever to seek a master's degree in creative writing at the university, Mrs. Wood does the washing and ironing for her family, which includes her husband and two elementary school age daughters and declares that keeping up with her studies is just a matter of 'getting up a few hours earlier and studying a few hours later.'"

The reporter may have misunderstood Anna's age, then nineteen, but Evelyn very likely misstated it. Caring for one young child wasn't much of a feat, and it would have been assumed that an older daughter pitched in. The mother-of-two descriptor served Evelyn's purposes under the headline "Busy Mother Finds Time to Work for MA Degree," but this was her last public mention of her second child.

Evelyn was still working toward a degree in 1946, when her father died during surgery at age seventy-six. His obituary mentioned only one grandchild, Carol. In the same year, Anna married Montgomery "Monte" North, returned from service in the Pacific. According to her son Scott, the Woods' gift was supposed to be a wedding photographer, who never materialized. The relationship, already "at arm's length," in Scott's words, grew ever more distant.

Postwar, there was little public appetite for lectures about friendly, peace-loving Germans. Evelyn's brother, Ariel, had served with the US Army in Germany as the Nazi death camps were liberated. Evelyn was still in school, but not working toward a master's in creative writing. She was taking graduate courses in the University of Utah's speech department, chaired by C. Lowell Lees.

Evelyn's encounter with Lees would shape her future. Her identification of him as a naturally rapid reader marked the genesis of her Reading Dynamics program. Years later, she'd still be talking about the day she'd turned in her master's thesis and how astounded she was at how fast he could read it. It would become the commercial equivalent of faith-promoting literature, boilerplate for thousands of newspaper ads.

First, however, she had to write the thesis. Anna was gone, but Carol was old enough to stay home herself, perhaps minded at times by grandparents. Evelyn became the director of the American Junior Red Cross's Salt Lake County chapter. This was a big job: Utah led the nation in percentage of students enrolled in the Junior Red Cross. But as always, Evelyn found a way to harness youth to her purposes.

Evelyn's thesis was essentially a description of a yearlong Junior Red Cross project she'd developed. At her behest, dozens of teachers had worked with children to write radio plays marking the centennial of Utah's settlement by Mormon pioneers. Performances, involving three thousand students at thirty schools, were recorded on heavy disks. Five radio stations were persuaded to broadcast these amateur productions over a span of several months.

It was an ambitious undertaking that demonstrated Evelyn's formidable administrative, teacher-training, and promotional skills—augurs of things to come. She encouraged teachers to take a cross-curricular approach, taking trips to museums and supplementing book research with oral histories. She recommended a local focus. A mining community, for instance, might produce a play about miners. Children were to contribute ideas and participate in the playwriting.

Arguing for her project, Evelyn described textbook histories of Utah as "boring," "uninteresting from a child's point of view," and insufficiently focused on individual communities. Ever the show woman despite her nonshowy personal presentation, she wrote that school superintendents "have felt the need of Utah material with glamour."

If Evelyn could not inject glamour, she could at least register astonishment. The submission of her thesis spurred a life-changing revelation. In words that would be stamped thousands of times from boilerplate, she wrote, "I turned in my thesis to Dr. Lowell Lees and watched in amazement as he read my eighty-page paper as fast as he could turn the pages; he read, graded, and returned the thesis within a matter of minutes. Tests which followed this remarkable experience proved that Dr. Lees could read over 6,000 words per minute—with outstanding comprehension."

Thus, Lees became the first of the high-velocity readers whom Evelyn would scrutinize for the next four years. She was determined to learn their secrets and share them with the world. Her thesis had been approved, and she'd found her life's work.

The professor's preternaturally swift reading of Evelyn's work would become central to her mythmaking, but this soon-to-be-famous story raises some questions. A copy of the thesis was preserved with Evelyn's other papers. It is ungraded, and lines designated for the signatures of her dean, department head, and thesis adviser are blank. Clearly, it was not the copy submitted to Lees. This version of the thesis fills three hundred pages, not eighty. Other than Evelyn's twenty-page introduction, which describes the Junior Red Cross project, it consists of scripts produced in the schools under the supervision of teachers trained by Evelyn. Page 80 is a random point in the compilation.

No matter how the thesis was presented to him, Lees would have been familiar with its contents before reading its first page. As usual, Evelyn had reached out to the media, aided this time by the American Red Cross. The organization's formidable public information office sent a photographer from San Francisco to Utah. He shot pictures of Native American teenagers as Evelyn accompanied them from the Uintah Indian school in Whiterocks, Utah, to Salt Lake City, about three hours west. She shepherded them through a gala Centennial-themed tour of the schools and monuments of the state capital, including a meeting with Governor Herbert B. Maw. As Evelyn acknowledged in her thesis, her radio project had not gone smoothly at the Uintah school, where students had not been eager to write or perform. Failing to examine why Native people might have hesitated to join in the Centennial hoopla, she focused instead on her strategies to eke a script out of them anyway.

It's possible that Evelyn organized the field trip to bond with students she'd had trouble reaching. But any benign purposes were lost in her quest for publicity. Alerted by the Red Cross press office, which sent out photos to the media, the *Salt Lake Tribune* ran a front-page story about the trip and Evelyn's radio project. In racially insensitive terms, the feature described the Uintah students as "diffident," "shy," and "saucer-eyed," poking fun at a Native boy who flinched as a camera flashed because he "thought it was lightning." Evelyn's work was also noted in the national magazine of the Junior Red Cross.

It's unlikely that Lees, her thesis adviser, had slept through all this. The thesis was essentially a detailed narrative about the effort and some of its outcomes. There were no quantitative analyses or references to scholarly work. Quite possibly, the professor had decided on a grade for his enterprising student even before flipping through the pages. In that case, he would have been glancing or—the dreaded word—skimming. However, Evelyn insisted he'd asked her questions about the paper that wouldn't have arisen without a close reading.

Lees apparently never contradicted his graduate student's account. But it was publicity, and Lees was in the theater world. Moreover, speaking of Lees in another context, a man who'd worked with him wrote, "Lowell Lees was a strange man. No matter what he said, it was the truth. To him, it was the truth; he really believed it, even though it might not have been the truth."

Moreover, Lees was not a disinterested party. A former theatrical director, Lees had built up the university's drama offerings. Now, however, he was looking beyond the footlights. In the quickened pace of life following the war, colleges around the country were exploring reading-improvement courses, and the U was no exception.

Around the time that Lees graded Evelyn's papers, his department began offering the university's first remedial reading courses. These were required of the lowest scorers on a standardized test for incoming freshmen, who regarded them with animosity. No one enrolled voluntarily. But by 1951, students across campus were vying for seats in a new type of reading class. Its title was Silent Reading for Speed and Comprehension, but everyone knew it by its course number: Speech 21.

Although not created by Evelyn, Speech 21 would eventually be assigned to her and launch her career. But a university appointment didn't fall into her lap. At any rate, despite scoring an instant hit with students, the course got off to a ragged start. With remedial courses sapping his department's resources, Lees temporarily withdrew it from the listings.

The students objected. "Statistics prove that over seventy percent of students double their reading speed and increase their comprehension after completing Speech 21," wrote the campus paper, reporting that students were petitioning for its reinstatement, an effort that proved futile. Lees could not fit it into the schedule.

Doubling reading speeds was small potatoes to Evelyn, who claimed to have clocked Lees reading twenty times as fast as the average mortal. While the U found a way to settle Speech 21 into the catalog, Evelyn continued researching "with Lees," as she later wrote. She spread the word that she was searching for preternaturally fast readers. She said she found fifty such gifted people, including a housewife and a sheep herder. All could read whole paragraphs at a glance with total recall, said Evelyn, also claiming to have found commonalities in their reading methods that she could teach to others.

Postwar prosperity had afforded Evelyn the time to spend on her project. The Woods had moved to a larger house in Salt Lake City's upscale Sugar House section at 2464 Fifteenth Street East (now designated 2464 S 1500 E). Doug had established himself in the appliance business, where he saw visions of the future. He and Evelyn were thinking of investing in something that promised to speed women through their chores.

Three years into her study, she was ready to launch her own futuristic product. Weber College, her alma mater, wanted her to teach and not charm this time. She'd hold a weekly night-school class for adults and teens who wanted to improve their reading. Her course was called Oral Reading, a throwback to a time when the best readers were thought to be those who read aloud fluently. But times had changed. A newspaper item said Evelyn would show that "the faster a person reads, the better his comprehension."

The notion was catching fire. A decade earlier, a report about an experiment conducted at Yale and Harvard had drawn unexpected attention. Among academic studies, it stood out. The Ivy institutions lent cachet, and the technology used was straight out of Hollywood. Reading materials were filmed and edited so that phrases projected on a screen soon vanished. The experimental subjects strained to read the words before they dissolved. The study concluded that, trained in this way, many (but not most) students could double their reading speed without loss of comprehension.

It was a tepid conclusion for a researcher who'd hypothesized that faster reading improved comprehension, perhaps by allowing "more time for thought." A footnote mentioned that the films produced by Harvard to teach speed reading, as the study called it, might soon be available for rental.

That was prescient of Harvard. After the war's end, orders poured in without need for advertising. As Evelyn inaugurated her night-school course, a wave of reading-improvement courses was beginning to rise.

The ranks of middle managers had swelled, and new printing technologies were piling paper on their desks. Students whose parents toted
lunch pails to work were enrolling in universities. General Motors was
about to organize reading training for executives. Banks and insurance
companies were scouring their local colleges for Speech 21–type courses
and sending executives back to school.

A for-profit company misleadingly named the Foundation for Better
Reading was fanning the flames, inviting people to take a course and
flaunt their outcomes. "The slow reader often does not understand or
retain as much of what he has covered as does the rapid reader," wrote
Jack Cooper of the *Chicago Tribune*. He reported trebling his own reading rate at a Foundation for Better Reading course. Expected to keep
up with events while beating deadlines, journalists were often hopeful
that speed-reading worked.

"Many Chicago corporations have sent key officials to the Foundation . . . and are gratified with the results," wrote Cooper. New teaching
methods "could result in a revolutionary change in American reading
habits," he added. A few years later, his paper would intensify the competition by printing that a Chicago lawyer had finished a Foundation
course reading 3,600 words per minute (wpm). In the era of the rat
race, the game was on.

As the Foundation spread to more cities, it filled thousands of mail
orders for pocket-sized tachistoscopes. These were home versions of a
device used in the company's classrooms to flash words or numbers
on a screen. Like the Harvard films, training with the tachistoscope
was said to increase a reader's fixation span, or the number of words
that could be seen in one glance. Images appeared on a screen for a
fraction of a second, and viewers wrote down what they'd seen, with
more letters or numbers added gradually. The training was designed
to reduce the number of stops, or fixations, needed to read a line of
print.

In these early years of the speed-reading wars, Evelyn was barely a
combatant. With her master's degree in hand, she'd left the Red Cross
for a job with the Jordan School District in Sandy, Utah. For the rest of
her life, Evelyn Wood would be known as a Utah schoolteacher, except

at Jordan High School, where her title was girls' counselor. Early in her nine-year career at Jordan High, she appeared in the school yearbook, *The Beetdigger*, on the faculty page over the words, "English, counseling." But in subsequent editions, covering nearly all her years at the school, she was grouped with out-of-classroom personnel, such as the boys' counselor.

In a résumé written years later and in interviews, Evelyn said she'd initiated, taught, and supervised a remedial reading program at Jordan High School. She was certified in high school teaching as well as counseling and guidance—not unusual for counselors, who sometimes fill in for absent teachers and help students with their studies. Still, counselors are not accountable for students' academic progress in the way teachers are. Moreover, her résumé lists no special credentials in reading instruction other than a summer certificate program at Columbia University's reading clinic, her own research, and a special certificate in teaching remedial reading, awarded just as she left her high school job. The idea of Evelyn as a veteran teacher was a cultivated misconception.

Within a short time of her hiring, she was organizing a fashion show at Jordan High, teaching students to be "slick chicks," according to the ensuing publicity. Christian Dior's New Look hadn't made much of a splash at Jordan High, where the hot items were white blouses and flannel skirts. Evelyn may have organized the event as a way to reach the school's lowest-performing students. She was said to have taught "troubled girls" who read slowly, and this is plausible. Struggling students often end up in a counselor's office.

But in Evelyn's world, problem students could become stars too. With names changed and narratives fictionalized, the reluctant readers of Jordan High would be profiled in the introduction of *Reading Skills*, cowritten by Evelyn and Marjorie Wescott Barrows. The phrase "speed-reading" does not appear in the book. It is a textbook, accompanied by a teacher's manual, purporting to teach poor readers new "habits." It was advertised for "below-level readers and the junior-senior high school level." But it laid down the principles of what would later become *Reading Dynamics*.

The book was published in 1958 by Holt, Rinehart and Winston, where coauthor Barrows was an editor. Barrows held a doctorate in education, but her classroom experience didn't extend beyond student teaching. She'd moved directly from graduate school at Columbia University's Teachers College into publishing. For Evelyn, the book was a labor of seven years. The lessons and activities were first piloted in schools around Utah, then in twelve additional school districts from Oakland, California, to Hartford, Connecticut. Curriculum supervisors for the New York City and Philadelphia school districts, among others, reviewed the manuscript before publication.

In her acknowledgments, Evelyn thanked Lowell Lees, "who urged the writing and insisted on the standards," although it's unclear what standards Lees was applying. He oversaw reading instruction at the U, including remedial classes, but his background was in drama. His nickname, "Doc," arose from a belief that Lees was the first person in the nation to be awarded a doctorate in theater. Lees, with whom Evelyn conducted research from 1947 to 1950 at the University of Utah, was not only a subject in her study of rapid readers but also the supervisor of it. Lees lent her research the university's imprimatur, apparently without administrative involvement.

An introduction for the teacher promises that the book will help students "correct faulty eye movements," "enlarge eye span," and see words "as meaning groups." Evelyn's signature contribution—the use of the hand as pacer—is graphically depicted as a zig-zag line. Teachers are told to call out, "Swish-back, swish-back," as students slide fingers along text, somehow gleaning meaning from it as their eyes move backward.

The method "requires no special equipment," the publisher assured cash-strapped school districts in an ad aimed at teachers of students reading below grade level.

Lacking the capital with which to court the corporate market, Evelyn had at least exploited the red-hot demand for reading-instruction books. Every publisher was on the hunt for them, wrote the *Wall Street Journal* in an overview of the speed-reading craze. Noting the brisk sales of Rate-O-Meters, Perceptoscopes, and the like, the *Journal* quoted one unnamed reading instructor as saying, "We have them around in case the men get bored studying and want to play with the toys." Taking a somewhat skeptical look at the phenomenon, but very likely fueling it with its front-page coverage, the *Journal* observed, "No one yet understands just how the eye and the brain combine to get meaning from the printed word."

No matter. Evelyn claimed that she did, and her manuscript had passed muster with reading experts and more than a dozen school districts. Sales of the book might not have been spectacular, but its publication elevated Evelyn to the rank of reading expert. The former girls' counselor for an obscure school district now had a place on the national stage.

She'd later aim only at proficient readers, caution others against using her methods with strugglers, and develop separate products for remediation. For now, her target market was teachers who'd presumably recognize the students profiled in her introduction: "Herman," the newspaper boy with the out-of-work father, and "Carl," the child of migrant farmworkers, neither of whom read well. A full page was devoted to each, followed by discussion questions.

Not all the names were changed. There was also "Anna," unmistakably modeled on Evelyn's daughter and bearing clues about the parent-child estrangement. Other characters in the section lived in shanties or hovels, but the drawing on Anna's page resembled the Wood's spacious colonial: "Anna is a very pretty girl. . . . Her cashmere sweaters are the envy of other girls. Both of her parents are college graduates. They live in a nice house in the best part of town."

Yet, despite private tutoring, the fictional "Anna is the poorest reader in her class." Busy with "clubs," her mother is rarely home. Her father, an executive, carves out time to listen to her read but often loses patience. "Anna wonders if perhaps he doesn't like her because she isn't as smart as he wishes she were." The parents are at a loss. "They have given her everything a girl could need or want." Sometimes they are ashamed of her, and "Anna knows it."

However, the story ends by blaming its victim. If Anna really tried, "maybe her parents would stop spending so much time with her. They'd be busier and busier. It was safer, she decided, to go on being a poor reader.. . . As long as her parents worried about her, she knew they loved her."

The reading problems of the story were invented, said Anna's daughter, Barbara North Smith. They're stand-ins for other deficiencies that Evelyn perceived in her older daughter. The real-life Anna did well in school, both in Germany and at Salt Lake City's East High School. Valuing her high school studies, she saved her notebooks. Her children remember her as an excellent reader and speller. But, as for the story in Evelyn's textbook, Barbara said, "I'm sure it was a stab at my mom. She never could make Evelyn happy. Otherwise, she would not have denied my mom's existence." By the time of the book's release, the Woods had essentially written Anna off.

Doug owned an appliance store in Salt Lake City. Anna and her husband, Monte, found themselves in the area one day, with their young son Scott in tow. They decided to drop by. They got a frosty reception, Scott recalled. Both Evelyn and Doug were in the store that day, and Scott felt no familial warmth from either of them. Evelyn was "snobby," he said, clearly giving Anna the message, "I'm better than you and your family."

He added that Carol sometimes bumped into Anna and acknowledged her but not with sisterly feeling. Carol, at least, had met parental expectations. After graduating from the U, she enrolled in a graduate program at Columbia University's Teachers College. While in New York, she met Ray Jay Davis, and the two became engaged. Already holding one law degree from Harvard, Ray was pursuing another at Columbia, intending to teach law. What's more, he was an observant Mormon. The Woods' ideal daughter had found an ideal match.

In a photo taken at Carol and Ray's wedding, Evelyn has shorn her curls. Sporting a head-hugging pixie haircut, she looks happy. However, it had been an intense year, with more changes to come. The Jordan School District had been paying Evelyn an annual salary of $5,812— about $51,759 in 2019 terms. But, now an author and expert, she had bigger fish to fry.

Doc Lees had offered Evelyn Speech 21, previously taught by Mabel S. Noall, who was leaving for a position in Boston. Noall held a doctorate in education from the University of Southern California, where she'd written her dissertation on the University of Utah reading program. Under her, Speech 21 had managed to become popular without promising outsized outcomes. Concerned about the effects of speed on comprehension, Noall would later write, "We are very much at risk of becoming a nation of rapid non-readers."

Evelyn, though, was ready to pull out all the stops.

4

We Have Liftoff

EVELYN'S NEW, IMPROVED SPEECH 21 hit the U like a lightning bolt. Students queued up for hours waiting for registration windows to open. Some camped out in sleeping bags on the campus lawn. Or so said a reporter, decades later, quoting unnamed university officials who supposedly recalled this. They'd probably at least heard about it. The sleeping bags were part of the Evelyn legend.

At the time, the papers didn't always get her name right. The *Salt Lake Tribune* breathlessly reported that the average student came out of "Mrs. M. George Wood's" class reading ten times faster. The same piece quoted course completers who said they'd needed less than twenty-five minutes to finish the bestselling novel *Peyton Place* (now estimated to take the average Kindle reader more than eight hours).

At this early stage of her career, Evelyn said she used "several methods for developing speed," depending on the reading matter. She was even using machines. Three were available to her and, as she attracted media attention, two news photos showed them in use in her classrooms. Her predecessor had been particularly fond of a mechanical pacer. Evelyn said she used mechanical aids to start students off, perhaps because the university didn't want its expensive purchases to gather dust. However, "they are too slow once speed has been developed," the *Salt Lake Tribune* report continued.

That didn't take long, according to the piece. After just a few weeks of instruction, several students were said to be reading at 1,500 words per minute with 85 percent comprehension. "Comprehension is stressed," the report assured.

The chain reaction had begun. Evelyn made fantastic claims, and her satisfied students spread the word to others. Among the smitten were sons of US senator Wallace F. Bennett. They were studying in Utah while their father spent much of his time in Washington. Bennett had just published his own book, *Why I Am a Mormon*. In it, he mentioned the growing community of Latter-Day Saints in the Washington metropolitan area. Virtually no Mormons lived in the DC area at the start of the century, but now there were five thousand, he wrote. Washington's LDS community was still a small world, but a highly influential one, including people with clout in government and industry.

The Woods had various connections to that world. Supposedly, the Bennett boys' glowing reviews of their speed-reading class alerted their senator father to the existence of Evelyn Wood. Most likely, though, the Bennetts knew the Woods before their sons signed up for Speech 21. Senator Bennett was active in church education in Salt Lake City. Even after election to the Senate, he sometimes taught Sunday School, and his wife had served on a church school board. Given that Doug and Evelyn were longtime seminary educators, it's likely their paths had crossed.

The Woods also had a close friend in the Washington area, Frederick W. Babbel, whom they'd met at the Frankfurt mission. "I sure liked him a lot," Evelyn told her parents. A former secretary to the Berlin mission president, Babbel wasn't assigned to Frankfurt when the Woods arrived, but he often dropped by to lend a hand. When he was released from his mission in the spring of 1939, Evelyn asked him to take some tablecloths she'd bought to her parents and in-laws. "If Brother Babbel comes with [the gifts], talk to him a bit," Evelyn urged her parents in a letter.

Babbel discharged his errand. In the course of doing so, he took Doug's parents out for a ride. Learning of this, Doug wrote them that such consideration was typical of Babbel. "It was certainly a thrill to hear that Brother Babbel came to visit you," Doug wrote. "Yes, he certainly is a fine boy. He has such a sweet personality and everyone who knows him just loves him a lot."

Babbel had also taken Anna to see *La Bohème* at the Frankfurt Opera, undoubtedly out of sympathy for the lonely teenager and not for romantic reasons. The journal he kept at the time leaves no doubt of his love for June Andrew, who was then serving a mission in France. The two married while Babbel served in the army during the war. After it ended, he returned to Germany with church leader Ezra Taft Benson to distribute food and medical supplies to war-distressed Mormons.

That assignment led to Washington. Eisenhower had appointed Benson secretary of agriculture. Benson had grown close to Babbel in their travels through war-torn Europe, and he hired him as his assistant. But a conflict arose, and Babbel left the Agriculture Department after two years. He found work with another co-religionist, J. Willard Marriott, then starting to build his business empire with a restaurant chain called Hot Shoppes. The restaurants began carrying cigarettes, which offended Babbel's religious principles. When they started serving alcohol, he quit.

Through all this, Babbel had stayed in touch with the Woods. In business, he was prized for his organizational skills. From his two years working closely with a cabinet member, he knew his way around Washington. He was interested in what Evelyn had to offer.

Babbel had convinced the Woods to come to Washington and explore the commercial potential of Evelyn's method. But first, they established a foothold in a smaller market, their own Salt Lake City. In the fall of 1959, Evelyn left the U, as she and Doug launched their own so-called "rapid reading" courses, to be taught by others trained in her method.

From the start, the Woods called the program Evelyn Wood Reading Dynamics classes. "The average person reads 150-200 words per minute," began one ad, lowballing things a bit. "Now over eight hundred people in Salt Lake City read 1,000 words per minute with greater comprehension." In addition to Speech 21, Evelyn had taught noncredit courses through the U's adult education program, which may have helped pad the total. The ad listed no address, only a phone number.

It was a telephone line in Doug's appliance store, where the first classes met. The store was named Wood's Ironrite, for a cumbersome machine that was supposed to replace hand ironing. It was designed for sit-down operation, and during sales promotions, Doug threw in the "health chair," a recommended accessory, for free. The manufacturer claimed that one woman had pressed an entire shirt on the Ironrite beautifully in under two minutes—blindfolded. This was speed ironing, advertised with the slogan, "The wife you save may be your own." There were even in-store demonstrations, with customers invited to bring in wrinkled laundry.

The machine has faded from memory, although one of its modernist health chairs is preserved in New York's Museum of Modern Art. But while it lasted, the Ironrite became the engine of a business battle that plunged Doug into a black hole of humiliation, anger, and revenge seeking. The episode, which occurred in 1957 and 1958, while Evelyn taught at the U, explains why the Woods were eventually willing to pull up stakes and go to Washington. It also offers a preview of business strategies they'd use to undermine competitors.

"Gordon wants to sell Ironrites, but why should he have half of my territory just to get even? . . . He quit of own will and free accord," scrawled Doug in private notes covering several sheets of paper. Preserved with Evelyn's papers, these notes could be a rough draft of a letter or perhaps were meant only for himself. Written as a stream of consciousness punctuated with dollar signs and percentages, they offer a window into a worried soul. "All of my lifetime earnings are in Ironrite, my reputation as a dealer," Doug wrote on angled lines, with cross-outs and ill-formed letters revealing his agitation. He mentioned "business associates to whom I can't explain the whole story."

Doug saw no future for his business after the territorial division. "This is elimination squeeze," he wrote. He'd already looked around for another partnership, but "not one of my friends who was familiar with our industry held out a ray of hope." On one page he jotted the phrase, "a feeling of insecurity."

Doug shook this off long enough to threaten legal action against the new competitor given half his territory. Grounds for these charges are not known, but in his inked ravings, Doug charged the man with stealing phone numbers of potential customers. Sharing the Woods' faith, the man had named his new dealership Deseret Ironrite, using a term from the Book of Mormon that refers to the honeybee. Doug's competitor wrote him: "I fear no character assassin, either in or out of the courtroom . . . . Doug, I think the thing you need is to get on your knees and ask the Lord to create in you a clean heart and to renew a right spirit within you. If you go to court I'm quite sure you'll regret it as long as you live. Your very eternity could conceivably be in the balance."

The letter was signed simply "Gordon." No records survive of further action against him. Either the threats of perdition had had the desired chilling effect, or perhaps the case was weak because Doug had failed to have employees sign a noncompete agreement—a mistake he and Evelyn would avoid in their reading business. However, Doug did take steps against the distributor who'd split up the sales area, Rollo Andersen. ("It will be almost impossible for Rollo to treat me decent [*sic*]," he'd written.) With Andersen placing less merchandise in pared-down Wood Ironrite, Doug sent him an order for fifty-two additional machines, with check attached. Unlike their conventional arrangement, he was paying in advance. Andersen refused to fill the order.

This time, the threat of a lawsuit worked. A letter from Doug's attorneys warned Andersen that his refusal was a violation of state and federal laws prohibiting restraint of trade and unfair marketing practices. The machines were shipped.

Nonetheless, the Woods could see no future for them in Ironrite. In other ways, too, their ties to Salt Lake City were weakening. Carol had moved to Phoenix with Ray. She was enrolled in a doctoral program while he taught law at the University of Arizona. However, Evelyn's mother, now in her early seventies, was a concern. She'd remarried but was now twice widowed. As before, Rose had married a man much older than she was. Just a few years after the wedding, he was diagnosed with the heart condition that eventually killed him.

Still, Rose chose to stay in Salt Lake City rather than move back to Ogden. Evelyn always said it had "much more doing" than the smaller city, and Rose seemed to agree. Her son, Ariel, had married and was practicing medicine in California. But the church provided Rose with plenty of work and social activities, and she seemed content in her own apartment.

The Great Depression was long over, but, for those who lived through it, it left an indelible impression. Evelyn had never experienced the suffering that Anna had—something she seemed to forget while criticizing Anna's perceived deficiencies. But she'd watched her parents worry during Elias's late-life bouts of unemployment, and she wanted nothing of that for herself. Ironrite was the wrong bet on the future. An iron and ironing board worked fine, cost little, and occupied less space. Moreover, the Ironrite was an expensive toy for women. "If Dad did the ironing, every home would have an Ironrite," proclaimed one ad, but that was just a fantasy. Men did read, however, and, increasingly, they did it at work.

"Rapid Reading for executives, businessmen, students, housewives," read the Woods' first ads, listing their markets in order of priority, adding, "Only authorized teachers to teach this method."

Evelyn had trained teachers before, for the Junior Red Cross project and for the piloting of her textbook. One of her first speed-reading trainees was West C. Hammond, a bishop with an interest in education. With their first authorized teacher in place, the Woods prepared for the move to Washington after collecting testimonials from students who'd studied with Evelyn in the summer. The manager of a local insurance agency thanked Evelyn for the "privilege" of having studied with her for five weeks. "My speed improved and is more than ten times as fast," he said.

Another letter anticipated a joke that the comedian Robert Klein would tell on college campuses years later. He imagined a patient wheeled into an operating room, only to find that his surgeon was using the Evelyn Wood system to review the surgical procedure. This wasn't too far from the truth. A letter arrived from Wallace L. Chambers, MD. "General and chest surgery" appeared after his name on the letterhead. The surgeon, who had taken Evelyn's summer course, wrote, "It is most impressive that you have discovered that the human eyes and mind have a much greater capacity than has been utilized." He added, perhaps fortunately for his patients, "I was somewhat hampered during the course by being unusually busy and not having enough extra time to read. I am still working on it." This suggests the method hadn't really worked for him. He blamed himself, as so many others would.

Evelyn, of course, would encourage students to blame themselves for their failures, just as she had blamed Anna. She believed people could decide to be successful. Habits could be changed, and they should be, if they were holding you back. Evelyn sometimes likened the demands of her reading method to training a right-handed person to write with the left hand.

However, what she called habits were sometimes deeply rooted in the self. In his missionary journal, Babbel wrote of attending a conference with the Woods, where the same topic came up. "I was chided for a little habit I have developed and felt deeply hurt," wrote Babbel, without specifying the habit or naming the source of the chiding. Clues emerged in an entry made two days later. "Sister Wood took a short walk with me alone and gave me lots of constructive criticism as to my behavior and speech." More charitable toward Evelyn than Blake, the other diarist, Babbel continued, "Some suggestions cut me deeply, but I am grateful for them and hope to profit thereby."

At some point in her life, Evelyn bought a recording made by the Dale Carnegie Service titled *How to Correct People's Mistakes Without Making Them Sore*. Perhaps she'd learned this lesson by the late 1950s, or maybe Babbel had forgotten the incident. The mature Babbel was encouraging Evelyn to change a nation's habits.

He'd even found financial backers to help her do it. Doug and Evelyn made ready to leave. Salt Lake City was too small to contain Evelyn's revolution. As for Doug, he very likely felt destined for better things than storekeeping, even if he'd had more success with that. Doug's letters reveal his class consciousness. Learning that a nephew wanted to grow up to be a fireman, Doug jokingly imagined the family's shock if the boy actually took such a "lowly" job.

Even before they'd pulled up stakes in Utah, the news of their decamping leaked to Washington. First to herald the arrival of the Evelyn Wood system was a crackpot newsletter called the *Little Listening Post*, which regularly reported flying saucer sightings in excited capitalizations. In the era of Sputnik and the Mercury space program, there was a new interest in science, of both the real and pseudo varieties. True to its mission of keeping an "ear to the sky" amid "today's unprecedented Conflicts and Confusions," the newsletter carried this report in the fall of 1959: "In last issue we promised 'news of a startling new discovery to SPEED ENLIGHTENMENT!' Deals with NEW SCHOOL, HQ Salt Lake City, they teach people to READ WITH PHENOMENAL SPEED . . . BASED ON EXTENSION OF PERIPHERAL VISION, also ability to comprehend. . . . One woman read 32 books in 2 days (retained it). All info not yet in. On small-class basis yet. D.C. may have School."

The same newsletter observed, in anxious tones, that a record number of new books were coming out, causing the Library of Congress to add another building. Promising to help Americans cope, the Woods and their backers felt sure of finding a receptive audience.

But they were annoyed that the *Little Listening Post* had jumped the gun. For once, Evelyn didn't want publicity. Reading Dynamics was to start small in the DC area while developing enough staff to expand elsewhere. The Woods would harness their mission experience in identifying and training the right teachers to carry the message. In the meantime, a lawyer was drawing up papers to incorporate Reading Dynamics in business-friendly Delaware.

Doug and Evelyn didn't plan at first to be shareholders. They might have intended to earn income as officers without buying a stake themselves. That notion changed. In a letter to Doug, a lawyer indicated that a small group of men were intended to own shares "before you and your wife came into the picture." In addition to Babbel, Byron Dixon and Carleton C. "Mac" McEachern were named. Dixon was a prominent member of the LDS Church in Washington, where he was also president of business-oriented Benjamin Franklin University.

Mac McEachern brought no business acumen to the enterprise. Instead, he was one of those ideal instructors that the company needed, although one with an unlikely background. In World War II, McEachern had been a tail gunner in the atomic bomb squadron. His training might have included practice with a tachistoscope. The US military had used the speed-reading gadget during the war, believing that it accelerated plane spotting.

McEachern had been on the regular crew of the *Laggin' Dragon*, replaced by alternates on August 9, 1945, when the plane flew weather reconnaissance for the devastation of Nagasaki. Peacetime had returned him to a quieter life. McEachern had a master's in speech from the University of Alabama. As Reading Dynamics incorporated, he was teaching sixth grade near his home in Arlington, Virginia, close to the nation's capital.

While the Washington insiders laid the groundwork, the Woods sold their house, continuing to lease the Wood Ironrite site. It was the first-ever Evelyn Wood "institute," as they'd decided to call the storefront school. Although undoubtedly sorry to see them go, Rose sent them off with the phone number of her kid brother, Leo LeGrande Stirland. He was closer to Evelyn's age than to Rose's. She was the second oldest of twelve children, while he was second youngest; twenty years separated them. LeGrande, as the family called him, was active in business circles in Wilmington, Delaware. Rose thought he might be able to do something for Doug and Evelyn's enterprise.

Arriving in Washington, Evelyn and her partners decided on a marketing strategy. Her reading theories weren't the stuff of scintillating conversation. People could stand just so much talk about fixations, regressions, and subvocalizations—the jargon of the field. Reading rates, expressed in wpm (words per minute), left some people cold. Like Doug's Ironrite machines, Reading Dynamics had to be seen in action. It needed the drama only demonstrations could provide.

Because of her theatrical training, her background in church youth activities—or from sheer instinct—Evelyn chose adolescents. Her decision was in perfect sync with the times. It was the era of the teenager and the teenage consumer. What's more, youth conveyed her revolutionary message. Young people represented the future.

There was one immediately handy. Fred Babbel's daughter, Bonnie, was already an avid reader. The fourteen-year-old immersed herself in the Reading Dynamics method with the encouragement of both her parents. They engaged her in repeated practice, urging her to whip through books and discuss their contents. "I was super-drilled by my parents on what to do and how to recall," she remembered. Another plus was her penchant for performing. Ever since coming across *A Boy's First Book of Magic*, she'd been entering magicians' competitions.

Magic was about to happen to Evelyn Wood Reading Dynamics. The demo that Bonnie most clearly remembers was held in a congressional office building. Ten books new to her had been plucked from the Library of Congress. A large number of people must have turned out because there were complaints from some that they couldn't see. To oblige, she stood on a chair, but "I was afraid that people could see up my dress."

Members of Congress enrolled. There weren't enough of them at first to justify a class on Capitol Hill. They had to share classrooms with real estate agents and homemakers at the institute in the Sheraton Building, as the commercial building at 711 14th Street NW was called then. This was no appliance store. An impressive Italianate brownstone, it was only two blocks east of the White House.

The DC classes filled up fast, thanks perhaps to paranormal forces, or rather those interested in them. The *Little Listening Post*, the UFO-spotting newsletter, claimed that its premature announcement of Evelyn's "far out front" discovery inspired twelve New Zealanders and several Australians to "throw slippers and toothbrushes into bags and sky-hop to Washington." Company documents confirm that the first classes enrolled students from those countries, India, and all over the United States. Even while the company was still training teachers and filing for incorporation, things were going well.

But then an unexpected controversy arose—in Delaware, of all places. Following her mother's advice, Evelyn had been in touch with her young uncle in Wilmington. A small city about a two-hour drive north of Washington, it was mainly notable as the headquarters of E. I. du Pont de Nemours and Company. In Wilmington, a school, hotel, hospital, auditorium, and street were named for DuPont, the state's dominant employer.

Raised in Utah, Leo LeGrande Stirland was a plant pathologist and botanist. But above all, he was a salesman. As a product manager for

DuPont, he shared his niece's conviction that few people had reached their full potential. L.L., as he was known professionally, had recently married an attractive widow, with whom he lived in rural Pennsylvania. However, he spent most of his time in town, advancing ideas about sales professionalism.

As vice president of Wilmington's Sales Executives Club, L.L. had been shaking up the town with sales "blitzes" and "clinics." One recent event featured a motivational speaker, Armand J. "Gary" Gariepy. Thanks to L.L.'s ticket-selling campaign and support from the mayor, twelve hundred businesspeople and curiosity seekers came to see this sales evangelist. Pacing with his microphone cord trailing behind him, leading the audience in chants, and hurling chalk at a blackboard for emphasis, Gariepy previewed ideas he'd package in a book, *How to Sell on Purpose Instead of by Accident*. Among his aphorisms: there's no such thing as aptitude. The audience was electrified.

The stage was set for Evelyn. In December 1959, the Sales Executives Club announced that it was hosting two demonstrations of the Reading Dynamics. It noted that, at the same time, two hundred people were completing the same course in Washington, including "top business executives, key government officials, military personnel," as well as students and housewives.

The Wilmington classes took off slowly, enrolling forty-three students in a night class and thirteen in a daytime group. Far more impressive were the reading rates claimed by course completers. After only six weeks of two-and-a-half-hour weekly meetings, most reported reading nearly 4,500 wpm with 90 percent comprehension.

That warranted two-thirds of a page of coverage in *Salesweek*, a trade publication put out by the National Sales Executives organization in New York, of which L.L.'s club was a part. Less than a year old at the time, the biweekly magazine sometimes printed short items with club news. Most of the magazine was devoted to multipage features— either how-to pieces about increasing sales effectiveness or discussions of topics like the threat of government crackdowns on deceptive advertising. The report on Reading Dynamics broke the mold, occupying two full columns. A photo showed Evelyn standing before her students.

Propped against a blackboard were poster-sized blowups of her detailed lesson plan.

The piece stated that Evelyn's "page perception" method trained the eyes and mind to read down a page, rather than across lines, extracting meaning from patterns rather than from individual words. Without a trace of doubt, it reported that her course completers could finish books in thirty minutes and dispatch entire professional journals in an hour or less. "It is one of the most outstanding projects we have ever sponsored," the Wilmington club's president, William Mahood, told *Salesweek.*

The piece about Evelyn appeared near the back of the magazine. It wasn't featured on the cover or listed on the contents. That didn't prevent it from attracting notice at Harvard's graduate school of business administration. There, a staff member who himself taught reading development found the claims utterly outrageous. He wrote a letter to the editor that touched off a small firestorm.

"Claims of fantastic achievements in reading speeds and comprehension crop up periodically," wrote George W. Gibson, Harvard Business School's director of audiovisual education. But he clearly felt that Evelyn took the cake. It was inconceivable, he said, that anyone could read whole professional journals "in depth" at 4,000 wpm. "In my opinion, you do your publication a great disservice by printing an article making claims of this sort without first making a thorough investigation of the material being so reported," Gibson concluded.

Far from feeling insulted, *Salesweek* seemed to revel in its unexpected attention from Harvard and was loath to let it drop. Evelyn stayed above the fray, allowing her uncle to rush to her defense. An angry L.L. fired off a letter of his own. Before printing it, the magazine's editor showed it to Gibson and solicited a response. The exchange occupied a page of the magazine headed "A Salesweek Debate." In a boxed comment, the editor brought readers up to date on the controversy sparked by "a short article" published five months before.

L.L. began by stating that Gibson had, "in effect, questioned the integrity of the Wilmington Sales Executives Club and the Evelyn Wood Reading Dynamics Institute." He claimed that he'd become aware of the Wood course by making a "study" of the results it had achieved at the University of Utah and in Washington. After comparing these outcomes to those of "'run-of-the-mill' speed reading courses (including Harvard's), the club had chosen Reading Dynamics." He said the program had graduated three hundred students, many of them reading 4,000 wpm with improved comprehension, and that the program would soon offer classes daily. He ended by inviting Gibson to attend a demonstration.

In all this talk about evaluating and comparing competing programs, L.L. failed to say that Evelyn was his niece, not just another vendor bidding on a job. Few people may have known that the DuPont executive, less than three years older than Evelyn, was her mother's brother. In this letter and to the local press, he presented their relationship as purely professional.

In his reply, Gibson said he was interested only "in the accuracy of the claims" and denied having questioned anyone's integrity. The Harvard educator continued: "There is always the possibility that these claims are true, in which case I would be most happy to become one of Miss [sic] Wood's enthusiastic supporters. On the other hand, there is also the possibility that these claims are not supported by research of acceptable reliability and validity and are thus open to question."

The inclusion of Harvard in the run-of-the-mill category struck a nerve. Gibson told L.L., "I'd be most interested in learning the source from which you learned information about my program." He continued, "So far as I know, the only accelerated reading course ever conducted at Harvard University is mine," and "I have never released any of my data to anyone."

L.L. might have been bluffing about knowing the Harvard results. If so, it was a safe bet, based on what Gibson himself had let slip in his first letter to *Salesweek*. The Harvard administrator said he'd never heard "anyone conducting an accelerated reading course in a college or university" make claims of "fantastic achievements" in reading speed and comprehension. L.L.'s big reveal—that "Miss" Wood had taught at the U—must have caught Gibson off guard, although one can guess how much weight the University of Utah carried in the hallowed halls of Harvard.

Invited to see for himself in Wilmington, Gibson threw down a gauntlet: "I trust you would not mind if I supplied the test materials to be used in one of the forthcoming demonstrations."

The Harvard vs. Evelyn match never came to Wilmington. Still, *Salesweek* wasn't ready to let it rest. Two weeks after staging the full-page debate, the magazine ran yet another letter from Wilmington. Signed R. H. Darling, it was from Robert H. Darling Sr., a DuPont chemical engineer and father of the teenager who'd soon be known in Reading Dynamics circles as the master demonstrator. Rushing to the defense of Evelyn, whom he called "one intrepid individual," the elder Darling reported the results of his adolescent son's studies with her. "Can he read at 4,000 wpm? Let me tell you. At three to four times that speed he can describe the plot and subplot of a novel . . . describe the characters and their relationships with each other and to the story. At two or three times that speed he can read highly technical materials . . . and discuss what he has learned from the treatise with an expert."

Anyone churlish enough to quarrel with this would be impugning the integrity of not only Evelyn and L.L.'s club but also an earnest teenager and his affectionate father.

Letters kept coming in after that, from people wanting Evelyn's address. "We've been deluged with such requests," *Salesweek* wrote, adding that the latest were from a refrigeration sales office in Pennsylvania and an ad man in Ohio. Referring future inquiries to the Evelyn Wood Reading Dynamics address in Washington, the magazine finally let the matter drop. Seven months had passed since it ran the article about Evelyn.

Reading about her no longer required a subscription to an obscure trade publication. In early August, the *Washington Post* ran a four-column feature about Evelyn under a large photo. "We don't feel we have succeeded if a student reads less than 1,000 words per minute at the end of the course," Evelyn told the *Post*, alluding to senators she'd taught without naming them.

Time magazine jumped in two weeks later and pumped up the volume, elevating "Teacher Wood" to rock-star status and even nicknaming her followers. "A Woodman can mop up *Dr. Zhivago* in an hour," declared *Time*, quoting Evelyn's explanation of the method. "You don't see the words as words," she said. "The story rolls on to you." For perhaps the first time, one of her senatorial students went on the record. Calling his own progress "fantastic," Senator Herman E. Talmadge, a Georgia Democrat, said he'd like to see it in all his state's schools.

"Washington has seen nothing like it since the days when Teddy Roosevelt read three books a day and ran the country at the same time," *Time* marveled.

It was 1960. The country would soon choose a new occupant—another prodigious reader—for the White House.

5

The Kid Farm

John F. Kennedy was inaugurated on a blustery winter day in 1961. His voracious reading habits became legend before the snows melted. For those too far from Washington to hear Capitol gossip, *Life* magazine ran a lengthy feature on the subject. It included photos of JFK reading while standing, the ten newspapers and sixteen periodicals that comprised his daily diet, and lists of his preferred books—everything from Anthony Trollope novels to a photostat of Che Guevara's book on guerrilla warfare.

According to *Life*, the president devoured reading material at a rate of "at least" 1,200 words per minute. His fast flips through dense reports sometimes appeared to be "mere skimming," the article acknowledged. But Kennedy's astute questions and comments about the material proved he hadn't missed a beat.

The author of that article, Hugh Sidey, later wrote that he'd invented Kennedy's 1,200 wpm rate. It seemed about right, he explained, and he didn't expect a US president to submit to testing. The rate may have been concocted, but Kennedy's interest in rapid reading was real. As a freshman Congressman, he'd enrolled in a course offered by the Foundation for Better Reading in Baltimore. An old prep school pal taking the class for job reasons had invited Kennedy to join him. After a few sessions, JFK dropped out but not from disillusion. Believing he'd "picked up" the rapid-reading knack, he continued on his own. As *Life* noted, those around him were scrambling to catch up.

"If you don't read and understand 3,000 to 4,000 words a minute, you're definitely 'out' of the New Frontier," announced a newspaper in Texas, where an Evelyn Wood Reading Dynamics institute was about to open in Dallas.

Two prominent Democratic lawmakers had gotten the message. Senators William Proxmire of Wisconsin and Stuart Symington of Missouri were finishing up their courses at the DC institute, where a milkman reportedly also was enrolled.

It is unclear whether the two Democrats were in the same class. Symington, at least, was taught by one of his former Missouri constituents, Maurice Nugent. Nugent shared Evelyn's love of theater and had directed some productions in Kansas City. Whoever taught Proxmire, it was not Evelyn. She was far too busy to teach at the institutes or in Wilmington. She was now an assistant professor at the University of Delaware, but the title burnished her reputation without requiring a heavy teaching load. Before the year was out, there'd be Reading Dynamics sites in New York, Chicago, Cleveland, Detroit, Philadelphia, Baltimore, Seattle, San Francisco, Los Angeles, Kansas City, Dallas, and New Orleans. When not touring the nation with student demonstrators, Evelyn was giving interviews, attending professional conferences, or training instructors.

A secretary arranged Evelyn's hectic schedule from the headquarters of Evelyn Wood Reading Dynamics Institutes of America in Arlington, Virginia. Doug also had an office there. Any plans made by the institutes required the approval of M. D. Wood, the company president. He'd come a long way from selling ironing machines.

Things were about to go farther. The new duo of senatorial enrollees caught the eye of an ABC news show, *Roundup USA*. Symington, in particular, had national name recognition. His fellow Missourian, Harry S. Truman, had backed him in his bid for the Democratic presidential nomination that ultimately went to Kennedy.

The televised presidential debates of the previous fall had helped Kennedy defeat Nixon. *Roundup USA* was anchored by Bill Shadel, moderator of the third of those historical debates. This respected newsman introduced the segment about Evelyn Wood Reading Dynamics, speaking earnestly into the camera next to a title card reading, "Mental Frontiers," before cutting to an ABC reporter in Washington. There, the camera discovered a roomful of mostly male adults moving hands down text and flipping pages rapidly. To the fascinated reporter, Evelyn briefly explained it all. In close-up, Proxmire reported his phenomenal new reading rate. Senators Symington, Talmadge, and Bennett completed the chorus.

The *Roundup USA* segment aired on March 26, 1961, and was rerun several times. According to a television columnist for a Pittsburgh paper, NBC's Chet Huntley and David Brinkley presented their own version in June, focusing on Proxmire. If so, Evelyn made no mention of it, although she repeatedly reminded print journalists of the ABC program. It's possible that Brinkley raised a quizzical eyebrow and some tough questions while interviewing the Wisconsin senator; the Pittsburgh columnist described their exchange as "amusing."

Roundup USA never enjoyed the popularity of Huntley and Brinkley, but its Evelyn Wood report eventually reached a vast viewership. By aiming a movie camera at a TV monitor, Reading Dynamics made a film, or kinescope, of the show. Copies of the kinescope were screened for years at the company's demonstration sessions. The ABC report became a vital sales tool.

Proxmire, known for his fitness mania, seemed to be everywhere, talking about his reading speed. The "trim, tanned physical culturist," as one columnist described him, declared that twelve weeks of Reading Dynamics had pumped him up to 12,000 words per minute. (He conceded that he "slowed down" to 1,200 wpm for highly technical material.) Interviewed in his office a half hour before a meeting with Treasury officials, he said he planned to read three books before they arrived.

Boasts made by Symington and Talmadge were somewhat less astronomical but still mind-boggling. In comparison to the claims they made, the president's rate seemed tortoise-like. Bennett mainly sought credit as the talent scout who'd discovered Evelyn. He also served another important function. The Utah Republican's presence in the otherwise Democratic group elevated speed-reading above petty partisanship.

The endorsements of the four senators—unpaid, as Proxmire would eventually reassure the Federal Trade Commission—became an essential element in the marketing of Evelyn Wood Reading Dynamics. Headshots of the senators would run in her ads for years.

Moreover, Evelyn had a chance to stick it to Harvard again. Some ads used Proxmire's photo only next to his quote: "I must say that this is one of the most useful education experiences I have ever had. It certainly compares favorably with the experience I've had at Yale and Harvard."

Yet, in what would become a pattern, Evelyn couldn't shake off Gibson's slight and looked for ways to nettle him further. The Harvard educator had been silent in the pages of *Salesweek*, but he'd published a piece about speed-reading courses for Harvard Business School's monthly publication, the *HBS Bulletin*. The subheading was provocative: "You can increase your reading speed—but beware of charlatans!" However, other than warning against mail-order courses and those that "guarantee phenomenal increases in speed and comprehension," Gibson named no methods to embrace or avoid. The piece ended with the tepid advice to "check with your nearest college or your state university" (unless, presumably, you lived in Utah).

Before that article came out, the *Roundup USA* program had aired. Since then, Evelyn's acclaim had been sealed further by an adulatory feature in *Family Weekly*, a Sunday supplement distributed in more than one hundred small-city newspapers, reaching millions of readers. The piece quoted people, presumably Evelyn's students, who described "breakthrough" moments in the Reading Dynamics course as quasi-religious experiences. According to these devotees, jaws ached or vision suddenly sharpened before whole pages were comprehended at a glance.

Family Weekly allowed Evelyn to rave—in every sense of that word—about a literary high she said she'd attained while reading W. H. Hudson's *Green Mansions*, a romance set in a Venezuelan rain forest. "All at once, I was living that story," Evelyn said. "I was walking around among the characters.... Even now, if I let myself go, I can hear the flames crackling and feel the heat as that child burns in the treetops."

The burning sensation returned in the *Detroit Free Press*, which ran a glowing report of Evelyn and her method, saying, "One student, speed-reading through the Chicago fire cried out, 'My God! I'm on fire.'" Compared to these media powerhouses, the Harvard Business School publication was invisible.

Nonetheless, as before, Evelyn had a white knight gallop to her defense. This time her cavalier was George M. Ferris Jr., a prominent Washington banker and Harvard Business School graduate. Ferris wrote Gibson to chide him for failing to recommend Reading Dynamics in his *HBS Bulletin* article. The banker said he'd made tremendous strides using the Evelyn Wood method, in contrast to the time he'd wasted years earlier in an HBS reading improvement course (not taught by Gibson).

Gibson, as unwilling as Evelyn to let matters rest, said the omission was deliberate. He added that he'd written to Evelyn directly, challenging her to let him test her students, after issuing the same challenge in *Salesweek*. Her reply, according to Gibson, was, "Inasmuch as our students are adequately tested, it will not be necessary for anyone else to do the testing."

Gibson added that he'd read "sensational" media coverage of Evelyn's method and her "spectacular" demos of it, none of which validated it in his eyes. Nor did, he added, the endorsements of "undoubtedly well meaning, but categorically unqualified, individuals who hold positions of considerable stature in high governmental and education circles," even if their approval seemed to "cast an aura of erudition" on the claims. Gibson told Evelyn's defender that he'd remain unconvinced until the program allowed an adequate sample of its graduates to be tested by standard measurement instruments.

Gibson had no way of knowing that Ferris was not just another satisfied Evelyn Wood Reading Dynamics student. He would eventually own shares in the corporation and sit on its board.

Lenders were playing an important role in the company. It was expanding rapidly through the formation of wholly owned subsidiaries with geographically specific names, such as Evelyn Wood Reading Dynamics of San Francisco, of Chicago, of Cleveland, of Minneapolis, and so forth. The subsidiaries were tightly controlled and directed by the parent company in Arlington, but shares were issued, and local banks might be involved. The Woods and their original partners comprised the board of Evelyn Wood Reading Dynamics of Dallas, for instance, and three officers of Dallas's Republic National Bank were the incorporators.

The country was divided into five districts, each with its own manager, sales supervisor, and instructional supervisor. Districts managed the institutes in their jurisdiction and tried to develop enough business for new ones. Evelyn was fond of citing the company's motto, Knowledge Through Reading, but Reading Dynamics was basically a sales machine. Reporting his activities for the week, a district manager mentioned Kiwanis Club luncheons, one Lion's Club dinner, and a talk with a corporate executive group. Promotional assistants paid on commission set up reading demonstrations and urged attendees to put down deposits. For this job, Doug recommended hiring former insurance or encyclopedia salesmen.

Setting up an institute wasn't cheap. With each institute required to have two full-time instructors, personnel was the major expense, around $40,000. Real estate had to convey the "aura of erudition" noted by Gibson. The New York institute occupied the entire ninth floor of a building on West Forty-Fourth Street, just off Fifth Avenue. In Lansing, Michigan, district administration offices occupied space in the new Stoddard Building (now the Farnum Building), a modernist structure glistening with plate glass. Lucite coffee tables, Danish Modern armchairs, framed posters, and towering potted plants completed the iconic midcentury look.

There were also the costs of Evelyn's kid farm, the fees and travel expenses of her young demonstrators. She'd finished with the free services of Bonnie Babbel, on whom she'd run a series of experiments. ("She gave me pistachio ice cream as a special treat. It was nasty," Bonnie recalled.) Evelyn now had a stable of high schoolers and a few college students. On school vacations or when excused from classes by administrators, they toured the country.

District offices alerted the local media of their arrival. Popping flashbulbs and whirring TV cameras greeted them at each stop. Bob Darling said he was paid "way over market price" by Evelyn, with whom his parents maintained a friendship that endured for several years past his demonstration days. They were less comfortable with Doug, whom Bob remembered as having a "fierce mustache." Doug had little in common with the Darlings, making his visits to their home awkward. By contrast, Evelyn and Bob's mother found plenty to chat about. They discovered they both belonged to the elite P.E.O. sisterhood, a national organization so secretive than even members' husbands didn't know what the initials stood for. (They're rumored to stand for "Protect Each Other," but only the initiated know for certain.)

Bob said his father would negotiate only with Evelyn, suspecting that her husband, the former Mormon bishop, might cut corners. By contrast, Bob said, Evelyn insisted that her young demonstrator travel first class. However, business letters and expense logs that he preserved from that time indicate that luxury wasn't always an option. They document a punishing summer schedule of eight cities in twenty-six days. Some stays were at Hiltons, but one was at the home of a Wood relative, and a winter demonstration at the National Conference on Higher Education required a shared room in a convention venue. But there was also a roomette on a Boston–Philadelphia train, a flight from Philadelphia to Chicago by tourist jet—not first-class, but costlier than non-jet—and an extra night at a Chicago hotel, not for sleeping but for resting.

Bob's fees for several West Coast demonstrations totaled $650 (equivalent to more than $5,000 in 2018.) "We didn't need the money," said Bob, who attended a private school in Wilmington before enrolling in public Mt. Pleasant High. He described his parents as well-off, even if not so much as the "sea of millionaires" surrounding them in DuPont's home base. He knew his family could cover costs when he went away to college. Still, he enjoyed watching his personal bank account swell to nearly five thousand dollars.

"I had a feeling of achievement," he said. The money financed two grand tours of Europe during college summers, and, he added, "I liked being applauded."

A swing through San Francisco also afforded him a chance to indulge his sexual curiosity. A New Zealand paper had written that Bob was "a 16-year-old all-American boy who likes baseball, girls, and reading," an obvious presumption of heterosexuality. In reality, Bob had already had a boyfriend and was eager to explore the San Francisco scene.

He'd brought a sailor back to his hotel room. "It was fantastic," he remembered, until there was a knock on the door. He was being summoned for business reasons by either Evelyn or one of her assistants. It was not a propitious moment to open the door, so he didn't answer. Feeling awkward about this later, he said he decided to come out to Evelyn even before he'd told his parents.

He said, "I thought, 'This is the end of my association with the Woods,'" Instead, Evelyn said only, "Don't tell Doug." Recalling the conversation decades later, Bob said Evelyn had added words of assurance, including, "Don't change," and "You'll have a great life." As remembered by him, the devoutly religious Evelyn was decades ahead of her time. In the early 1960s, the police in San Francisco regularly arrested men for homosexual acts, publicizing the men's names and their places of employment. Evelyn would have been condoning a criminal act conducted in a room she was paying for.

Another demonstrator was Louise Mahru, who walked onto the set of the hugely popular TV game show *I've Got a Secret* holding a copy of *Gone with the Wind*. The object of the game was to stump a panel of intellectuals with some information hidden from them but flashed in a caption to viewers. The secret was her claim to have read all 1,037 pages of the book in an hour. To the delight of the studio audience, the panelists failed to guess it.

With the secret disclosed, the segment evolved into a lengthy plug for the Evelyn Wood reading system. Evelyn, seated in the audience, rose to take a bow to loud applause. The host of the show, Garry Moore, appeared personally interested in speed-reading, observing to one of the panelists, "We were just talking about this." He was a major pop cultural figure of the era with a variety hour, *The Garry Moore Show*, as well as the game show.

For the millions of Americans watching coast to coast, Louise demonstrated the Reading Dynamics method. In the verbal equivalent of a drumroll, Moore announced she'd have one minute to read *The Last of the Southern Winds*, a not yet released novel. In the standard format of Wood demonstrations, Louise was granted a few minutes to preview the book, making notes as she glanced at the book jacket and examined the front matter. Then a timer was set, and it was off to the races. The audience gasped as Louise ran her fingers down the sides of pages before quickly turning them.

At the end of a minute, Louise had covered twenty-seven pages— twenty-six more than the average reader could have covered in that time, as Moore noted. Next, the author of the work, David Loovis, entered to applause from stage left. Introducing him as the "final authority," Moore asked him to listen to Louise's summary of the portion she'd read, then verify or deny its accuracy.

Louise's synopsis bore the hallmarks of a parlor trick. She correctly named the setting, Key West, and the full name of the protagonist, which was mentioned only once in the pages she'd covered. All this could have been lifted from her previewing of the book jacket. She recalled a few random details, like the silver bangle bracelets worn by a character, and confused a few others. But her summation completely missed the point. The protagonist, recently fired from another job, was assessing a struggling restaurant for its business potential. Louise said he was at a friend's house.

"That is very accurate indeed," said the author. This falsehood would have been obvious to anyone who'd read the book, but why would Loovis spoil the fun? His book was about to be published, and this was priceless publicity. Everyone won this game, especially a middle-aged woman in the audience wearing a patterned dress with a waist-length shawl collar. Moore ended by saying, "Louise, I tell you you're incredible, you tell me it's the system. I'll have to take your word for it."

Watching the show from a rural town in Maine, a young girl had failed to catch Evelyn's name. Because John F. Kennedy was synonymous with speed-reading, she wrote to the White House, confident that the president could help. The letter read:

Dear Mr. Kennedy,
My reading is very poor and as a result my school work isn't top-notch. . . . On the Gerry [sic] Moore show this week, a woman

displayed her ability to read 27 pages of a book in one minute. My
mother told me that you also had this unusual ability. Could you
give me the <u>name</u> and <u>address</u> of the woman who perfected this
new system for reading?

A response was signed by Ralph A. Dungan, special assistant to the
president: "In reply to your query the President attended meetings of
the Foundation for Better Reading, a speed-reading course which he
took in Baltimore. After going to the classes a few times, the President
picked up the idea himself. His speed of reading is estimated at about
1,200 words a minute. Perhaps you could contact your local librarian
for further information. Good luck!"

The White House reply contained no information not previously
reported. It's worth noting, however, that the Kennedy aide ignored
the girl's inquiries about a specific woman who'd "perfected" a system
showcased on a national TV show.

That omission raises questions about Evelyn's association with the
Kennedy White House. In years to come, although not during that
administration, she and her company would cultivate the JFK-and-
Evelyn connection. Millions of Americans would see ads declaring that
top aides to Kennedy and his joint chiefs of staff had studied the Evelyn
Wood system. The implication, sometimes directly stated, was that JFK
had summoned Evelyn to the White House to conduct the lessons.

Evelyn would reinforce the advertising narratives in interviews. In
one, she recalled trying to teach the joint chiefs of staff at the time of
the Bay of Pigs invasion. "They were gone too much of the time," she
lamented.

Yet only three months after the failed action in the Bay of Pigs, the
White House was unable or unwilling to identify Evelyn for the Maine
girl. Possibly this was to avoid the perception of a commercial endorsement. To be sure, the Foundation for Better Reading was also a business, but by the time Kennedy became president, it was defunct. Or so
said JFK's personal secretary, Evelyn Lincoln, replying to a query from
Colorado that followed the one from Maine. The White House made
no reference to the Wood method in that letter either.

In the ads and interviews that have survived from that era, Evelyn unfailingly hyped her Congressional endorsements but said nothing about working for the executive branch. It's conceivable that the administration had requested her confidentiality. More likely, Evelyn's legendary White House classroom was a myth, based loosely on the truth. National security adviser McGeorge Bundy took the course, according to a news report of the time, and so did two of Kennedy's senior military aides, General Godfrey McHugh and General Chester V. Clifton. Neither general was a member of Kennedy's joint chiefs of staff, however, and it's unclear who taught them and where they attended classes. Courses offered at the institutes were open to all.

As we shall see, one member of the Kennedy family would take an Evelyn Wood Reading Dynamics class in a government building, with JFK's documented encouragement and perhaps at his suggestion. However, Evelyn would not be the teacher.

Evelyn did instruct members of the military in the spring of 1961, although not the top brass. She flew twice weekly to the US Air Force Academy in Colorado Springs to teach her method to the academy's instructors. The officer who secured the air force contract for her, Captain John C. M. des Islets, was a foreign-language instructor at the academy with a master's in educational psychology.

Without a doubt, Evelyn's techniques were popular with the legislative branch. To meet congressional demand, a classroom opened on Capitol Hill. Every Tuesday, two dozen US Representatives studied with a company-trained instructor. An amused press described how "solons" had been sent back to school, practicing their finger-reading on Hardy Boy juvenile mysteries and hoping to eventually rip through the Congressional Record.

It was an irresistible topic: lofty lawmakers relearning one of the three R's. A lengthy AP report on the classes ran in papers around the nation. For once, Evelyn's company was making a splash without even paying rent: classes were held in the blue-and-gold hearing room of the House Ways and Means Committee.

The name Evelyn Wood didn't consistently appear in the coverage. The version of the wire story printed in some major papers called the company simply Reading Dynamics. In its first two years, the Washington institute was owned by the partnership Wood, Wood, Babbel, McEachern & Alexander. Babbel ran the DC institute, where Proxmire and his senatorial colleagues had studied, and where generals and milkmen were also welcome. Babbel, who eventually owned the franchise to the institute, had likely arranged the Capitol Hill classes. Talking to the press, he may have neglected to push the Evelyn Wood brand, reflecting growing tensions among the partners.

But Evelyn was the face of the company, which hadn't forgotten its corporate roots. Identifying herself as "Evelyn N. Wood, executive vice-president and director of education, Reading Dynamics Institute," Evelyn contributed a series of four articles to the *American Salesman*, a *Salesweek* rival. A photo of her with short hair and a spit curl on her forehead accompanied each installment. A caption said her institutes "have been attended by many company presidents, senators, and others." There was no hint of a White House connection.

The articles crystallized the method into a few simple steps. As always, subvocalization was discouraged. She equated all phonological response to reading with whispering to oneself or moving the lips. Diagrams of hand movements were provided, and a short list said it all:

- Use the *fingers* to guide and prod the eyes along;
- Read down—not across—the page, unless the lines are very long;
- Avoid *fixations* and *regressions*;
- Read *phrases*, not *words*;
- Try to grasp whole *pages* at one time.

The advice to *avoid* fixations, or pauses in eye movement, seems bizarre. Reading is generally understood to occur when the eye looks at print, although Evelyn's advocates were about to challenge that definition. Writing how-to steps for the trade magazine, Evelyn probably meant that readers should try to reduce the frequency or duration of fixations, not eliminate them altogether. That was also the aim of courses that trained readers with machines or images projected on film.

The problem with these suggestions, according to Gibson and other critics, was that the research of the time already indicated that eye movements, including frequent regressions—reversal to a previous word—were symptoms of reading problems, not the cause of them. But Evelyn had developed her method apart from other researchers. Her theories on eye-brain connection could take wild flight, as when she wrote in the student manual, "Your mind doesn't register what's in front of your eyes. It is your eyes that register what is in the back of your mind."

Basically, though, she was using the *American Salesman* editorial pages for free advertising. Like all good salespeople, Evelyn anticipated resistance and wrote, "In the course at Reading Dynamics Institute, we *don't use* any of the three most common methods for reading short articles—scanning, skimming, or looking for key words. None of them result in reading speed with good comprehension."

Evelyn disclosed her trade secrets knowing they'd only increase enrollment in her courses. No one reading these how-to pieces was likely to achieve a speed of 1,000 wpm or above. However, exposure in another sales trade magazine heightened her profile with corporate training departments.

Corporate interest was keen, and not just among sales divisions. Inquiries were pouring in from aerospace and tech companies on the West Coast. An official from General Electric's Defense Electronics Division begged Evelyn to come to Santa Barbara. "See you in Washington, and we'll see what we can work out," she responded. Meanwhile, Boeing was asking the Seattle district office to set up a "pocket institute"—a small site with some permanent staff—for its Tacoma workforce. This was red meat: corporations typically reimbursed employees for classes they took on their own time.

"I believe that Boeing should account for from $50,000 to $90,000 worth of business next year," the director of the Seattle subsidiary told Doug. He outlined plans to open institutes in Spokane, Portland, and Vancouver in the coming year, "and then there's always Hawaii." He continued, "The Reading Dynamics iron is hot, and I believe that the sooner we strike the better results we will have."

Now in thirty American cities, the company was going international. Evelyn spent early December in Copenhagen, checking on an institute that had opened there and touring two public schools at the invitation of the minister of education. Her Danish-born father, born in or near Copenhagen, would have been amazed. As a missionary in the American Midwest, he'd had to beg a brother for a pair of shoes.

With obvious affection, Evelyn wrote to Bob, inquiring about his parents, whom she called "wonderful friends," and asked what he'd like as a gift from Denmark. (He recalled that she brought him a heavy sweater.) "You should see the Danish people read down the page. It is remarkable that anyone can read this funny language. . . . Some of the people are beginning to get pretty good results. My, how I wish I had you over here."

She also wished for more women customers. Showing off her Danish press clippings to a Washington reporter, Evelyn injected "some other revolutionary ideas in the field of education," in the words of the female journalist. "I'm not a feminist," Evelyn said, using a term seldom heard at the time, "but if I had a son and daughter, and could send only one of them to college, I would choose the girl." In an era when most Ivy League schools, including Harvard and Yale, excluded women from undergraduate admissions, this was radical talk. Tempering it, Evelyn continued, "I feel very strongly that our culture depends on women because of their role as mothers." In keeping with her elitist attitudes, Evelyn went on to suggest that only a well-read woman could inspire her children to learn.

Frustrated by her lack of female companionship in Germany, Evelyn was still surrounded by men. All of her business partners were male. Women were hired as teachers, secretaries, and receptionists but not as institute or area directors. The most striking gender disparity was in the Reading Dynamics classrooms. A statistical report made later in the 1960s showed that 74 percent of course enrollees were men.

Employed men were more likely to enroll in corporate groups or qualify for employers' tuition-reimbursement programs. On college campuses, where men had long predominated, the gender gap was slowly starting to close. Yet Reading Dynamics enrollment remained overwhelmingly male. The course was a luxury, and as Evelyn remarked, men were thought worthier of the investment.

It's possible that her mixed feminist message was meant to lure in more women and, hence, tuition dollars. But the course's popularity with men ultimately helped it. Women's pursuits were viewed as frivolous. The endorsement of the senators, all male, and the ensuing national news coverage linked Evelyn Wood's feminine name with power and success.

One particular male, Bob Darling, was clearly an asset to the company. He'd followed Louise onto national television, turning in a more assured performance. Scheduled to appear in a three-minute spot on the widely viewed *Art Linkletter's House Party*, Bob had so fascinated the host in rehearsals that the segment was extended for ten more minutes. Bob read forty-nine pages of Irving Stone's *The Agony and the Ecstasy* during a one-minute commercial break. The book is a fictionalized treatment of Michelangelo's life. Bob had an interest in Europe, where he ultimately spent his speed-reading earnings. His solid schooling may have provided him with background about Florence in the Renaissance, which he used in his cogent, authoritative-sounding summary.

It was an impressive effort but not equivalent to test-taking. The only questions posed by the genial host, Art Linkletter, were about Bob's reading speed (2,000 wpm to 10,000 wpm, depending on the material) and whether he'd really gotten "the flavor of what the man's writing—the color, the shading." Predictably, Bob insisted that speed only enhanced such enjoyment.

Oh yeah? A voice of dissent arose from the University of Florida at Gainesville. "Reading Dynamics Hit by Dr. Spache," read a headline in the campus newspaper. The director of the university's reading clinic, George D. Spache, was issuing a fresh challenge to Evelyn.

"Mrs. Wood claims that her speeds can soar up to 25,000 words per minute," Spache told his student interviewer. "We have over one hundred years of testing to prove that 900 words is the average individual's maximum of speed for a 100 percent comprehension." Except for the simplest materials, Spache continued, "all reading over 900 words per minute is skim reading."

Ominously, Spache indicated that reading experts had been conducting tests on Reading Dynamics graduates. "In every case tested, after
an individual leaves her reading clinic, they have only increased their
reading rate 10 to 20 percent and even in those totals there is a loss of
comprehension."

Announcing that he was about to publish a paper about this, Spache
concluded, "I hope to be able to put a stop to Wood within the next
two years."

Loud alarms sounded at Reading Dynamics headquarters. Spache
was a past president of the International Reading Association, based
at the University of Delaware, where Evelyn taught under Russell G.
Stauffer, the current president. The association published a journal, the
Reading Teacher, for which Spache said he was writing his anti-Evelyn
screed. The same journal had published an article by Evelyn just one
year before. Spache was poaching on her territory.

The University of Florida professor had an obvious interest in stop-
ping Evelyn. Alongside his interview in the *Daily Alligator* was an item
about a student-initiated drive to persuade Reading Dynamics to open
a site near the campus. A petition was quickly gathering signatures, the
Gator reported.

Regardless, Evelyn wouldn't let the matter rest. This time, a letter to
the editor wasn't going to be sufficient. She sought to silence her critic.

A letter from a lawyer representing her and her company threatened
Spache with a lawsuit unless he retracted his statements and refrained
from making similar claims in the future. The lawyer said his clients
had no desire to stifle free speech. But, referring to the *Gator* piece and
other "reports which have reached our clients," the lawyer wrote, "Your
charges appear to transcend legitimate criticism."

The lawyer said that Spache had made "startling charges" and "libel-
ous attacks" on Evelyn and her company. He continued, "Our clients
have no desire to cause any trouble for you nor are they anxious to file
a lawsuit if it can be avoided. However, they feel you must be advised
that they may be compelled to file suit to protect their interests."

In an attempt to bolster his threat with congressional powers, the lawyer concluded by referring to the "individuals in responsible positions"

who'd been satisfied by the course. "To permit untrue attacks . . . to go unchallenged," he wrote, would "impugn the reputation of these men."

Undeterred, Spache continued working on his article. As for Evelyn, she'd officially become a bully.

6

Bunk and Debunkers

FAR FROM BEING INTIMIDATED BY the threats, George Spache ambushed Evelyn at a reading conference. Bob Darling and two other students had just finished demonstrating, to the usual oohs and aahs, when Spache stepped forward. He pointed to an adjoining room where a device used to test eye movements was set up.

Before an audience of two hundred, the University of Florida professor asked if he might test Evelyn's demonstrators. "The confusion on her face when it was proposed indicated she didn't know just for a moment what to do about it," wrote William Liddle, a University of Delaware graduate student who was present. Liddle was an acolyte of Evelyn's but no callow youth: he was a former secondary-school supervisor for the Colorado Springs school district. Both Liddle and Evelyn recognized the device in the next room as a Reading Eye Camera. Spache clearly intended to photograph her demonstrators' eye movements as they read and test them on comprehension.

It took Evelyn only a moment to compose herself and refuse. Her grad student admirer said this elicited some "snide remarks" from Spache, who suggested she was afraid. Other observers probably agreed with Liddle's assumption—that Evelyn would have been agreeable if only Spache hadn't sprung it on her.

These events took place at the National Reading Conference at Texas Christian University. They probably supplied plenty of conversation for late-night sessions in Fort Worth's Loring Hotel, when conference-goers kicked back, wrapped brown bags around their "beverages of choice" (in a journal's sly phrasing), and gathered to discuss the day's events.

Earnest Bill Liddle had tried to make peace between the adversaries, but Spache declined an offer to breakfast with Evelyn. Eggs and toast did not go down well after threats of lawsuits. Moreover, she was threatening not just him but the future of all college-based reading clinics.

Spache made that point in the pages of the *Reading Teacher*. A month after the ambush, he carried out his own threat and published a full-out attack on Evelyn. Her article for the same journal had been titled "A Breakthrough in Reading." Spache called his, "Is This a Breakthrough in Reading?"

Spache presented Evelyn's claims in brief: that individuals could learn to read thousands of words a minute, and that this could be accomplished with improved comprehension. He also focused on her insistence that large groups of words—as much as half a page—could be read with a single fixation, or pause of the eyes, as they followed a hand moving vertically.

If these claims were true, "then practically all present methods of training intended to improve rate of reading are, by comparison, antiquated and ineffectual," wrote Spache in a wake-up call to his counterparts on other campuses.

As in his interview with the University of Florida student newspaper, Spache stated that it was physiologically impossible to read above 900 words per minute. To substantiate his point, he produced research from an optometric journal and other sources. He cited findings that the human eye could see a maximum of five to six words per fixation, and that even within this span some letters would be blurred. He presented other research showing that "processing" the meaning of two-word phrases flashed by a tachistoscope required at least seventeen hundredths of a second.

The weight of these arguments, Spache recognized, "hinges on the definition of the word 'reading'" and whether it was, as commonly thought, "reading most words on a page." If so, Spache continued, then graduates of Evelyn's institute were not reading at all. They were skimming.

If Evelyn refused to produce students for experimentation, experimenters would do it themselves. Spache had contacted Reading Dynamics hopefuls even before they enrolled at an institute, testing them with the Reading Eye Camera both before and after the course. On completion, they handled a book at between 1,800 and 2,400 wpm. But Spache declined to call this "reading." He said their photographed eye movements were consistent with skimming, showing they'd made about one fixation a line before jumping down a line or two. These patterns were interrupted by brief attempts to read horizontally. Comprehension, measured by a true-false test, averaged 50 percent.

The article concluded with Spache's impressions of the demonstrators at the Texas conference where he'd set the Evelyn trap. As usual, the youths were allowed to preview the book cover and the contents before the clock started. Spache dismissed their "facile oral reports" as based "on the information gained during the pre-'reading' survey or . . . on their previous familiarity with the field of the book they 'read.'"

With Google and other search engines still decades off, not everyone agreed that this wasn't reading. Reacting to the experiment conducted on Reading Dynamics course completers, Bill Liddle suggested that what Spache called skimming might actually be "versatility" in reading. He also thought Spache set the bar unnecessarily high for comprehension.

In a letter to Stauffer, director of the Reading-Study Center at the University of Delaware and Evelyn's guardian angel there, Liddle considered the case of someone looking through pages of a telephone directory before finding a particular number. "Is this to say he has skipped over hundreds of words? No. He has seen, but he has rejected what he's seen because it was not the particular thing he wanted." As for demanding high comprehension levels, Liddle countered that people reading for relaxation might be content with far less than that. Perhaps they just wanted to look at pictures or captions.

Of course, Evelyn had repeatedly insisted that her method was not about skimming or scanning. But Liddle's remarks about comprehension signaled a shift that would occur, at least within the company. In a conference paper that Evelyn presented, a subheading declared, "Meaning is Inside People, Not Words," and these Orwellian pronouncements cropped up in a Reading Dynamics instructor's manual: "There is no meaning on any printed page. Meaning exists only in people. . . . Any test made by another person to test your 'comprehension' of material you read can only test a very narrow range of the many things you may get out of the material."

Spache wasn't the only researcher using Wood alumni as guinea pigs. Liddle himself was experimenting. A certified Reading Dynamics instructor trained directly by Evelyn, the former Colorado high school administrator was writing his doctoral dissertation about her methods. With his work not yet completed, he wrote of suspecting that the speeds she quoted were "overly enthusiastic" when "tied down to comprehension levels," but added, "My mind is open."

Most of America kept an open mind too. By spring of 1962 fifty-six Evelyn Wood Reading Dynamics institutes were enrolling people across the nation. Few saw Spache's article or an even more devastating paper by Stanford E. Taylor that appeared in the published proceedings of a midwestern reading conference. Longer and more technical than Spache's work, the article included images of film produced by reflecting beads of light off the eyes of forty-four Reading Dynamics graduates. Taylor said they produced arrhythmic patterns consistent with skimming.

Taylor wrote, "Mrs. Wood has frequently stated that her students read so rapidly that they cannot be photographed by an eye-movement camera. Obviously, they can be photographed." Regarding her assertion that General Electric was at work on a special camera for her purposes, Taylor said he'd investigated the effort. He found it was initiated by a GE engineer who'd taken a class with Evelyn but was not a reading expert. Taylor dismissed the man's efforts as unworkable.

Debunkers Taylor and Spache traveled in the same circles. They'd both been present at the aborted ambush of Evelyn in Texas, for which Taylor might have provided the Reading Eye Camera. Similarities in their experiments suggest they'd tested some of the same Wood graduates, although neither man cites the other's work.

Evidently, Taylor had gotten a heads-up about Evelyn's litigious nature; his paper concludes, almost comically, "The presentation of this data is in no way intended to discredit Mrs. Wood or those who advocate her methods." Spache, too, ended his article with a timid disclaimer: "This article is not written to disparage the efforts of the Reading Dynamics Institute or any of its personnel, for it is apparent that they do produce some degree of reading improvement in their pupils," though that point was hardly apparent in his article. The lawyer's letter may not have stopped Evelyn's detractors from publishing, but it had had the intended chilling effect.

Evelyn still had no problem enlisting advocates. In New York's Nassau County—not far from the Educational Development Laboratories that Taylor directed in Huntington—the bar association had organized a Reading Dynamics class, enrolling superior court justices, district court judges, and county commissioners of both major political parties.

But skepticism was creeping in, and not just from professional circles. A *New York Times* feature titled "2,000 W.P.M.—But Is It Reading?" surveyed the speed-reading craze with one eyebrow raised. Tracing interest in the topic back to the early 1950s and noting it was now as popular as Monopoly, the lengthy think piece raised the question of whether speed-enhancing instruction was effective. For the answer, it quoted university-based educators, who said there was "evidence" that modest gains in rate and comprehension, in the 50 to 150 percent range, could be attained.

Reading Dynamics was left till last. The *Times* turned a jaundiced eye toward its claims of producing reading speeds to up to 20,000 wpm, writing that some "reading authorities" who'd witnessed "such high-velocity word gulping" urged that the demonstrations be "regarded with reservation." A professor at Columbia University Teachers College was quoted as saying she'd like to see some scientific testing.

Moreover, the *Times* added, "at least one member of the Reading Dynamics staff has acknowledged the need for more proof of comprehension." For Evelyn, this was notice that she was unwittingly harboring an enemy. The *Times*'s unnamed source was a member of her own staff, or rather, the staff of one of the subsidiaries.

The rapidly growing company was becoming difficult for the Woods to control. There were now twenty-four separate Reading Dynamics subsidiaries operating institutes in fifty-six American cities. Doug and Evelyn had been voted the sole directors of the company. The other shareholders were no longer on the board.

In April 1962, the Woods began converting the business to a franchising operation, but change came slowly. A detailed agreement spelled out the terms under which franchisees could offer courses under the Reading Dynamics and Evelyn Wood banners—her name had been trademarked separately. After paying a franchise fee, which varied with the market, franchisees would pay a royalty on each course sold to the Woods' Arlington-based company. The parent company would provide manuals, books, and teacher training, setting rules for promotion of instructional staff and reserving the right to observe classes. The franchise would pay for nearly all its own advertising costs, with headquarters kicking in only 10 percent.

Franchisees were also required to sign a noncompete agreement valid for three years that forbade the disclosure of proprietary knowledge of the Evelyn Wood Reading Dynamics method. Such agreements were common at the time, but this company added a new wrinkle: students also had to sign a nondisclosure agreement.

Franchising would bring in capital while reducing costs, but royalties didn't amount to much unless the franchisee hustled. The licensing agreement didn't give the Woods a big stick to ensure that. It was a tough year for Doug and Evelyn, who were seeking a professional manager. Later, the Woods would say that the company was facing bankruptcy because rapid expansion had made it hard to find qualified teachers.

That statement contradicts the portrait presented by company lawyers in a California trademark infringement case decided that year. In those proceedings, Evelyn Wood Reading Dynamics was found to be a thriving operation that, in less than two years, had enrolled 17,500 people in fifty-six cities. With courses normally priced at $150, that indicated revenues of about $2.5 million. However, sleek offices, large staffs, and promotional costs devoured income, as the founders discovered.

Certainly, the Woods' own financial affairs were a mess. At the start of the year, Evelyn and Doug each still had $9,715 in the five-person partnership that owned the Washington institute. Seven months later, all that and more was gone. Each of the Woods was posting a loss exceeding $6,000. Fred Babbel and the other partners were deep in the red too. A $56,000 loss had been distributed equally among the five. In addition, all the partners had made withdrawals from the partnership, essentially using it as piggy bank and deepening their losses. The partnership apparently relinquished the Washington institute at this point. The corporation franchised it to Frederick W. Babbel & Associates, a corporation formed by Babbel to operate several sites under license to the parent company.

The Washington institute, where senators and milkmen had studied together, was practically a vanity operation. An itemized statement for the first half of 1962 shows that revenues, almost purely from tuition, were dwarfed by expenses. Not enough people were enrolling to justify the high rent and large instructional staff. Small, subtle ads in Washington papers avoided mention of a growing problem. Skepticism was in the air, and brasher Evelyn Wood operators met it head-on.

Evelyn Wood Reading Dynamics of New York announced a demonstration in the Barnard College newspaper, ending with, "You have nothing to lose but your skepticism." A Pennsylvania licensee went further, taking out an ad in the September 12, 1962, issue of the *Philadelphia Inquirer* that read:

Speed Reading Is a Lot of Bunk!

Some people insist that speed readers skip words. But thousands of Americans have learned to read 3 to 10 times faster by taking the Evelyn Wood Reading Dynamics course. They read downward on the pages, taking in whole sections <u>without skipping a single word</u>. Contrary to popular myth, their understanding has actually improved.

For almost all of her career, Evelyn never referred to her method as speed-reading, using only the phrase *dynamic reading*. But the ad reflected deeper problems than that. It was a response not to popular myth but to a popular magazine, the *Saturday Evening Post*. The *Post* had recently run an article, "Speed Reading Is the Bunk," with the subheading, "Beware of 'experts' who claim they can teach you to read thousands of words per minute. Nobody can read that fast."

Again, the attack was launched from the Ivy League. The author of the piece, Eugene Ehrlich, taught reading-improvement courses at Columbia University's School of General Studies. He also provided such programs through contracts with corporations. In one of these, Ehrlich found willing lab rats. Three engineering executives had finished Reading Dynamics courses and boasted of reading rates that Ehrlich believed impossible. A fourth was about to sign up.

The four agreed to be tested on rate and comprehension. Ehrlich gave them nonsense to read. He'd inserted lines from one engineering text into another text without regard to meaning or punctuation. He let his subjects read through the mash-up three times. Showing off their best speeds, none of the Wood-trained readers noted anything amiss, but their untutored colleague protested, "Whoever typed this must have been nuts."

Written in an accessible narrative style, with just a few quick references to fixations and eye movements, the piece offered brilliant insights into Evelyn's sales techniques and the psychology of her followers. The author had seen her present a paper at a College Reading Association conference. Afterward, he said, she turned aside critical questions by stating that skeptics needed to see one of her demonstrations before accepting a system "as revolutionary as hers." Turning the tables, she was suggesting that the questioners were close-minded.

Ehrlich attended two demonstrations, one live and one taped. At the first, Evelyn was seated at a long table with four demonstrators. She made the usual to-do about pulling books at random from a carton. After the usual preview period, the young people read for three minutes. The only male was a young lawyer who summarized the three dozen pages he'd covered at better than 4,000 wpm.

Evelyn had asked if anyone in the audience wanted to examine the book—a step in the procedure not mentioned by Spache or perhaps more recently instituted. Ehrlich raised his hand. He concluded that the young lawyer "had borrowed from the summary I found in the book jacket, had embellished this with some of his own thoughts and was warmly applauded." He found that the youth had also "turned the thesis of the book upside-down."

But Ehrlich had no chance to tell this to the audience. Evelyn had deftly moved on to the next demonstrator.

Evelyn did not appear at the next session that Ehrlich attended, in New York City. The only live people were sales prospects, watching a kinescope of the ABC news show that had catapulted Reading Dynamics to fame. Ehrlich wrote in his magazine article that many in the cosmopolitan gathering "tittered" as a "high-school lad," most likely Bob Darling, reported having read five thousand books in a year. Ehrlich pointed out that these volumes would require a bookshelf the length of a city block. Another high schooler's testimony also drew laughs, he reported.

But the giggles subsided as the tape continued playing. "There was no laughing off three United States senators," Ehrlich wrote. "Obviously these men honestly believed they could read that fast. But so did my engineering executives. The way their hands glided down the swiftly turned pages reminded me of playing a Ouija board. . . . Indeed, the whole speed-reading approach smacks of autosuggestion."

The efforts of Spache and Taylor paled next to this. The *Saturday Evening Post* reached some seven million readers, and the experiment with the mixed-up text was a stunt worthy of Evelyn herself. As before, a pawn moved to protect the queen. Someone who'd been disappointed by Ehrlich's methods but delighted by Evelyn's was found. This person typed a lengthy letter to the *Saturday Evening Post*. The magazine didn't include it in an assortment of four brief responses to Ehrlich's piece, two positive and two negative, that appeared on its Letter page four weeks later.

The unpublished defense of Evelyn shows how her promises played on American insecurities. The lament began, "I left Mr. Ehrlich's classroom 'by the same door wherein I went' . . . with a fatalistic sense that I was destined to read slowly, meticulously, and retentively the few books which I would be able to wade through in the next fifty years . . . always something of a cripple surrounded by the four-minute milers of the world of books, and always stung with envy."

It was an era of record setting. Americans celebrated as astronaut John Glenn orbited the Earth, but the USSR's Yuri Gagarin had done it first. An Associated Press story linked Evelyn's success to Cold War jitters. It quoted a psychiatrist who said, "People ask: 'Is Russia ahead? Or are we?' They don't know. . . . Reading becomes an area for improvement in seeing what is unknown. Some try speed reading for reasons of fear rather than a healthy interest in knowledge."

Fear and insecurity kept customers coming and institutes opening. In the professional community, however, Evelyn lost some of her fan base. Her company's tentacles were spreading into more college towns, threatening reputations and enrollment at university-based reading clinics. Some big shots on the reading conference circuit, like Nila Banton Smith, were questioning Evelyn's claims. Smith, director of the New York University Reading Clinic, told the *New York Times*, "The eye simply cannot see thousands of words a minute."

Academics who once lauded Evelyn's revolution were now more likely to consider it a theory. A paper presented by one of her admirers probably hurt more than it helped. A year after Ehrlich heard Evelyn speak at the College Reading Association, Bill Liddle spoke to the same group. At the University of Delaware, Evelyn's former colleague had been testing his own Reading Dynamics students and comparing them to a control group, still working on his dissertation.

Liddle's Wood-trained readers had scored significantly lower in comprehension than the control group when reading fiction. In nonfiction, he had not found significant differences between the groups. "This investigator is admittedly not an authority in the field of test construction," Liddle wrote of himself in his paper, and, indeed, his multiple-choice questions seem faulty—too focused on picayune details for fiction, and too easy to guess at in nonfiction. Still, he was a doctoral candidate at the University of Delaware and a former assistant school-district supervisor. He'd worked with Evelyn on a program to train other college faculty in teaching the Wood method. Liddle's name had been linked with Evelyn's in papers presented at conferences and published in journals, making his findings hard to ignore.

They could, however, be half ignored. Citing Liddle's findings, Evelyn wrote—accurately—that he'd found no difference between his experimental and control groups in the comprehension of nonfiction. She said nothing at all about fiction.

Evelyn used those redacted results to face Ehrlich in the ring. Some months after his article appeared in the *Saturday Evening Post*, the National Education Association's *NEA Journal* ran a double-page spread bannered, "Opinions Differ on Speed Reading." On the left was Evelyn's piece; on the right was one by her Columbia-based nemesis.

"There is no trickery or chicanery," wrote Evelyn, evidently on the defensive. Ehrlich pulled his punch a bit at the end. "Is there nothing then to speed reading? Is it a complete hoax? By no means," he wrote. However, in the non-hoax category he included only courses that promised modest gains, like his, as well as self-help techniques like vocabulary building. "No tricks, no secret formulas, no magic, no need for fantastic claims," he wrote.

Evelyn no longer wore the crown she'd won at the NEA's Atlantic City convention. Her name appeared side by side with Ehrlich's, as if they were on the same level. With the permission of the *NEA Journal*, his piece was subsequently reprinted—without hers—in newspapers like the *Quad-City Times* of Davenport, Iowa. And he'd effectively called her a scam artist.

To his question "Is it a hoax?" Ehrlich might have added, "Did Evelyn know it was a hoax?" The deft redaction of Liddle's results indicated she knew something was amiss. As we shall see, his continued work yielded even more damning results, ultimately shaking his faith in Evelyn's system. But it took years for Liddle to complete his dissertation, which was never published. At any rate, Evelyn's instructors were told that no comprehension test was valid.

Meanwhile enrollment was apparently falling below expectations. The Woods laid the blame on the subsidiaries. An item in the company newsletter, the *Evelyn Wood Reading Dynamiker*, tried to rouse them from lethargy. An item titled "Evelyn Goes West," announced that Evelyn, "our founder," would again swing through San Francisco and Los Angeles, as well as Denver. She and Bob were scheduled for media spots and demonstrations. Evelyn would travel anywhere, the item said, but subsidiaries had to lay the groundwork: "The next move is up to you."

In over their heads, the Woods needed someone to shake up the troops. In late summer, Evelyn returned from her jam-packed tour of the West, leaving Bob to finish his summer vacation with a Colorado friend. In the fall, he returned to high school for his senior year, and the Woods found their savior.

"We have a tremendous man working for us," Evelyn wrote Bob the following January. "I am so relieved to have him managing the business end." Writing to Bob on company letterhead, she'd crossed out the Arlington address of the corporate offices and replaced it with 4000 Massachusetts Ave. NW, the address of her Washington apartment.

It had taken a malignancy to keep Evelyn at home. In fact, even after diagnosis, she'd attempted to keep on going. A goiter had appeared on her neck. As the holidays approached in early November, she consulted a Washington doctor to show him the enlargement. She also complained of nervousness and swelling of the lymph glands. He advised surgery, but instead she proceeded with her plans to spend Thanksgiving with family in Salt Lake City.

She went but fell ill. Asserting that she hadn't even had a cold in seven or eight years, Evelyn still refused to believe that anything was seriously wrong with her. According to her self-diagnosis, the hiring of the manager gave her permission to let go. It was all related to her mission, the reading revolution. She told Bob, "After seeing what he could do, and knowing that we were going to be able to do what we set out to do, I relaxed and let the tiredness show through."

Her physician in Salt Lake City was not so sure. The Utah doctor "convinced me" to have the goiter out, Evelyn wrote her young correspondent, apparently still not entirely convinced of the necessity. She'd had the surgery in Washington shortly before Christmas, and recuperation was taking longer than expected. Almost a month post-op, she was still in bed most of the day.

"My throat has been so sore," she managed to type. "Everyone asks my husband how it feels to have a wife that can't talk. We get a big kick out of it. . . . I have very little energy. This too, is a change. I guess I was tired." Now that 1962 was over, she made an uncharacteristic confession. "Last year was a most difficult time for me," Evelyn acknowledged, although she couldn't help adding, "but we accomplished many things."

The girl from the Beehive State had stopped buzzing, at least temporarily. However, others were rushing in to pick up the slack, knocking one another over in the process.

7

Civil War

EVELYN WASN'T MISSING ANY ACTION at the corporate headquarters in Arlington, because it had closed. The "tremendous man" hired by the Woods was running the show from his own offices on Connecticut Avenue in Washington. Evelyn's postsurgical voice loss didn't make much difference. Neither she nor Doug had much of a say over business affairs anymore, and that suited them perfectly.

They made one last announcement: "We are very happy to inform you that our arrangements with the bank went through, and we now have a three-year program free of financial worries," the in-house bulletin informed all its far-flung branches.

That arrangement was most likely made not by Doug and Evelyn but by their consultant, George C. Webster, and a group of investors he'd assembled to take the company off the Woods' hands. In financial terms, these men aspired to become Evelyn Wood.

Evelyn's illness had convinced the Woods to shed the tension and worry. They were prepared to sell out, at a price described as thirty cents on the dollar. Any riches they'd dreamed of remained elusive, but Evelyn's fame was now incontrovertible: in Hy Gardner's syndicated gossip column about Hollywood and Broadway, her name occasionally appeared in bold type. She and Doug were making their exit "to stop the bleeding and have enough for their retirement," according to their grandson Stanton Davis.

However, there was one obstacle. Fred Babbel had always considered himself a cofounder of the business. Now he was just one of many sponsors, as the organization called its franchisees. Under Webster the company had become principally a franchising operation, and Babbel had licensed several Evelyn Wood branches in the Washington area. He'd been willing to do so while his old missionary friends, the Woods, were in charge, but he balked at sponsoring George Webster.

The two men immediately locked horns. Reading Dynamics franchising agreements had always included a noncompete clause banning former employees from the reading business for three years after the contract ended. Babbel, however, hadn't signed, perhaps because as cofounder, he was exempted. It's also possible that Doug Wood had overlooked this detail. Webster produced a pen and a deadline. As the investment group moved toward acquiring the firm, Webster wanted Babbel under his thumb or out of the picture.

The two men couldn't have been more different. Webster had a Harvard MBA, two law degrees, and membership in a Chevy Chase country club. The son of a successful Washington plumbing and heating contractor, he'd worked under his father before becoming a consultant. Before Evelyn Wood Reading Dynamics, Webster's biggest client had been his family's firm. His wife raised funds for the National Symphony, socializing with the wives of the bankers and lawyers whom Webster had convinced to invest in speed-reading.

Babbel was a self-made man with a hardscrabble upbringing. Second-eldest of nine children, he'd grown up in a two-bedroom house in Twin Falls, Idaho, sleeping with four brothers on a glassed-in porch. At age five he was a walking billboard, dressing in a miniature suit to advertise his father's tailoring business. Much of his education took place in the newsroom of the *Idaho Postman*, where, mentored by an editor, he advanced from paperboy to writer, learning grammar and typesetting along the way.

Two different routes had led the rivals to the same destination. Known for the organizational skills he'd demonstrated in his LDS church posts, Babbel, like Webster, had consulted to industry. Although not a native of Washington like his nemesis, Babbel had lived there so long that his and Webster's circles overlapped. It must have particularly galled Babbel that his co-religionist and former boss, Milton Barlow of the Marriott Corporation, was on Webster's investment team. Webster didn't share their faith.

All dissension was put aside in early 1963, when Babbel briefly became the face of Reading Dynamics and the focus of the press. His Washington institute had been contracted to teach a group of prominent senators inside the Capitol building. The House already had its on-site classroom, but Senators Talmadge and Bennett had previously failed to establish one in the upper chamber. Behind the latest successful effort was the company's most illustrious student to date: presidential sibling Edward M. Kennedy, just sworn in for his first term as Massachusetts senator.

Fascination with the Kennedys was at its height. Every movement made by young Ted generated media interest. From his days assisting Agriculture Secretary Ezra Taft Benson, Babbel knew how to craft quotable quotes. He informed a Pittsburgh paper that speed-reading helped politicians "confound the opposition," adding, "We've told the Democratic senators they'll be able to skin the pants off Republicans."

Ted Kennedy had recruited eight other senators of his party to the class, including George McGovern, Birch Bayh, and Abraham Ribicoff. Sessions were held near to the Senate chambers, allowing lawmakers to slip out for a quick vote. They were expected to practice on their own for an hour daily, perhaps speed-reading each other's bills and speeches, their teacher suggested. She was Elsie Carlson, who'd previously taught the bipartisan group that met in the House of Representatives.

"Not one of my students was defeated last fall," Carlson told a reporter.

Evelyn Wood Reading Dynamics had come to be viewed as a political tool, and Babbel deserved much of the credit. Classes continued in the House, taught by another of his employees. They met in an Agriculture Committee hearing room, undoubtedly secured through Babbel's connections. He'd brought Evelyn's method to both chambers of Congress, and the media was taking notice.

A newspaper editorial praised the younger Kennedy's bold initiative, albeit with a quibble:

> We can't quarrel with Senator Ted Kennedy's bid for leadership of this sort, since members of Congress do need some special reading talents to keep abreast of their homework and the day's news. It is significant, however, that he continues to follow so assiduously in the footsteps of his elder brother, the President, who was responsible more than anyone else for having started the rapid reading craze. . . .
>
> One wonders when he is going to strike out on his own.

Indeed, JFK didn't intend to leave his kid brother alone, at least when it came to doing homework. A taping system that the president had secretly installed in the White House captured a bit of fraternal scolding on that subject. A transcript of this phone conversation between the two Kennedys was only recently made available to the public:

JFK: How's your reading going ahead?
TED: Oh, well, I'm right after . . .
JFK: You reading more?
TED: What?
JFK: You reading more?
TED: I'm reading about, uh, 325 words so fast [JFK laughs] but now with about forty percent comprehension.
JFK: Have you speeded up?
TED: Uh, I really have. Yeah.
JFK: Have you? Have the others?
TED: Yeah. Everyone has.
JFK: Yeah.
TED: The problem was we had about a two-week break in there . . . where uh . . .
JFK: Yeah.
TED: . . .where we went back.
JFK: You got to go back, don't you? It's like doing push-ups, you know, you have to keep doing 'em every day.
TED: But it's, it's really helpful.

JFK: There's no magic, though, is there?
TED: No, it's just a matter of going right down that . . .
JFK: Page . . .
TED: . . . page on the right . . .
JFK: . . . and hanging on every minute . . .
TED: Yeah.
JFK: . . . and just keeping your mind on it.

Convinced that speed-reading was a matter of putting one's shoulder to the wheel, the president sided with the system over the senator. No teacher could have asked for more support from an older family member. As it happened, Ted's instructor would eventually start her own company, snagging government contracts and becoming a significant player in the Washington speed-reading market, at least for a short while.

That type of competition was precisely what Webster sought to avoid by tightening his vise on the franchises. Carlson never promised not to compete with Evelyn Wood Reading Dynamics. Babbel wouldn't sign Webster's agreement, and he advised Carlson and his other employees not to sign either. Webster was determined to bring Babbel to heel.

Some reading professionals believed Reading Dynamics's hasty expansion was spurred by fear that others would "steal" Evelyn's method. It wasn't necessarily *Evelyn's* method to Babbel, who'd nurtured it from the start. Indeed, though all course texts were supposed to be purchased from the parent company, Babbel wrote his own materials and copyrighted them under Frederick W. Babbel & Associates, the entity that owned his franchises. With titles like *Rapid Reading Course: Instructor's Manual*, these books made no reference to Reading Dynamics or Evelyn Wood. As Webster clamored for his signature, Babbel's publishing efforts reached fever pitch. In June and July of 1963, he registered twelve separate volumes of homework activities with the Library of Congress. No prison break was more elaborately planned.

As summer arrived, Evelyn rose from her sickbed to stand again behind the footlights. She had her voice back, and she was using it, demonstrating at the annual meeting of the American Society of Newspaper Editors. The editor of Washington's *Evening Star* hosted the demo, suggesting that "supersonic reading" might encourage newspaper consumption. Bob Darling came down from Princeton for the event, sharing the stage with an impressive addition to Evelyn's stable. Her new demonstrator was no excitable adolescent prone to literature-induced nightmares. He was Dr. Floyd E. Bloom, a twenty-six-year-old researcher for the National Institutes of Health with a medical degree.

More challenging than the usual demo, this one required both men to read the same 3,000-word piece in ninety seconds. According to the *Evening Star*, neither "quite finished" before offering a summary, meaning that Bob had slowed his usual breakneck pace. Not content with Evelyn's customary selection of books from a box, the editors most likely had copies of the piece in their hands. Still, the *Star* indicated there had been general satisfaction with the summaries. A tinge of skepticism crept into questions about whether rapid reading captured "the beauty of the English language," but predictably, Bob issued assurances.

The UPI wire service reported the presence of "Mrs. Evelyn Wood" at the event while skipping the details about the demo. The report characterized it as "shop talk," in the same category as a lighthearted mock debate about whether newspaper culture critics should be launched into orbit. Evelyn and her young men were just opening acts before the main event: an address to the organization by President John F. Kennedy about steel price hikes and the nation's economy.

The skeptics hadn't sunk Evelyn yet, or even made much of a dent. She was booked through July for reading conferences in Rhode Island and New Jersey. In August, she'd make her first trip to Hawaii, where a Honolulu woman named Hilda Takeyama was introducing Reading Dynamics to the islands. While recovering from surgery in Michigan, Takeyama had met Evelyn and promptly bought a franchise. Announcing Evelyn's upcoming demonstrations to educators, business groups, and the military, a Honolulu paper ran a picture of a slim, beaming Evelyn with Senator Daniel K. Inouye of Hawaii, a recent Evelyn Wood graduate. Although a caption described the senator as Evelyn's "pupil," the two might never have met before the photo was taken. As a classmate of Ted Kennedy's, Inouye had been taught by Babbel's choice of instructor, Elsie Carlson.

With Webster's new sales expectations in place, the sponsors seem to have awakened from their slumbers. Financial responsibilities were clarified. There was no charge for Evelyn's time, but sponsors had to cover her local expenses. She no longer had to beg for bookings. First come, first served, warned the company bulletin.

The deadline for Babbel's signature was set for the fall of 1963. But the date passed, and the line was still blank. By this time, Evelyn and Doug had moved back to Utah, leaving things in Webster's hands. Evelyn's mother put them up at her apartment while they looked for their own place and relaxed at their cabin canyon. They were gone fishing—until a letter arrived from their lawyer. It warned that hostilities between Babbel and Webster could endanger the impending sale of the company, which had yet to be formalized.

The lawyer warned that Babbel and his allies "have been telling some pretty wild stories about George Webster throughout the country," and "George is ready to sue them for slander if he can get sufficient proof."

The letter writer was Ronald E. Madsen, the attorney who'd threatened University of Florida professor George Spache with a libel lawsuit. More recently, the politically wired attorney had backed the unsuccessful bid of the University of Utah's far-right president, Ernest L. Wilkinson, for a seat in Congress. Now he was issuing a wake-up call to Doug and Evelyn, urging them to find a third director for their company, as legally required, and schedule a shareholders meeting to approve the sale.

"Hope you catch a big one," Madsen wrote the vacationing Woods, assuring them he'd reel Babbel in. However, he said it might not be easy. Babbel, he wrote, "has an attorney, and we are working on it."

Despite the cheery valediction and mostly confident tone, the letter was unsettling. It suggested that Babbel could sour the deal with Webster even though he had little voting power. The Woods had recently convinced another partner, Mac McEachern, to sell them his shares. Owing heavily to the Woods, among other creditors, McEachern eagerly agreed to wipe the slate clean with stock instead of cash. The Woods' stake was greater than ever.

Still, it was possible that Babbel would file a minority shareholder's lawsuit. Were that to happen, Madsen recommended suing Babbel for breach of contract and terminating his franchise. "Quite frankly, this is something I did not think he would do," wrote Madsen, slipping from cautious legal syntax into the familiar. "Even [if] we terminate Fred's franchise contract, it may be possible for him to go into direct competition with Reading Dynamics here in Washington. I don't think he could do it without Reading Dynamics' name and publicity; I think he is dead."

Still, Babbel wouldn't roll over. Armed with his own manuals and volumes of homework assignments, he prepared to strike out on his own. Ads appeared in the *Washington Post* for "Evelyn Wood Reading Dynamics, sponsored by Frederick W. Babbel & Associates Inc." In those few inches of newsprint, at least, he and Evelyn were on nearly equal footing. In another section of the paper, a legal notice signed by "Evelyn Wood, secretary" announced a special meeting of the stockholders of Evelyn Wood Reading Dynamics Institutes of America in April 1964 to decide whether to dissolve the company. As required, the Woods had found a third director. He was someone with no prior connection with the company, who'd presumably agreed to raise his hand with theirs.

Fred Babbel might have been braced to watch the company change hands, but he wasn't ready to give up speed-reading. The father of five had nearly sacrificed one child to the cause. Tracing her own route to success, Evelyn had told a reporter of staging her first demonstrations in Washington "with the help of a friend's teen-age daughter, taught during odd hours." That was Bonnie Babbel, who today still believes she'd reached the speed of 60,000 words per minute, a record beaten by a medical student "who cheated," tearing his own book apart and mounting pages on the wall so he didn't have to turn them.

Her family's immersion in the method continued after hours. Bonnie said that about a month after her supercharged reading of *The Count of Monte Cristo* she woke up laughing and crying. "When you speed-read it's like a movie, the emotions don't surface until later." That was not an uncommon view of how the method worked. Mulling how

Wood-trained readers could appreciate Jean Kerr's bestselling humor book, *Please Don't Eat the Daisies*, a reporter wrote, "Read now, laugh later, say the experts." But after Bonnie's nocturnal outburst, her parents halted her demonstrations. "They got scared," she recalled.

Fred and June Babbel were having a new home built, facing this considerable expense just as Webster issued his nonnegotiable orders. Clearly, the Woods had abandoned Fred Babbel, the old friend who'd eased them into their jobs at the Frankfurt mission, delivered gifts to their families in Salt Lake City, and taken Doug's parents out for a spin. The "fine boy" with the "sweet personality," as Doug had described him, was evidently expendable.

The directors' meeting was held in Washington, but the Woods didn't have to attend. Their lawyer had assured them they could cast their votes by proxy. There were 223 shares outstanding at the time, and the vote for dissolution passed, 184–0. By that time, Babbel might have sold his stock to the Woods, or perhaps his were the missing votes.

Evelyn Wood Reading Dynamics was reborn as a subsidiary of Webster's investment group, called DEAR for Diversified Education and Research Corp. Despite the name, it had formed for the sole purpose of acquiring Evelyn Wood and would never diversify beyond that.

There's no way to know how much money the Woods made from this transaction between two private companies. Beyond their gains from the sale, Evelyn became a consultant to the national company with a guaranteed monthly paycheck of $1,000. In all likelihood, she was guaranteed that amount, $12,000 annually, for just sixty days of work per year. Her first consulting contract has not been preserved in its entirety, but the sixty-day limit on her time appeared in subsequent versions of her consulting contract and seems to date from the initial one. In the first months after the sale of the company, Evelyn made only a few appearances on behalf of the company, including one at New York's Biltmore Hotel and another at a Holiday Inn in Newark, New Jersey.

The Woods were also granted lifetime rights to the Utah-Idaho franchise, royalty free and not subject to sales or transfer. It was a sweetheart deal. Evelyn Wood branches graced places like Carroll, Iowa, and

Corsicana, Texas. Yet Utah, with its prosperity and large universities, lay fallow. The Woods' first institute, in Doug's old appliance store, directed for a while under their chosen successor, had long since closed. They'd never licensed a subsidiary or franchise in their home state, likely saving it for themselves.

This time, they wouldn't need to run classes amid ironing machines and dishwashers. If the sale of the company hadn't left them rich, they were surely comfortable. Moreover, the lifetime contract granted them freedoms unavailable to other franchisees. Now a director and company president, Webster was guiding with an iron hand.

The licensing agreement he crafted for DEAR eventually became a model for the franchising business, booming since the end of World War II. The contract would be published by a respected business-research group, the Conference Board, and reprinted for decades in business textbooks with dollar amounts and percentages redacted. It was a masterful document, airtight for the licensor and stifling for the licensee.

As spelled out in the Evelyn Wood agreement, the franchisee, or sponsor, was responsible for nearly all expenses involved in offering the reading courses, including renting facilities, hiring teachers and staff, and advertising. The parent company provided teacher training, textbooks, plus "information," "assistance," and "advice" on running the business. Most valuable of all, it provided the Evelyn Wood and Reading Dynamics trademarks, registered separately. In truth, that's why the franchisees signed on. They were buying the right to use Evelyn's name.

In addition to franchise fees, sponsors paid the parent company a royalty for each student enrolled. Royalty terms would change over the years, and with these changes came additional promotional pressures. Franchises failing to meet specific sales targets could face termination.

The Woods' lawyer, Madsen, apparently made good on his threats. Even before the Woods held the shareholder meeting, an ad appeared in the *Washington Post* for a new enterprise called Reading Inc. Promising to triple reading speeds, its address was the same Sheraton Building office where Frederick W. Babbel & Associates had previously sponsored an Evelyn Wood institute. His link to the famous name was over, yet he stayed in the same coveted real estate, probably unable to get out of the lease.

As if sensing that "Reading Inc." was a less than scintillating name, Babbel described his as the "Conceptual-Visual Method." His small ads included a slogan, Knowledge Is Power, suspiciously like the Evelyn Wood Reading Dynamics trademarked motto, Knowledge Through Reading. It also followed its mammoth competitor's example in providing a photo of its founder. But Fred Babbel, unlike Evelyn, didn't have a face known to millions, nor could he claim the Danish queen and Madame Nehru as pupils.

Babbel was truly a lone wolf now, having shed even the "associates" of his franchise. One of them might have been Elsie Carlson, the teacher who started her own business after teaching in both wings of the Capitol. She hired teachers and ran operations from a small office in Arlington, perhaps within her home. Interviewed there by the *Washington Post*, she didn't refer to the senators and representatives she'd taught, nor did Babbel in his advertising. The licensing agreement prohibited former sponsors from deriving commercial advantage from their Evelyn Wood pasts. Babbel and his former associates might have been advised by their own lawyers to tread cautiously on that ground.

While Babbel promoted his Conceptual-Visual system, Carlson dubbed hers Vicore, short for visual-conceptual reading. A mother of two, Carlson boasted to the *Post* of overseeing twenty teachers. Carlson's company thrived at least into the early 1970s, landing contracts from the local government and becoming the second-largest provider—after Evelyn Wood—of reading-improvement courses in the DC area. However, neither her system nor Babbel's ever posed a serious threat to the Evelyn Wood juggernaut.

The last *Post* ad for Babbel's Reading Inc. ran in May 1964. His son, David F. Babbel, said his father was left in debt to various creditors, including the *Post*. As David heard it, these debts had been run up by the Woods—although perhaps it was the partnership—but his father settled them, partly with proceeds from the sale of the other franchises he'd owned in the Washington area. The son said Babbel's next job was at a cosmetics company, and some of his salary there went toward wiping out Evelyn Wood debt.

David's sister Bonnie recalled that the new house her family had hoped for was never built. Lacking funds to complete it, her father ordered construction stopped. Evelyn had once advised Fred Babbel to change some of his habits that she thought were holding him back. As it turned out, she had quite an effect on him.

8

Consulting the Oracle

EVELYN'S FIRST DEMONSTRATOR was old enough for college now. Bonnie Babbel left Washington for Brigham Young University to study broadcasting. With her father, Fred, reeling from the Washington franchise mess, she knew she'd have to work at school. Bonnie the Magician appeared on a Utah TV show for kids, with other characters called Carrot Top and Uncle Wagwinkle. She was a pro now; Evelyn had always known how to spot talent.

George Webster and his partners were performing some magic too. Working out of a national franchise office in New York, Webster kept a sharp eye on the sponsors and their sales quotas. Nonperformers were out, replaced by new ones likely to meet their sales quotas. With DEAR in charge, Evelyn Wood Reading Dynamics conquered new territory in the West. Branches sprouted over Northern and Southern California, and Colorado was opening new sites to accommodate record enrollments.

Elsewhere, new blood replaced dead wood. Webster lured a Lutheran pastor from his church and sent him to reinvigorate Cincinnati, Columbus, Indianapolis, Louisville. There were now ten institutes across the breadth of Canada and groundwork for more in Japan, Australia, and South America.

In newspapers and on the radio, the name Evelyn Wood became inescapable. Full-page newspaper ads—resembling news pages, with columns and headlines—recounted the origins of Evelyn's "discovery." The four senatorial endorsements had been trimmed to two: Proxmire and Talmadge. Readers were again told that the late John F. Kennedy had brought in Evelyn to teach (depending on the version) his top aides, his joint chiefs, or his top administrative aides. A mock op-ed about the importance of speed-reading to democracy was bylined with the name of the local sponsor, and a "feature" reported the exceptional reading gains made by a graduate of the nearest institute.

Invariably, the ads included a photo of Evelyn, head tilted to the side as if listening. Appearing less often in public under the consulting arrangement, she was slipping into mythical status, like the fictitious Betty Crocker.

But there was a brand-new element too. As directed by DEAR, all ads prominently displayed a money-back guarantee to students who failed to at least triple their reading rate—provided they'd attended all classes and done all homework.

Evelyn and Doug were in no rush to open their Utah franchise. Their move back to the West had brought them closer to Tucson, where Carol and Ray had a new baby, Stanton. But "Mimi" and Grandpa, as they were known to their grandchildren, were still wrapped up in work. Stanton would remember Mimi as a "busy, busy businesswoman, at a time when there weren't many." After the sale of the business, the Woods spent nearly a year living out of suitcases, much of that in California. Webster placed Evelyn on a special assignment to develop new lesson plans, while Doug was contracted to help a new sponsor grow business in Southern California. Doug himself bought the Orange County franchise and its sole reading institute in Tustin.

The couple rented temporary quarters in Los Angeles, near the Evelyn Wood Reading Dynamics institute on Wilshire Boulevard. They chose the Towne House apartments, a sleek new luxury building with balconies, sundecks, Formica counters, and subterranean parking. "East Meets West" was its developer's slogan, promising a combination of Eastern efficiency and relaxed Western living.

East and West also met at an Evelyn Wood Reading Dynamics conference in Washington called to address instructional problems. Held in the Shoreham Hotel, it was billed as a teacher training meeting. Evelyn and Doug flew in and hosted welcome sessions. Evelyn's name was emblazoned on every pen and handout, but Webster set the tone. He said he wasn't qualified to evaluate instructional methods, but he did know this much: the company had to come up with a product that produced better word of mouth.

Enrollment problems were evidently brewing at the older institutes in the East. Webster laid the blame on lesson plans that had been "patch-worked by various people" over the years. He said results had been better in places like Denver, Phoenix, San Francisco, L.A., and Hawaii. The company president said he looked at results "not from a speed standpoint because that is not my interest. My interest is, how many referrals do we get? How many people are satisfied?"

Webster's remarks revealed nary a trace of doubt about the product or its inventor. Evelyn, he said, had been working "day and night" on creating new lessons. But it couldn't have escaped his notice that skepticism was settling like a cloud on the older eastern institutes and would inevitably move west. Behind the scenes, DEAR was exploring new options, including a promising new test-prep method developed by a Brooklyn man named Stanley H. Kaplan.

Webster then relinquished the floor to DEAR's new educational director, Dan Theodocion, a former Evelyn Wood instructor. The brawny Theodocion had played football for Georgia Tech. But he'd never encountered as much resistance on the field as in a Nashville classroom, where he'd assigned a book on evolution for speed-reading. With that anecdote as a springboard, Theodocion opened the floor to comments.

The purpose of the meeting was to help Evelyn develop a national lesson plan. Scheduled to meet later with smaller groups, Evelyn stepped out of the room. This probably came as a great relief to many in the gathering: in accordance with the Mormon Word of Wisdom, Evelyn prohibited smoking at meetings where she was present. In her absence, attendees unleashed a litany of grievances, which were audiotaped, tran-scribed, and given to Evelyn. It's possible that not all the participants knew they were being taped. In startlingly frank terms, sponsors and company educators exposed their frustrations about "the skill," as the method was sometimes called.

An employee named Jackie Horner Colson said Chicago had had "some rather black years" since 1961, when she joined the company. She said staff there had to deal with constant criticism from the city's many colleges and universities. "Professors will simply get on the phone, and say, 'Your course shouldn't be allowed to operate because you don't do this and this and this." She'd found she could stop the callers in their tracks by informing them that Evelyn Wood Reading Dynamics did, in fact, have a testing program.

But did it? Testing at Evelyn Wood reading centers was often based on subjectively scored "tellbacks"—students orally recalling what they'd read to partners or a teacher—or essays. The institutes also made liberal use of fill-in-the-blank diagrams, often in fishbone or pyramid patterns. Now known as graphic organizers, these asked students to categorize whatever they remembered. A line to be labeled with a character's name, for instance, might branch out to other lines for descriptors.

The transcript of the conference made clear that testing was left to the individual institutes. "You don't want a test that will discourage them," said the teacher trainer for New York, referring to tests suggesting that speed gains came at the cost of comprehension. One major sponsor proposed leaving it up to self-evaluation. "A man can tell you how well he is reading by using his own set of values and saying, 'I am reading great, I am reading well, I am not getting it,'" he said. Theodocion rejected the suggestion, noting that after a lifetime of schooling, consumers wanted a numerical score. The days of autosuggestion, which had worked so well with the senators, was over.

But Evelyn hadn't changed much. Three years earlier, she'd opposed testing in a paper presented at the University of Delaware. She'd taken the same stand in writing the teacher's manual. At the Washington no-holds-barred session, she'd delegated one of the sponsors, her coreligionist Howard Ruff, to speak for her.

"There is no good test of comprehension," Ruff said, adding that no test measured the ability to connect the beginning and end of a lengthy text—something a fast reader might do better than a slow reader. He said the University of Southern California's psychology department was eager to research this. The university, he said—delivering a message from Evelyn to DEAR—was "just waiting for someone to advance the money."

Promising that research would be done, Theodocion noted that a standard test would need to reflect standard materials. But reading tastes had changed over the years, and, lacking direction from the parent company, sponsors had chosen their own texts. The juvenile novel *Old Yeller* was too corny for New York, which replaced it with *The Stranger* by Camus. Another institute ditched *Goodbye, Mr. Chips* and *The Old Man and the Sea* because everyone had seen the movie versions. Theodocion asked everyone to send him their tests, perhaps hoping to somehow cobble them together.

Perhaps the most sobering comments in the session came from the University of Delaware, where Evelyn had become an assistant professor despite her lack of a doctorate. Russell Stauffer, still praising Evelyn in academic circles, was not at this commercial conference. Nor was the disenchanted grad student Bill Liddle, finally nearing completion of a dissertation that would refute Evelyn's claims, at least in regard to reading fiction. However, another Evelyn—Evelyn Dew, supervisor of the university's speed-reading program—was present.

Dew taught a credit-bearing course that combined "Wood Dynamic" instruction, as it was called on campus, with a list of required books on which to apply it. Having surveyed students who'd completed the elective, she had unsettling news. Of seventy polled, only ten reported that they used the method to a great extent. The largest number, forty, said they used it sometimes but with varying enthusiasm. In that group, and of the ten reporting nearly no use, many said they didn't feel confident that they could actually apply the method.

Some lukewarm students thought the method had great "potential" and was "a great tool," but that they'd only use it "if pushed." One who seldom or never used it blamed himself for lack of practice.

Dew said Theodocion had given her carte blanche to report her findings, and the sponsors listened, rapt, allowing her to talk past the start of the lunch break. Unlike the other conference participants, Dew was not a company employee, and she was telling hard truths.

Evelyn Dew was one of the people most responsible for Evelyn Wood's quick ascent on the academic ladder. Her husband, Walter, a DuPont executive, had emerged starry-eyed from an early Reading Dynamics class hosted by the Wilmington sales executive club. Possibly at Walter Dew's suggestion, University of Delaware president John A. Perkins had appointed Evelyn to the faculty. Walt Dew was in charge of DuPont's corporate giving to nonprofits, including universities.

A year later, Walt and Evelyn Dew had lauded the Wood method at the reading conference held on the U of D campus. Now the bloom was off the rose.

But none of this truly threatened DEAR's business model or the Woods' plans. With Stauffer bearing the torch, Evelyn could slip away from the halls of academe and their reading confabs. Any traveling for DEAR was to launch new institutes or shore up tottering ones, not to present papers. Moreover, the results of the University of Delaware survey could hardly have come as a shock to them. Self-recrimination and belief in the system's potential—for someone else—prevented the disillusioned from seeking refunds. Conditions attached to the guarantee were another deterrent. Consumers of the era had few places to turn other than Better Business Bureaus.

As for those reporting they lacked the confidence to use the Wood system, its creator had a ready answer. As Evelyn told a student who expressed doubt that she could speed-read, "Young lady, if there is any doubt in your mind about ultimate success, I promise you that you will fail. You must have perfect confidence in yourself." The student manual put it in capital letters: "You must have a desire to try and the WILL to succeed."

This was eerily similar to themes in the Broadway show *The Music Man*, released in a movie version around the same time that Evelyn wrote her manual. The story follows a salesman promoting the "Think System" of music education. Parents buy the lessons, persuaded that their children can learn to play an instrument by "thinking" the notes. It was a well-known work, about a salesman who was clearly a con artist.

But the franchisees responded well to Evelyn's faith-based system. The major ones had organized into a sponsors' council led by Howard

Ruff, a franchisee who was also a Mormon. The sponsors rallied around Evelyn, insisting on a wider role for her, while rebelling at the financial demands of Webster and his executive committee. While collecting a 10 percent royalty, DEAR had allowed sponsors to raise the cost of the course to $175 from $150. Those choosing not to raise prices were nevertheless responsible for paying a royalty of $17.50 per course sold.

Alarmed, the sponsors council wrote to Webster, arguing that an increase not based on percentage violated the franchising agreement and, perhaps—as their lawyer had suggested—antitrust laws. Webster, however, did not back down.

Other grievances presented by the sponsors council demonstrated their high regard for Evelyn. They asked Webster to free her from most of her promotional responsibilities, so she could devote more time to "research and development of the Wood method," and visit any institute requesting her presence "for the inspiration of teachers."

The franchisees were clearly concerned about teacher quality, also asking that Evelyn organize a cadre of skilled teacher trainers who could fly around the country. In their eyes, any consumer dissatisfaction sprang from teacher inadequacy. The method and its creator were blameless.

Evelyn hadn't lost her touch since those days at the Frankfurt mission when she'd enchanted the young missionaries. The sponsors ranged from Robert Boles of Missouri, a teacher who'd once had reading problems, to Arthur C. Kramer of Pennsylvania, the owner of a company called the Lyceum, which operated institutes in Philadelphia and New York City and was valued by a potential suitor—at least for a while—at nearly $1 million. Kramer listened intently while Dew presented the survey results from the University of Delaware, urging her to continue speaking through part of the lunch hour. Still, his faith in Evelyn remained unshaken. His signature was on the sponsors' council letter asking that she spend more time with teachers.

That letter also asked Webster not to collect royalties for refunded sales. In public pronouncements and in advertising franchise opportunities, the company said that less than 2 percent of sales were refunded. By raising the topic in their letter, the sponsors seemed to regard refunds as more of an issue.

Despite Webster's disappointment with word of mouth, enrollment was growing. If referrals were lacking, advertising could pick up the slack—expensive as it was—or sponsors could plunge into new markets. The faux news articles in the full-page ads announced record enrollments in places like Denver and Northern California, where many institutes were less than a year old. College towns like Colorado Springs were a favorite market. Campus newspapers and radio stations offered relatively low ad rates, and where else did people have to do such heavy reading?

With Bob Darling retired from the demonstration circuit and Evelyn's promotional schedule pared down, the company increasingly relied on the filmed news and game shows. In Ramada and Holiday Inns around the country, footage from *I've Got a Secret* and *Art Linkletter's House Party* still rolled, along with the senators' testimonials. But even in parts of the country not gripped by anti–Vietnam War protests, hairstyles and skirt lengths had changed. In Austin, Texas, a new Evelyn Wood Reading Dynamics demonstrator claimed to have read *War and Peace* in eighteen minutes. Among the irreverent, such statements would eventually invite ridicule.

Still, there was plenty of business to tap. The corporate sector remained robust. Ad copy shared by the sponsors listed the major corporations that had run Evelyn Wood classes, at least in the past, like International Paper, Bendix, Boeing, General Electric, and IBM.

Despite the burgeoning counterculture movement, office life was still cutthroat. In California, Howard Ruff exploited the fear factor. "Has the New Man Already Tried Out Your Desk?" was the headline over a warning that "your promotion potential" requires keeping up with all the reading about new developments. A small photo of Ruff's head floated over the copy, replete with masculine pronouns and references to businessmen. An image of Evelyn was nowhere to be found.

In early 1966 it was Doug Wood's turn for a picture in the paper. He appeared in an ad for the two institutes that he and Evelyn were opening, in Provo and Salt Lake City. Before taking the leap, Doug had spent some time as a salesman for a firm specializing in butchers' supplies, perhaps ambivalent about going into business again. The Woods had rerooted in Salt Lake City, buying a house at 1812 Harrison Avenue in the Wasatch Hollow neighborhood. It was hip-roofed, like the house they'd bought after returning from Germany with their children. Anna still lived nearby with her husband and four children, but her adoptive parents had only a few brushes with them.

The Salt Lake City franchise soon moved from rented quarters to a small office building not far from their home. Here, the Woods were their own landlords. They'd leased the space as a partnership, then rented it to their corporation. Their franchise sites were ideally situated near college communities, Brigham Young University in Provo and their own alma mater in Salt Lake City.

But the U had changed in their absence. The students who'd queued up for Evelyn's Speech 21 class were gone, replaced by less reverent youths. The campus newspaper, the *Daily Utah Chronicle*, was a prime beneficiary of the Woods' return to Salt Lake City. But as Evelyn Wood ads became a fixture in the *Chronicle*, her name drew laughter—and fire—in the news pages.

Less than a year after the Salt Lake City institute opened, the *Chronicle* ran a scathing indictment of Evelyn Wood Reading Dynamics on its front page. Announcing his intention to debunk the "unbelievable" claims made in Evelyn Wood ads that had run in the *Chronicle*, a staffer cited the alleged results of an undercover 1961 investigation into Evelyn Wood Reading Dynamics by two representatives of an unnamed "major automobile manufacturer," one of whom was a reading expert. The two were said to have enrolled surreptitiously in an Evelyn Wood course. In a brief note, the newspaper editor clarified that this had occurred somewhere other than in Utah.

These industrial spies had allegedly discovered fraudulent measures of reading speed and comprehension, designed to give students an inflated idea of their progress. A test timed for three minutes actually lasted four minutes and ten seconds, the article claimed, and students were told that a book averaged 375 words per page when the actual count was 250, producing a distorted picture of rate gains. Another finding, according to the piece, is that comprehension tests were based mostly on material covered in untimed "previews." Not unsurprisingly, the carmaker decided not to offer or sponsor the course, or so the *Chronicle* reported.

By journalistic standards, it was a weak effort. The name and location of the auto manufacturer weren't specified, but there was no explanation for this. Were these details unknown to the reporter, or was he told them on the condition of confidentiality? If the latter, then how had the *Chronicle* obtained the information? Appearing out of nowhere, five years after the alleged events, the report could have been fabricated.

Evelyn's response, however, made it seem credible. Five days later, the *Chronicle* allocated its entire letters to the editor space to her lengthy rebuttal. Headlined "Charges Untrue, Says Evelyn Wood," her attack would have been convincing if focused on editorial issues. Instead, she faulted the piece for covering events that happened five years earlier and, she stressed in boldface, "in a **different area**." This suggested that an automobile manufacturer had indeed sent investigators to an Evelyn Wood course—albeit not one run by her franchise—where they'd discovered bogus testing practices. It was a startling confirmation, but Evelyn swiftly countered with other evaluations of her method. She quoted Proxmire, flashed her University of Delaware credentials, and cited page numbers of books by academics who'd mentioned her work favorably.

Her letter ended with the company's most powerful weapon, the you-can't-argue-with-success defense. Since the Evelyn Wood method's "humble beginnings" in Salt Lake City, she wrote, it had trained three hundred thousand people at 61 large institutes and 150 smaller ones, recently tripling enrollments over the previous year. Case closed.

The business press would later adjust some of Evelyn's numbers. By 150 "small institutes," she seemed to be counting—and inflating—temporary workplace classrooms, and the claim of tripling enrollment was exaggerated. She may have also inflated the alumni count: company stationery was headed "Over 250,000 graduates," not 300,000. Without a doubt, though, the number was growing. By November of that year ads would boast 350,000.

Evelyn didn't have the last word. Another letter writer expressed astonishment that Evelyn herself had bothered to comment on vague and stale allegations. But the Woods continued with their heavy buys in the *Chronicle*, taking out full-page ads as if nothing had ever happened. Occasionally, other letter writers or columnists made snide comments about Evelyn Wood, but only to deplore the relentless advertising.

She was a battleship, easily absorbing the blows. At any rate, the *Chronicle* was invisible outside the University of Utah. Soon she was being interviewed by *Newsday*, widely read in Long Island, New York. Two institutes were opening there, and Evelyn had been summoned to help.

"I've been called a charlatan," Evelyn calmly told *Newsday*. Whatever image that conjured in the reader's mind, Evelyn probably didn't square with it. Photographed near a pile of books, she wore a large brooch—a fashion signature of hers—on a smart one-button jacket. In predominantly white, middle-class Long Island, she was eminently relatable.

In a departure from custom, Evelyn talked about the importance of previewing a book, which the reporter interpreted as "scanning it to get the gist" before plunging into reading. Preferring to call it "organizing," Evelyn said, "I spent twenty minutes organizing *Dr. Zhivago*, then I read it in twenty minutes." This new twist to Evelyn's spiel was clearly a response to detractors who'd characterized the previews as cheating.

With references to the senators and Kennedy growing stale, Evelyn had a new name—or, at least, a hint—to drop. She'd recently told the press of giving evening lessons to a "certain movie star" and his girl-friend after teaching the star's wife earlier in the day. This could have been a coy reference to Burt Lancaster. According to her grandson Stanton, Evelyn had no high opinion of Lancaster and enjoyed irritating him by repeatedly calling him "Bart." Apparently, she also liked spreading thinly veiled gossip about a celebrity customer, who might have asked for her discretion. While her franchise demanded that students, as well as teachers, sign nondisclosure agreements, Evelyn evidently thought herself above such strictures.

Meanwhile, the stockholders of DEAR had taken the company as far as they wanted to go. In February 1967 they voted to put it on the block. The financial press described DEAR as owned by eleven investors, most based in Washington.

Corporate filings show that Webster's partners included bankers, businessmen, and members of white-shoe law firms. Henry K. Willard II, a Morgan Guaranty vice president who socialized with Richard Nixon, was a director.

The directors also included the franchisee Howard Ruff. In his updates to other members of the sponsor's council, Ruff had indicated that some franchisees hoped to buy the company. Now he had a stake. Another DEAR partner was the banker George M. Ferris Jr., Evelyn's defender in the flap involving *Salesweek*, the courses in Wilmington, and the Harvard Business School. As evidenced in her recent newspaper interview, Evelyn hadn't forgotten George Gibson, the man who first called her a charlatan, albeit obliquely.

Evelyn's name was being tarnished at Harvard again, this time in a student newspaper. The *Harvard Crimson* ran a three-part series written by Jeffrey C. Alexander, a senior. This was student journalism for the Ivy League—clear, polished, and professional. The first two parts traced the history of the speed-reading industry and Evelyn's disruption of its norms. In fairness, Alexander observed that Evelyn's critics ran courses of their own and had much to lose if her theories proved correct. But the final installment summed up the message for consumers: "Most Just Waste the Money."

The *Crimson* described the decor at the Evelyn Wood institute in Boston's Back Bay: "Subdued colors. Thick carpets. Soft lighting. Pretty secretaries." A framed portrait of Evelyn hung in every classroom. Institute director John Kilgo sat for an interview, in which he mentioned that 95 percent of his customers "could, sooner or later, read more than 2,000 words per minute," but that "people who are conscientious enough to stick it out long enough are rare."

With so many consumers failing to learn the skill in eight weeks, as the ads promised, why were so few refunds given? The *Crimson* provided further details of fraudulent testing practices. Because indexes measuring progress multiplied reading rate by comprehension score, a loss in comprehension accompanied by a big boost in speed would seem like an overall gain. In Connecticut, a Yale graduate student was suing a Bridgeport institute claiming, among other things, that his entrance test was more difficult than the one he took on exiting.

The Yale student eventually settled his claim with the institute, whose records showed he'd missed a class or two. He was not alone. Kilgo told the *Crimson* that the course had shortened to eight weeks from ten because a flood of enrollees were leaving before the end. Now the average student attended only five of the eight sessions, the *Crimson* alleged without citing a source for that data.

The Harvard undergraduate left unclear whether he'd ever seen Evelyn in person. He said she had a "motherly smile" and was "deeply religious." Regarding that side of Evelyn, Kilgo told the *Crimson* that the company no longer encouraged talk of "breakthroughs," although Kilgo claimed to have had one himself. "My vision blurred and suddenly I could see the entire page in one glance," said the institute director, using almost precisely the same words attributed to "an executive" in the influential *Family Weekly* piece published six years before. The implication then was that the quote came from a student, not a franchisee.

Kilgo, who had done himself no favors in the interview, wrote a letter to the *Crimson* after the series ran, calling it erroneous and biased. His response lacked the clarity and panache of the *Crimson* piece, though he cleverly turned one passage to his advantage. Referring to speed-readers, the undergraduate had written, "They are everywhere. Walk into Lamont [Library] and you see three of four of them, hands tracing large 'S' patterns with their fingers down the pages. And there are many more to come."

Quoting the reporter's words back to him, Kilgo rested his case.

But, for all its prestige, the *Crimson* was just a campus newspaper. Copies may have reached Wall Street decision makers with Harvard ties from time to time. However, the student journalist's astute, thorough, and entertaining muckraking did nothing to diminish the company's investment appeal. In May, Famous Artists Schools announced that it would acquire Diversified Education and Research Corp. and its subsidiary, Evelyn Wood Reading Dynamics Institute, for stock valued at around $3 million.

The "schools" in the corporate name of Famous Artists were in the homes of its students. It was a correspondence school. Aspiring artists submitted work and received critiques by mail. Consumers were led to believe that these critiques would come from the celebrity faculty listed in the business's promotional materials, including company cofounder Norman Rockwell. In truth, Rockwell and the other name artists listed never communicated with students. All responses came from nonfamous employees. Huddled in cubicles at Famous Artists' headquarters in Westport, Connecticut, these workaday artists issued stock feedback to new enrollees, depending on their level. For students who stayed with it, they drew corrections on transparencies and dictated comments for transcription. It was art instruction by assembly line.

The Reading Dynamics acquisition was a marriage of compatibles. Like the Evelyn Wood institutes, Famous Artists advertised heavily, featuring rags-to-riches stories of its graduates' success, as in, "Don Golembia of Detroit stepped up from railroad worker to the styling department of a big automobile company—by showing his work with the school. Now he helps design new car models."

Famous Artists, traded on the American Stock Exchange, also offered correspondence courses in writing, photography, accounting, and languages. Like speed-reading, it profited from the American mania for self-improvement.

Webster and his partners were also profiting. The *Crimson* said that the Woods, teetering on the brink of bankruptcy, had sold out to DEAR for one-third of its value. Now Famous Artists was offering millions for DEAR, and Webster was to stay on as president.

Not everybody celebrated wholeheartedly. DEAR, whose sole business was Evelyn Wood Reading Dynamics, owned about 25 percent of the institutes. The rest were franchised to sponsors, who faced an uncertain future. They already had their differences with Webster, and now he and they would have new masters.

Evelyn, at least, got what she wanted. In August, she signed a new consulting agreement with Famous Artists, granting them use of her name and rights to her future "discoveries." Instead of $12,000 a year, she'd be earning $20,000 for a maximum of sixty days of work per year. Travel outside Utah would be reimbursed at $100 per diem plus expenses.

It was a fifteen-year agreement, with the guaranteed yearly salary to be paid to her heirs in the event of her death. The girl raised in Ogden who always worried about her father's employment now had a contract worth $300,000, to say nothing of the lifetime Utah-Idaho franchise, from which Famous Artists agreed to collect no royalties.

Famous Artists didn't even seem to want much from her. The agreement began by stating, "It is contemplated that the Employee will reside in the State of Utah, and in general, conduct her duties in the State of Utah." It was as if Evelyn had stepped into one of Norman Rockwell's idyllic paintings of American life.

In September, the ink was dry on Evelyn's contract. The Famous Artists acquisition was also going smoothly. The shareholders and boards of both companies had approved the acquisition, pending a tax ruling that was expected to be favorable.

Then there was some other Wall Street news.

9

Times Are A-Changin'

IT HAPPENED DURING THE SUMMER of Love and, in a way, was part of it. Thousands of young people had converged in San Francisco in 1967, eager to explore new thinking about art, sexuality, politics, and spirituality. Ira West, a twenty-one-year-old from Tucson, was there for another reason. He had a summer internship at the San Francisco bureau of the *Wall Street Journal.*

Clean shaven and short haired, West dressed for work in a jacket and tie. In his neighborhood, that was a curious getup. He lived in the city's Haight-Ashbury district, the epicenter of hippie culture, where flowing tresses, bell-bottomed jeans, and ethnic jewelry were the gender-free norm.

In high school, West had been an ardent follower of Barry Goldwater, carrying around the Arizona senator's memoir *The Conscience of a Conservative* as if it were the Bible. He'd also tried his own hand at right-wing commentary, writing antisocialist editorials for his prize-winning high school newspaper. "I loved pontificating," said West. A conservative Tucson radio station regularly read his work on air. He'd also worked for three summers on an Arizona daily newspaper.

West had changed since his Goldwater days. He'd finished three years at Occidental College in Los Angeles, and in college "you get radicalized," said West. By the time he arrived in San Francisco in his 1959

Chevy, he "was quite liberal." When the *Journal* told its interns that they could pitch ideas for features, he started looking for stories.

An editor shot down West's idea to profile a charismatic figure, Ashleigh Brilliant, whose open-air lectures in Golden Gate Park attracted crowds. (The self-styled guru was eventually profiled in the *Journal*, a quarter-century later.) West's other idea was a feature about the Evelyn Wood speed-reading method because, he recalled, "the ads were really pervasive. I was fascinated, and I thought, this was horseshit. How could anyone read 40,000 wpm?"

His editor was immediately enthusiastic. West spent about a month researching the article, which including taking an Evelyn Wood course in Berkeley, where he disclosed that he was a reporter on assignment. He was offered free classes, but the *Journal* insisted on paying the full fee.

"I did try to have an open mind about it, like, 'Well, I can't imagine this will work but I'll see if it does,'" said West, but "I got basically zero out of it." He summed up the method as essentially just "telling you to tell yourself to read faster."

Told that Evelyn was now just the company's public face, West quoted only Webster. He recalled interviewing an official—probably Howard Ruff—at the branch where he took the course. He added that the piece went through heavy editing and rewriting before running in the paper's most widely read spot: column 7 of the *Journal*'s front page.

When the story ran on September 27, 1967, the headline and sub-heading said it in a nutshell: "Evelyn Wood Schools' Speed-Reading Claims Spark a Controversy. Enrollment Soars, but Some Students, Out-side Experts Say Comprehension Suffers." The article lent a powerful megaphone to Evelyn's university-based nemeses. Once threatened for talking to the University of Florida's student paper, Spache now told the country's leading business paper about the miserable comprehension scores he'd obtained from Evelyn Wood graduates. Columbia's Ehrlich obviously relished his chance to talk about a $200 prize, yet unclaimed, that he'd give anyone who demonstrated effective reading at 2,000 wpm.

Issues mentioned by the Harvard student paper got a national airing. The institutes' fraudulent measures of before-and-after reading scores were exposed, and there were harsh words about the Evelyn Wood

LEFT: Evelyn's maternal grandparents, Rosina and Thomas Stirland, with her aunt Eliza. *Used by permission, Utah State Historical Society*

RIGHT: Evelyn's parents, Rose Stirland Nielsen and Elias Nielsen. *Used by permission, Utah State Historical Society*

Graduating from the University of Utah, 1929. *Special Collections, J. Willard Marriott Library, The University of Utah*

Evelyn and the only daughter she publicly acknowledged, Carolyn, nicknamed Carol. *Used by permission, Utah State Historical Society*

Evelyn and Doug at a Wood family reunion, ca. 1935. Doug, smiling broadly, is in the center of the top row (fourth from left). Evelyn is directly below him (small ruffled collar, no glasses). *Used by permission, Utah State Historical Society*

The European mission presidents and their spouses, 1939. The Woods are in the middle row, third and fourth from left. *Used by permission, Utah State Historical Society*

Evelyn, as pictured in the *American Salesman*, one of two trade magazines that were early promoters of her method. *Used by permission, Utah State Historical Society*

The Woods, left, at Carol's wedding. Carol's first husband, Ray Jay Davis, is next to her. *Used by permission, Utah State Historical Society*

LEFT: M. Douglas "Doug" Wood, undated. *Used by permission, Utah State Historical Society*

RIGHT: The face that sold hundreds of thousands of courses. Evelyn, as she appeared in countless ads. *Used by permission, Utah State Historical Society*

Speed-reading, Evelyn Wood style, with the hand as a pacer. *Used by permission, Utah State Historical Society*

George W. Gibson of Harvard Business School, the first of Evelyn's detractors. In 1960 he challenged her claims in the pages of *Salesweek* magazine, drawing sharp criticism from her supporters. *HBS Archives Photograph Collection: Faculty and Staff, Baker Library, Harvard Business School*

Evelyn teaching, ca. 1969. *Used by permission, Utah State Historical Society*

George C. Webster, the "tremendous man" who saved the company from bankruptcy and took it over. *Courtesy of DC Public Library, Washingtoniana Division*

The sleek reception area of an Evelyn Wood Reading Dynamics institute, from a 1968 company brochure. *Courtesy of DC Public Library, Washingtoniana Division*

Businessmen often took the course at company expense. Enrollment was predominantly male. *Courtesy of DC Public Library, Washingtoniana Division*

LEFT: Eugene Ehrlich, author of the 1962 *Saturday Evening Post* article "Speed Reading Is the Bunk." Of all of Evelyn's detractors, he irked her most. *Courtesy of Henry Ehrlich*

RIGHT: Anna Wood, born Anna Marie Pearson. Adopted by the Woods at age fourteen, but not treated or publicly acknowledged as their child, she felt connected only to her biological family. *Courtesy of Barbara North Smith*

President Jimmy Carter gave Evelyn Wood Reading Dynamics a needed boost by taking a course during his presidency. Here he chats with his instructor, Bernard Kelly, in 1977. *Used by permission, Utah State Historical Society*

method from the Yale grad student who'd sued a Connecticut institute. By now, he'd gotten his money back in an out-of-court settlement.

There was also a startling new revelation: the US Air Force Academy had withdrawn from Evelyn's fan club. Major John des Islets, who'd arranged her air force contract when he was a captain, told the *Journal*, "I was clocked at 4,000 words a minute, but I wasn't doing anything more than skimming." He added that academy instructors still demonstrated her technique to cadets, "but we don't for a minute tell them they're reading."

Moreover, a Dow Chemical facility had ditched the course after trying it on two dozen executives.

The senators' testimonials were provided as balance. The alleged instruction at the Kennedy White House got a mention, although the source cited was an Evelyn Wood ad. This was thin gruel compared to the weight of damaging evidence reported for the first time in the business press.

The article appeared five days after the board of Famous Artists approved the acquisition of DEAR, at the slightly sweetened purchase price of 60,500 shares, up from the 59,400 approved in May. The stock was now worth about $4 million.

Still awaiting a favorable tax ruling, the deal wasn't yet final.

Warmly congratulated at the *Journal*'s San Francisco bureau for his column 7 victory, West returned to college for his senior year. He interned again for the *Journal*, tried a doctoral program, and worked for the AP before settling into a public school teaching career. His spectacular debut didn't leave a lasting mark on West, who was more interested in teaching than finance.

The article also didn't make much difference to Famous Artists Schools, which was more interested in finance than teaching. Founded by the celebrated Rockwell and the illustrator Albert Dorne, the company, always a commercial enterprise, was straying even farther from its artistic roots. Of all the artists associated with the business, Dorne was the only one who'd actually run it as chairman and president. But a few years after taking Famous Artists public, Dorne had died unexpectedly. Rudderless but feeling flush, Famous Artists sought a successor.

The logical choice was Fred Ludekens, a founding artist who was also a businessman. Like Dorne, who'd risen from the slums of New York's Lower East Side to become a highly paid illustrator, Ludekens was a self-made man. Born in British Columbia, he'd worked on fishing boats and as a cowboy before one art course set him on a successful career path. Known for his dynamic depictions of the American West and animals in the wild, Ludekens was also a seasoned advertising executive, always well dressed, right down to the cuff links.

Ludekens was named board chairman upon Dorne's death. He was available for telephone consultations but plainly had no interest in running the company. "He always would have wanted to live in the West," said his grandson, John Stutesman. Referring to Famous Artists' headquarters in Westport, Connecticut, Stutesman said, "I can't see him living in a bedroom community in a suburb."

So Ludekens stayed in his stunning home on Belvedere Island in San Francisco Bay, while the company's former accountant, Gilbert K. Granet, took over the reins. Granet, named president when Dorne died, had nothing against Westport. Its artistic community defied the suburban stereotype, but it was decidedly residential. Famous Artists, in fact, was one of its largest businesses.

And it was getting larger. It was the era of conglomeration, and Granet was on a buying spree. According to a company insider, he believed that Evelyn had taught John F. Kennedy to speed-read, and he wanted her company—among others.

With the deal still pending, a confident Webster began empire building, advertising a new position for a financial vice president to oversee international expansion. Any investors rattled by West's story would have been reassured by the ad, which described Evelyn Wood Reading Dynamics as a "fifteen-million-dollar-plus" division of a listed corporation. The ad didn't mention that the reading company was mainly a franchising operation fed by 10 percent royalties.

In December, the *Wall Street Journal* carried an announcement: "Famous Artists Schools Inc. has acquired substantially all the assets of Diversified Education and Research Corp. including the name Evelyn Wood Reading Dynamics." It was a large display ad with a few lines of text centered in a large outlined box. Such ads are known as tomb-stones—a term that would turn out to be fitting.

Evelyn, already on Famous Artists' payroll, was in Atlanta to judge a Junior Miss competition. Beauty pageants, always insisting they valued brains as much as looks, were an ideal vehicle for awarding scholarships and garnering publicity. The women's section of the *Atlanta Constitution* devoted a full page to a profile of Evelyn, enliv-ening the hoary Reading Dynamics origin story with an assortment of Evelyn's recipes.

It was a time when even the most accomplished women had to demonstrate their domestic skills. That was not a problem for Evelyn, who said she'd won baking prizes in high school and junior college. The banana cream pies she baked in Frankfurt got rave reviews in mission-ary diaries. She was a recipe collector and "really good at cooking Ger-man food—cabbage and potato salad," said Verla Nielsen (no relation to Evelyn Nielsen Wood), who worked with the Woods in Salt Lake City. The Woods hosted picnics for the staff in their landscaped backyard that were a highlight of the summer. "They bought the most expensive steaks," one staffer remembered.

But it was winter now, even in Atlanta, and Evelyn gave the news-paper her recipe for a nonalcoholic version of hot wassail. It was a rare trip outside of Utah for Evelyn. Famous Artists no longer relied on her to revive flagging franchises or launch new ones. Sponsors remained responsible for their own advertising.

Some franchises went for a modern look. Copy appeared beneath the portrait of a recent Evelyn Wood grad, usually young and male, relaxing with a book. Names were given to enhance the impression of legitimacy. One began, "Meet Ralph Frey, Jr. He's a college junior. He can read 3,000 words a minute. He is NOT skimming." With clean lines and an updated font, the new ads strived for a late-1960s aesthetic, although plenty of verbiage remained.

One sponsor who clung to the old-school approach was Howard Ruff. Proud of having created the mock-news pages, he still used them to advertise his institutes. In addition to the Berkeley branch that had taught the *Wall Street Journal* reporter, these included Oakland, Palo

Alto, Walnut Creek, San Francisco, and San Jose. Ruff relied on the ads to list the dates and times of demonstrations, which at busy registration times, he held almost daily at various locations.

San Francisco rang in the new year of 1968. It would be a trying time for the sponsor and the city. Already in arrears with his royalties, Ruff had spent $25,000 on an eight-page supplement, to be inserted into a Sunday edition of the *San Francisco Examiner*. A strike closed down the newspaper for eight weeks, and the supplements ended up in the trash bin. By the time a wage settlement was reached, the dates of the demonstrations had passed.

It was a heavy blow to Ruff's house of cards. Social climbing and reckless spending had left him and his wife heavily in debt. He'd bought into the investment group that sold out to Famous Artists, possibly borrowing from friends to do so. Now he was only a franchisee, dangerously behind in his royalty payments. Up until now, he'd gotten away with it. Charisma and an operatically trained voice had made him a master salesman. He'd enrolled some ten thousand students in the Bay Area, setting a record, but he owed a half-million dollars.

Setting up a new schedule of demonstration sessions, Ruff resumed advertising after the strike was settled. But one day he went to work and found his office door padlocked. As Ruff, known for his rueful wit, put it, "I went to work rich (I thought) and came home broke. It ruined my whole day." As he told it, "The parent company, seeing an opportunity to grab off the business and resell it to someone else, abruptly cancelled my franchise and notified the sheriff."

Ruff went on to become a popular financial adviser with a bestselling book, a newsletter, and a TV show. He made millions from prophesies of apocalyptic financial disaster, inspiring followers to stockpile gold, silver, and freeze-dried fruit. His writings repeatedly recalled the shutdown of his Evelyn Wood franchise. Ruff portrayed it as a watershed moment that forced him to mend his ways—not by living more prudently but by making heaps of money to pay his creditors. In Ruff's version, he and his wife spent twelve years erasing their debts because bankruptcy was against their religious principles.

Whether that included the missing royalty payments is unclear. Evidently, Ruff was not the only franchisee that Webster wanted to replace. His ads for sponsors "with solid financial backing" asked applicants to name which market they were interested in. This was a stark departure from the preacquisition days, when only a few counties in a small number of states were available.

Prospective franchisees were promised up to 30 percent in profits, but advertising costs were rising. After taking two months to settle its strike, the management of the *San Francisco Examiner* warned that it would raise prices to cover wage increases. Meanwhile, television, also crucial for Evelyn Wood's publicity, was undergoing tighter regulation. The Federal Communications Commission stopped a station in Knoxville, Tennessee, from presenting a so-called "documentary," with fifteen minutes of praise for the Wood method from deans and professors at the University of Texas. The FCC ruled that it was really just one long commercial, and to present it otherwise was "inconsistent with the public interest."

The company found other ways to circumvent the FCC with commercials masquerading as programs. The bestselling author Arthur Hailey was a partner in this effort. Arriving at a TV studio with galleys of his not-yet-published novel *Airport* in a locked case, he challenged Evelyn Wood grads to tear through it. But Hailey's stunts were aired on UHF stations, associated with low viewership and poor reception. Not for years had a top-rated show with a national audience paid attention to Evelyn Wood Reading Dynamics.

Famous Artists head Gilbert Granet didn't seem bothered. Evelyn Wood was just one of a string of acquisitions. The former accountant was now, like Evelyn, a bold-faced name. A prominent society columnist reported that Granet had bought a new Westport house. Impatient to fill it up, the former accountant had asked Dong Kingman, one of the original Famous Artists, to paint furniture on the walls while he awaited shipment of the real thing.

With similar impatience, Granet took the company on a multimillion-dollar spending spree. In addition to Evelyn Wood, it now owned Linguaphone Institute, a self-study language concern; the International

Accountants Society, a correspondence school; and Welcome Wagon, which greeted newcomers to small cities and towns with coupons and promotional gifts from local merchants.

Doug probably paid close attention to these moves. He'd hired a consultant to look into the company's finances. The consultant had given Famous Artists a generally good review but warned of the unpaid correspondence-school tuitions. Undaunted, Doug sank nearly $6,000 into Famous Artists stock. Evelyn, however, had other things on her mind. Her mother, Rose Stirland Nielsen May, died at age eighty-two.

The end had come at a nursing home near the Woods' house. The letters Evelyn wrote from Europe are testament to a close and loving mother-daughter relationship. Very likely, Evelyn visited her daily in the nursing facility, but she couldn't have cared for her at home. The Utah-Idaho franchise was much too busy.

Like Famous Artists, the Woods were dabbling in a bit of expansion, although on a smaller scale. Evidently meeting Webster's requirements for new sponsors, Doug had bought the southern Arizona franchise. In Salt Lake City, he and Evelyn had made some promising hires. Verla Nielsen, who'd come to them as a temporary worker, soon helped to manage the office. "I was Evelyn's right hand," she said. There was also an educational director, Mary Gussman, an Evelyn Wood graduate herself. Tall and slender, Gussman towered over Evelyn. Nielsen remembered Gussman as invariably well dressed and put together—in contrast to Evelyn, who'd finally realized her long-ago dream of letting herself go.

"We had a parking lot," Nielsen recalled, "and one day Evelyn came in and said, 'My girdle was bothering me, so I took it off and put it in the car, but I guess it was the wrong car.'"

The impeccably groomed Gussman figured into plans for the Arizona franchise. For a year and half, she taught in Salt Lake City on the weekdays, then drove to Tucson to offer weekend classes there. It was a grueling commute of more than twelve hours each way, but if all went well, the Woods would let her take over the franchise. More than an employee, Gussman was a partner in the incorporation of Evelyn Wood Reading Dynamics of Utah, along with the Woods' younger daughter, Carol, who taught for a while at the institute in Tucson, where she lived.

Although twenty years Evelyn's junior, Gussman had already spent several years with the company, first in Philadelphia. There were some even younger faces around Salt Lake City too. Marlene Bennett grew up a few streets away from the Woods, who were friends with her parents. She remembered being disappointed when they gave her an Evelyn Wood course as a high school graduation gift. "My friends were getting cars." However, this soon led to a part-time job that paid twice as much as her old one. First assigned to help students with their practice drills, Bennett eventually moved into teaching.

With the office in good hands, Evelyn and Doug were spending more time at their cabin in Mount Aire Canyon, a short drive from their home, where they had a private pond. They also went to Europe for a summer vacation, letting Bennett and her husband, Mike, stay in their house while they were gone. The young couple enjoyed sleeping outside in the garden—until the sprinklers came on.

There was another catch too. Young Marlene Bennett was farther removed than Evelyn from Utah's pioneer heritage. As the house-sitting arrangement was made, Evelyn had mentioned offhandedly, "The raspberries will be coming along. If you could make some jam . . ." Bennett had to seek emergency canning lessons from her husband's grandmother.

Bennett eventually had six children but retained her part-time job at the Woods' institute. Weeping with emotion, she recalled how Evelyn was willing to rearrange her schedule after the birth of each of her babies, slotting her into night classes when Bennett's husband could take over at home. "My kids didn't even know I worked," said the younger woman.

An anomaly in her own time, Evelyn was witnessing the gradual acceptance of women in the paid workforce. She remained heavily involved in the LDS Church, which was fighting against the Equal Rights Amendment, but her grandson Stanton remembered her responding to comments about the brethren by retorting, "What about the sister-en?"— a term of her own coinage. Meanwhile, DEAR was exploring the market potential of the emerging women's movement. A large display ad in the *Hartford Courant* announced a new Career Directions course, to be piloted at the Evelyn Wood institute in affluent West Hartford.

Successful applicants would update office and job-search skills, with the goal of helping women get well-paid positions. But the idea apparently went nowhere.

The Woods also hired a young man named Richard Shipley as an instructor. Good-looking and personable, he was popular with the rest of the staff. The Woods promised him a quick trip up the career ladder if he could prove his mettle, and he quickly did. Although Idaho was covered by their franchise, the Woods hadn't developed business there. Shipley, a native Idahoan, eagerly embraced the challenge of spreading the speed-reading gospel to rural areas. Buying ad time on local radio stations for comparative pennies and handing out leaflets, Shipley knew how to market in towns with a few hundred inhabitants. Soon the Woods changed his title to promotional director.

Idaho was small potatoes to Famous Artists, which renamed itself FAS International in 1969 and moved from the American Stock Exchange to the New York Stock Exchange. Granet bought the first block of shares issued in the new name. He could well afford the purchase; his salary was now $125,000. Around that time, the Woods were also doing well, although not *that* well, jointly reporting an adjusted gross income of $85,000 from their franchise and Evelyn's consulting fee. Observing religious tithing rules, they contributed about one-tenth of that to the LDS Church.

At least for FAS's Evelyn Wood division, the term *international* was apt. Evelyn was famous in dozens of countries, as Carol and her family discovered. On a trip around the world, they visited far-flung institutes, where "they treated us like royalty," Stanton recalled. In the United Kingdom, where pirate companies had advertised as Evelyn Wood branches, there was finally an authorized institute. Other countries joined the list, including Mexico, Trinidad, Germany, Belgium, and France. Canada, where Evelyn Wood tuition was tax-deductible, had thirty institutes. The Toronto sponsor signed a new ad agency to a $100,000 ad contract, nearly matching New York's annual advertising budget of $125,000.

Gone were the days when the parent company supported franchisee-paid publicity with floods of positive news stories. Skepticism had taken a toll, and FAS International didn't score much coverage for its speed-reading subsidiary. Still advertising for franchisees, George Webster had moved from New York to his old management-consulting digs in Washington when a *Newsweek* wire-service piece appeared. Its ostensible purpose was to announce that speed-reading was now a $25 million business, but its main message was praise and awe for Evelyn Wood Reading Dynamics. Skepticism and the skimming question were addressed by one sentence, buried deep. Referring to Wood students, the reporter wrote, "Because they are instructed to read thoughts, not just words, their comprehension is supposed to grow with their speed." Other than that cautious "supposed to," all claims were reported as facts.

This was like old times—free publicity. Distributed by Newsweek Feature Service, although it might never have been published in *Newsweek* magazine, the article was printed in several major newspapers. Evelyn's origin story reached new generations of high school and college students, with her alleged ties to Kennedy pulled tighter than ever. In this version, she'd supposedly moved to Washington "with a push from Kennedy"—something never mentioned previously.

The problem with that assertion is that the Woods moved to Washington in late 1959. By early 1960, the Washington institute was up and running, and Evelyn was teaching in Wilmington. All this preceded Kennedy's presidency. Indeed, the then Massachusetts senator had not yet been nominated as the Democratic candidate.

For all its adulation, the *Newsweek* piece inadvertently exposed weak spots in the Evelyn Wood structure. Its list of celebrities who swore by the course began with the usual suspects: Proxmire, Talmadge, and Queen Ingrid of Denmark. But there were also two mentions of S. I. Hayakawa, a highly controversial figure who'd later represent California in the US Senate. As president of San Francisco State College, Hayakawa had used a strong arm against students in a four-month strike that had recently concluded. Joined by the Black Panthers, Students for a Democratic Society, and other community groups, the students had fought to establish an ethnic studies department, among other issues. Hayakawa became the darling of California conservatives by yanking out the speaker wires from a student sound truck.

The strike spread to other California state colleges and dragged on amid student arrests and convictions, injuries, and property damage. The students ultimately won many of their demands, but Hayakawa remained in his post, a symbol of authoritarianism to many. Yet Evelyn Wood Reading Dynamics continued to claim him as a celebrated course graduate. The *Newsweek* piece began by breezily noting, "S. I. Hayakawa can zip through the morning newspaper in twelve minutes."

Oblivious to social change, the company was also ignoring price resistance. The only other commercial speed-reading course named by *Newsweek* was shorter and cheaper than Reading Dynamics. The Joyce Brothers Reading Development Center charged $55 for four sessions, compared to $175 for the eight-week Wood course. This new competitor came charged with star power. Dr. Joyce Brothers was an enormously popular TV psychologist who'd attached her name to a so-called Read-Ability system, remarkably similar to Evelyn's method. The main difference was that students were taught to *imagine* the lazy-S pattern on each page instead of using fingers to trace it.

Despite her fame and good looks, Joyce Brothers was no serious threat to Evelyn Wood. Aside from licensing her name and face, Brothers did little to promote the business, leaving that to a national franchising concern. *Newsweek* reported that her namesake speed-reading business was in a dozen cities, operating out of church basements and community centers to control costs. Its prices crept up the following year but stayed below Evelyn Wood levels.

Although the Joyce Brothers chain soon disappeared, price resistance remained an issue at Evelyn Wood Reading Dynamics. By now, an army of full- and part-time instructors had been trained in the Wood method and could potentially offer their own discount versions. The company enforced its nondisclosure agreements. Teachers who quit the program were often sued if they stayed in the reading field.

Some renegades gave it a try, regardless. Shortly after the settlement of the strike at San Francisco State, the college newspaper ran an ad for bargain-rate reading improvement courses taught by a man claiming to be a former Evelyn Wood institute director. Ads for the same company popped up in Santa Barbara. There, they made no mention of Evelyn Wood Reading Dynamics but undercut its prices, offering six sessions for one hundred dollars.

In another college paper on the opposite coast, a professor questioned the credentials of Evelyn Wood–trained instructors. "Would they qualify, for example, for a Pennsylvania certificate as a reading teacher?" asked Ralph C. Preston, the director of the University of Pennsylvania's reading clinic. In a lengthy letter to the editor of the *Daily Pennsylvanian*, Preston declared that his eye-movement research and other studies indicated that the only value of speed-reading courses was to teach skimming.

Preston claimed to have written the letter in response to questions about privately operated courses in general, but his response repeatedly mentioned Evelyn. Several months later, longtime Wood franchisee Arthur C. Kramer wrote an even lengthier response. It began by declaring that, as a matter of fact, every Evelyn Wood instructor in Pennsylvania did have state certification in speed-reading. Leaving readers to decide whether such a credential existed, the letter addressed Preston's other criticisms. Research at one academic institution was countered by research at another, a cited study was said to have been found invalid, and eye-movement photography was challenged because, as Kramer wrote, "What the eyes do is not nearly as important as what the brain does."

Although printed in an Ivy League newspaper, the letter opened not with these tiresome scientific arguments but by dropping names of illustrious speed-reading alumni. Again, S. I. Hayakawa topped the list, probably doing the company no favors. But Kramer also mentioned a hipper personality, Marshall McLuhan. Famous for coining the phrase "The medium is the message," and popular among youth, McLuhan was an influential new entrant to Evelyn Wood fandom, whose son reportedly taught the method in Canada. The franchisee ended his letter by offering his U of Penn detractor a free course.

Preston responded with a second letter, rebutting some of Kramer's points and suggesting that the federal government test the "extravagant claims" of so-called speed-reading courses.

More a businessman than a reading specialist, Kramer may have had someone write portions of his letter. He'd outlasted Ruff as one of the largest and oldest Evelyn Wood sponsors. Kramer and a partner franchised institutes in Philadelphia and New York, also running test-prep courses through their company, the Lyceum. Around the time that he wrote the letter, a publicly owned company that manufactured forklift equipment was poised to acquire the Lyceum for $1 million. The deal, however, ultimately collapsed.

By spring of that year, 1970, the student press had other issues to air besides the speed-reading controversy. In late April, President Richard M. Nixon expanded the Vietnam War into Cambodia, and many campuses erupted in protest. At Kent State in Ohio, National Guardsmen shot and killed four demonstrators. A fellow student captured the anguish of the tragedy in a photograph of a young woman grieving over the body of a fallen student.

That picture was burned into the national consciousness when *Life* magazine used it on a cover. It was taken by a Kent State student named Howard Ruffner (not to be confused with Howard Ruff, the franchisee). Ruffner, whose work earned him the George Polk Award in Journalism for News Photography, had studied photography while in the air force. "[That] is where I really learned about film and composition," he said recently. But he'd also been a customer of the Famous Photographers School.

However, Ruffner's success was a fluke for FAS International and its correspondence schools, which were basically high-pressure sales operations. In July 1970, the *Atlantic* magazine ran a devastating exposé of the Famous Writers School. The piece, by Jessica Mitford, revealed that writers listed on the school's ads essentially sold their names but had nothing to do with instruction. The so-called talent tests for "admission" summoned salesmen who misled consumers before signing them to three-year contracts.

FAS, already watching its stock price slide, would never recover from this. The piece was widely read and discussed. Mitford, famed for her muckraking of the funeral industry, was a favorite guest of TV talk show hosts. On Wall Street, too, her investigation aroused great interest.

Banks had been financing FAS's mad expansion on the premise that each mail-order-school enrollment represented between $825 and $900, the fee for a full course. But Mitford found that the vast majority of customers made a down payment, then dropped out after a few classes. Threatening letters often failed to produce the balance owed.

The article sparked an investigation by the New York attorney general, forcing the company to cease deceptive practices and permit course cancellation with pro rata refunds. An analyst warned that the changes would significantly reduce earnings and affect the company's outlook for long-term growth.

The Mitford article had nothing to do with Evelyn Wood Reading Dynamics, which was separate from the Famous Schools division. But as 1970 drew to a close, and as FAS's stock was down more than 80 percent from its 1969 high, the analyst also noted problems in the Evelyn Wood franchising operation, though he also saw potential for improvement.

At least one franchisee wasn't so sure. Doug Wood got rid of his FAS International shares, taking a $5,000 loss.

Finances aside, the year had restored Evelyn Wood Reading Dynamics to some of its former glory. An invitation arrived from President Nixon's White House, requesting reading instruction for staffers. Apparently, it was not sent to Evelyn's address. Dan Theodocion, still the company's national educational director, chose two New York instructors to teach the Nixon aides and advisers.

Seventy students were on the roster, including some staffers' spouses. Among them were Ron Ziegler, press secretary; Patrick Buchanan and Dwight Chapin, special assistants to the president; and Leonard Garment, special consultant. Assistant White House physician Stanley H. Bear, and the First Lady's press secretary, Constance Stuart, were also in attendance, as was Nixon's personal secretary, Rose Mary Woods.

One teacher of this notorious group was Peter Kump, who would later achieve culinary prominence with a cooking school and his establishment of the James Beard Foundation. At thirty-two, Kump was a seasoned Evelyn Wood instructor, teaching while trying to break into theater. It's not clear whether the taxpayers or the company paid for the lessons, which were held on Monday and Tuesday evenings, requiring each instructor to commute from New York once a week.

"We hit a rather bad problem," Kump told a reporter. It was hard to keep the class on task through eight weeks that witnessed the invasion of Cambodia, an enormous antiwar march on Washington, the Kent State shootings, and the near-disaster of the Apollo 13 space flight. Nevertheless, he said, the average participant emerged reading seven times faster than at the beginning.

Nixon didn't take the course himself because he had no need for it, Kump told an interviewer. He didn't specify the president's reading speed.

If Ziegler, the press secretary, was satisfied, he didn't share his joy at news conferences or in press releases. If the media were aware of the lessons, they barely paid attention. There was one small item in the *New York Times*, citing the company but not the White House as a source. Erroneously identifying Evelyn as the company's current president, the *Times* wrote that Evelyn had taught at the Kennedy White House.

Several small-city papers interviewed Kump about the experience, but there was no major coverage. Some Evelyn Wood ads reprinted or invented a feature about the White House gig, purportedly by an obscure news syndicate. A photo of Kennedy bore the cutline, "Invited Mrs. Wood to teach at the White House in 1962," although in interviews she'd indicated this had happened in other years, either 1961 (during the botched Bay of Pigs invasion) or 1963 (as McGeorge Bundy left for India). An image of the White House was labeled, "Reading Dynamics Held Here Under Two Presidents." In fact, the class for Nixon staffers met at a site now named the Eisenhower Executive Office Building.

There was a place for Evelyn in all this. She went to the White House to present diplomas, or so the ads declared. The impression, however misleading, was that she'd also taught the classes. For the franchises that placed these ads, the Washington invitation was a welcome shot in the arm and a break from watching FAS's stock price plunge.

Evelyn could travel to Washington or anywhere else knowing that the office back home was in good hands. Mary Gussman had left Salt Lake City to take over the Tucson franchise. That had been the plan, though her move came somewhat suddenly. Unable to stand the punishing weekly commute from northern Utah to southern Arizona, she left in midwinter, when Tucson housing was scarce. She settled temporarily in a mobile home, happy to be less mobile herself.

Dick Shipley, the young promotions manager, was still doing well with the Idaho market. Despite Wall Street's worries about FAS, DEAR still hosted annual meetings for the Evelyn Wood division, and Doug was thinking of proposing Shipley as a speaker. His ideas for boosting business in small towns should be shared with others.

The only problem with Shipley, in the Woods' estimation, was that he valued himself as highly as they did. There'd been some discussions about money.

10

Snake in the Grass

A DECADE AFTER IT WAS TAKEN, Evelyn's photo with tilted head and butterfly brooch was promoting another product: Operation: R.E.A.D., brought to you by "Evelyn Wood, a name you can trust," declared ads inviting parents to bring their kids in for a reading test at six Utah locations, including a shopping mall. With the free test came a sales pitch, aimed at parents of children reading below grade level.

"How well does your child read?" began the ad, promising "much more than just a speed-reading program." Classes for adults with reading problems were also available. And for students on or above grade level, the Utah franchise offered Junior Rapid Reading, holding some classes in elementary schools.

The trade winds were shifting. Evelyn Wood Reading Dynamics, now claiming to have taught half a million people, said it expected to enroll one hundred thousand more annually. In the New York area alone, ten thousand people were expected to study speed-reading in one recent year. Students still poured into an institute in Manhattan, where framed portraits of a gray-haired Evelyn hung on every wall. In smaller cities, however, the river was beginning to dry up.

An economic downturn didn't help. In places like Washington, DC, enrollees typically made a $50 deposit on the $175 course, paying the balance at the first class meeting. Elsewhere, with credit cards not used as commonly as now, an Evelyn Wood institute might have to make its own credit determinations. Records preserved from the Woods' franchise indicate that their business manager, Ellen Gunderson, was often occupied with such matters. The Utah operation charged the same fees as big cities, although it was not bound to do so contractually. Doug spent liberally on advertising.

Dick Shipley, the Woods' protégé, summed up Reading Dynamics in one word: expensive. He knew cheaper ways to do things. In Blackfoot, Idaho, for instance, he'd persuaded a local TV station to price a bulk buy of one-minute commercials at $1.50 a pop. He was going to blitz the market with sixty of these—one hour of television advertising for ninety dollars.

Shipley shared some of his observations with Doug while keeping others to himself. The rest of the staff seemed content. Marlene Bennett said Evelyn started the remedial course, but she and Verla Nielsen developed it. That is not the impression given in ads for Operation R.E.A.D. that ran in Los Angeles, crediting Evelyn with creating the program and announcing her appearance at its California launch. Authorship issues aside, both Bennett and Nielsen said Evelyn had obviously viewed the teaching of reading as her calling in life.

"She was disorganized, she didn't care that much about what she wore, but she was a master teacher," Nielsen said, adding, "She could make the class believe anything she wanted to. She thought this was her life to do these things."

Evelyn once described her new dresses in letters from Germany and told Bob Darling's mother where to get the best European cashmere. Now, she was oblivious. Nielsen once alerted Evelyn to a broken front seam on her pants. In Evelyn's estimation, no needle, thread, or even safety pins were required: she just turned the pants around in the bathroom. She went to a spa every day, jumping from a hot tub into a cold one, then not always bothering to put on hose—as Doug reminded her on the day of a magazine interview. As cameras began to roll for a new Evelyn Wood video, the founder called out, "Is my wig straight?"

Peter Kump had come from New York to make the video, which mainly showed Nielsen teaching. The man who'd taught Nixon's aides was now national education director. The company needed to refresh its store of films. A memo had gone out to all franchises prohibiting the use in commercials of the senators' testimonials or the Bob Darling demonstration on the Art Linkletter show. New television regulations required permission for such use, said the memo. Evidently, the company didn't think it could obtain releases.

That was the least of Evelyn Wood Reading Dynamics's problems. Financial woes were worsening for its corporate parent, FAS International. Its Famous Schools division had never recovered from the Jessica Mitford debunking. Enrollment plummeted, accounting practices were forced to change, and debts mounted. In May 1971, the Securities and Exchange Commission suspended FAS International from trading while financial statements were audited. The stock price bottomed, and the board fired Gilbert Granet, found to have drawn a handsome salary as Rome burned. He could paint furniture on his walls somewhere else.

It was not yet clear how this corporate cataclysm would affect Evelyn Wood Reading Dynamics, still a subsidiary of DEAR. Despite its full name, Diversified Education and Research, it had never diversified, remaining the licensor of Evelyn Wood institutes. Around this time, the Conference Board business-research group published DEAR's franchising and licensing agreement, a sterling example to a nation bursting with Kentucky Fried Chicken outlets and Holiday Inns.

But Webster was no longer president of DEAR. He'd returned to management consulting in Washington, taking with him the whip he'd cracked over the franchisees. One laggard in upstate New York had recently been shut down, but sixty others hummed along. After Webster's departure, Doug noticed a change in a paycheck, probably for Evelyn's monthly consulting fee. A letter explained that FAS International and DEAR were now splitting the item between them. This could not have been reassuring news to the Woods. There were still eleven years left on Evelyn's consulting contract, which she'd signed with Famous Artists, now the tottering FAS International.

Doug might have feared that Evelyn's check would go up in smoke. Or maybe he was indulging in a friendly competition with young Shipley. For whatever reason, Doug's sales approach struck Nielsen as needlessly aggressive. When reading demonstrations held at the Hotel Utah attracted fifty or more people, Doug would pressure staffers to try to enroll every one of them, she recalled. "Mr. Wood could sell you his false teeth," said Nielsen, while Evelyn was "not a businesswoman."

"I think that Mr. Wood was pushing for the money, for the masses," said Nielsen. "I don't think that's what the program was designed for." She added, "Mrs. Wood had everyone hypnotized into thinking everyone could do it." Three decades after operating the franchise herself, Nielsen maintained that the method could have been taught to more people, given more time and more personal attention.

"I wish we could have taught more people on a one-on-one basis," Nielsen said. "People expected a magic wand—it's a difficult skill that took a lot of time and effort. The advertisements were true but didn't say you had to work your butt off." The course's testing of comprehension was inaccurate, she added, giving students an inflated view of how much they'd understood.

Jessica Mitford had sunk Evelyn Wood's entire parent company with a single magazine piece, but speed-reading itself seemed invulnerable. Ten years of challenges from the *Wall Street Journal*, the *Saturday Evening Post*, and academic experts had barely left a mark on the Wood method. The controversy had died down, with opponents agreeing to disagree. Or, at least, that was the pronouncement of a *New York Times* piece that described speed-reading as "no longer a fad but a solid fixture of American education." Distributed through the *Times*'s wire service, the article ran in papers throughout the country.

It was a boon to Evelyn Wood Reading Dynamics. Ostensibly about speed-reading in general, the article focused nearly exclusively on Evelyn's namesake company, making clear her reduced role in it. Like Ira West of the *Wall Street Journal*, the *Times* reporter observed classes at an Evelyn Wood institute—this time taught by a Mrs. Pike at the Atlanta institute. Unlike West, the *Times* reporter was willing to suspend disbelief. While noting a high dropout rate, the *Times* reported that for the final assignment, the surviving students would need to finish George Orwell's *Animal Farm* in twenty-five minutes.

"To finish in time, they would have to read at 1,400 words a minute, a speed many of those in the class had already reached," the *Times* asserted. Portions of the original article were cut from wire-service versions, including:

> Few controlled, scientific studies of the effectiveness of speed reading exist, and the findings of those that do exist appear to be contradictory. Nevertheless, results such as those apparently achieved by Mrs. Pike's satisfied students have enabled the Evelyn Wood institutes, the biggest and best-known of commercial concerns, to expand to more than 150 cities in forty-seven states and seven foreign countries.

In other words, results, rather than marketing, had produced growth. The *Times* piece concluded with a word from Russell Stauffer, still an Evelyn booster at the University of Delaware. As for the "non-believers," who associated the Wood method with "snake oil and patent medicine," the *Times* wrote, "While there have been some claims that students have been taught to read tens and even hundreds of thousands of words a minute, they are not generally taken seriously."

That would have come as a surprise to the large crowds who gathered each week in hotel suites around the nation to see demonstrations of the Evelyn Wood method. It was standard procedure at such events to screen the segment of the Art Linkletter show with Bob Darling presumably reading forty-nine pages of *The Agony and the Ecstasy* in sixty seconds.

The company didn't promise that every student could become a Bob Darling—now ten years older and embarked on a successful law career. But it was suggesting the possibility. Haircuts and suit styles had changed, but Darling's startling performance remained an effective lure.

More abreast with the times was the so-called news program, filmed at the University of Texas's engineering school, that the FCC had judged to be one long commercial. Nonetheless, the film was screened at a demonstration session in Washington, DC, where an experimental psychologist named Ronald P. Carver was in attendance. It began with an animation of ticking clocks and a narrated warning about reading slowly in the jet age. Carver was impressed by the production values. He described it as "psychedelic."

No sales pressure was needed to register Carver for an Evelyn Wood course. Like a fairy-tale hero determined to succeed where others had failed, he was there to slay the speed-reading dragon. Carver, a senior research scientist at the American Institutes for Research in Washington, enrolled to write a book. Titled *Sense and Nonsense in Speed Reading*, it was composed on an IBM Selectric typewriter and printed at his expense. Paying for the course himself, Carver took it incognito. Unlike Ira West and the author of the recent *New York Times* article, Carver was a scientist, not a journalist. Disclosure could change the thing he was observing.

Carver acknowledged he was biased from the start. He didn't expect the Evelyn Wood course to teach reading at all, but rather skimming. He said his opinion was common in the academic community. In contrast to the *Times*, which described two irreconcilable but "quiescent" camps of believers and nonbelievers, Carver saw unity. He wrote:

> What happened to the breakthrough in reading that Evelyn Wood wrote about and that received such public attention? . . . Most researchers seem to have accepted speed reading as a skimming activity. The research results are in and have been for more than a number of years. The ethics of the situation are being debated, but . . . nothing can probably be done until the public is informed sufficiently to read the advertising claims in a slow, plodding, and highly critical manner.

Carver's undercover status at the institute didn't yield any startling revelations. His instructor, a male ex-Marine working toward a doctorate in reading at the University of Maryland, conscientiously taught the lessons, as did a female substitute. Neither indicated in words or deeds that they thought the system was hokum. But Carver was observing the method, not hoping for a gotcha moment.

Expecting to request a refund, he'd intended to complete all homework. He scrapped that plan after the first lesson. The instructor asked everyone to read down the pages, guided by hands in a lazy-S or serpentine pattern. Paced by the teacher's progressively faster count, students hurried through the pages. They were assigned the juvenile novel *Black*

Beauty for at-home drills. Carver recoiled "in horror" from that first assignment and ditched his initial plan.

The rest of the lessons confirmed Carver's hypothesis. "Anyone who is moving his eyes down the page of an ordinary book is skimming, not reading, since he is not perceiving most of the words," he wrote. Carver stressed that skimming was a highly useful skill for deciding what to read carefully and what to skip. Skimming strategies could be taught, he added, but there was no need for an expensive course.

A session about what the Wood institute called "threading" struck Carver as one such strategy, but not an easy one to grasp. Students were told to read at three times their usual "comprehension" rate to get the gist of the material. After filling out a recall sheet they read the same pages again, this time at their usual speed-reading rates. A metronome set at high velocity pushed them through drills.

Students were told that threading would improve overall performance, as their regular reading rate would become one-third of their threading rate. This made no scientific sense to Carver, who noticed something else:

> During this class it occurred to me that those students who were having trouble doing the skimming probably thought that something was wrong with themselves, since the course goals are advertised as being achievable by everyone. . . . This might be called the "Look at the emperor's fine clothes" effect. Nobody wants to admit that he is the only one who cannot see the emperor's clothes or be able to speed read.

Written for the layperson, Carver's book briefly outlined medical research about the time required for an eye fixation, the number of words that could be perceived in one fixation, and the time required for the eye to jump to the next fixation. The writings of Evelyn Wood debunkers, including Spache and Ehrlich, were condensed into a few bulleted points. Summing up Taylor's discoveries with the Reading-Eye Camera, Carver wrote, "Eye movements are not the cause of good or poor reading." Evelyn's first detractor, George Gibson of Harvard Business School, had made that point a decade earlier.

The debatable point separating reading from skimming is whether the author's *intended* meaning is acquired, Carver wrote. Commenting on a recent article in an academic journal, which contended that an individual had "read" material at 1,200 wpm despite missing a few key points, he said: "Someone who covers reading material at over 1,200 word per minute could pick up knowledge about the written material and maybe also pick up a sprinkling of the thoughts the writer intended to communicate. If, however, intended meaning is taken to refer to most of the total body of thoughts (in the form of sentences) that the writer of the information intended to communicate, then it has not been scientifically demonstrated that the speed reading of material is possible."

The book then trained its sights on Liddle's claim that Evelyn Wood graduates had accelerated their reading speeds for nonfiction with no significant loss of comprehension. (Carver said he was "disturbed" by Evelyn's continued insistence that her method was useful for fiction after Liddle found it wasn't.) Armed with the test-design skills that Liddle lacked, Carver conducted some casual research on Liddle's nonfiction passages. He found that people who had not read the passages could, nonetheless, answer Liddle's questions correctly. Dubbing this phenomenon "clairvoyant reading," Carver credited it to inadvertent cues in the wording of questions or multiple-choice answer selections. Another possibility, he said, was that the reader used prior knowledge of the nonfiction topic to choose the right answer.

Carver ended by advising consumers to take an Evelyn Wood course only if $175 and seventy-two hours were "of little consequence" to them. People needing skimming instruction could "practice running your hand down a page on your own . . . and once you have trained yourself not to require that you understand complete thoughts as when reading, then you have accomplished almost all of value that the course teaches."

That withering conclusion was somewhat undercut by the results of Carver's customer satisfaction survey. Unmasking himself as an infiltrator after the last session, he distributed a questionnaire to the twenty-one classmates who'd made it to the end, mostly male college students. Either because they knew him or because Carver had clipped a dollar bill to each survey, all but one returned it.

His first question was about the students' progress. Pressured for years to use standardized tests, a few Evelyn Wood institutes, including this one, had thrown them in the mix. Carver's teacher had administered a widely respected assessment, the Nelson-Denny Reading Test, in the first and last classes. In addition, the Washington institute relied on the reading "index" that multiplied speed by comprehension score.

Looking for subjective answers, Carver asked his classmates, "Regardless of what your results on the standardized tests were, do you think that you were able to at least triple your reading speed with no loss in comprehension?" Sixty percent answered yes, and 30 percent said no. The remaining tenth were unsure.

On the one hand, nearly one-third of the class was dissatisfied—far more than the 2 percent companywide who were said to have requested refunds. On the other hand, most were content. Carver acknowledged that speed-reading classes had something to offer. They gave permission to skim, something that too many schoolteachers presented as sinful. But that wasn't what was advertised. The self-recrimination he'd noted probably explained why so many settled for less. He himself couldn't stand to do the homework.

Within a year, Carver had a far bigger megaphone than his self-published book. The magazine *Psychology Today* ran an abridged version under the title "Speed Readers Don't Read; They Skim." Carver began his piece with a joke attributed to Woody Allen, then unmarked by controversy and enormously popular: "I took a speed-reading course, learning to read straight down the middle of the page, and I was able to go through *War and Peace* in 20 minutes. It's about Russia." An image of a filthy bathroom wall illustrated the piece. Scrawled on it was, "Evelyn Wood Moves Her Lips When She Reads."

Peppered with pithy subtitles like "Farce" for the section on testing, the article provoked angry response. Bags of mail penned by Evelyn advocates and other speed-reading proponents swamped the offices of *Psychology Today*. Citing research that seemed to contradict Carver, readers urged the magazine to conduct its own unbiased research. The publication declined, but one researcher accepted. Wheels were set in motion for a follow-up piece that the magazine would print several years later.

At DEAR's Atlanta headquarters, the drawbridge was raised, and the archers took their places. The monthly bulletin sent to Evelyn Wood employees, usually a sheet or two, swelled to fourteen pages. Bracing the staff for questions from the public, Peter Kump rebutted Carver's anti-Wood arguments, point by point.

Kump said he was disturbed not only by Carver's attacks in the widely read article but also by the description of his lessons at the Evelyn Wood institute in Washington. "Some of the theories and techniques which Ron Carver was taught have long ago been abandoned by RD [Reading Dynamics] and they are contrary to what we know about the theory of efficient reading," wrote the national education director, without offering details. Recommending that franchisees review their teacher training manuals, he reminded them of their contractual duty to keep up to date.

Kump observed, "If Ron Carver had been taught RD as it is officially prescribed, we would most likely not be facing this problem. Any deviations from current theory cannot be considered to be Reading Dynamics." Underlining the words seemed to be a substitute for action. Would the Washington, DC, franchisee be held accountable? Beyond issuing a warning, the national education director gave no indication of consequences.

Evelyn Wood Reading Dynamics apparently had reverted to the "patchwork" that Webster had deplored years before. Even testing seemed to be a local decision; Kump mentioned that only a few institutes used the Nelson-Denny test that Carver had taken, but he had no objection to it.

Rallying the franchisees to stay current, Kump announced, "Evelyn Wood's latest lesson manual will be available for your fall classes."

By the time the bulletin arrived in Salt Lake City, Evelyn had other things to think about besides Ron Carver. Shipley had been behaving strangely, producing less and sometimes not showing up for work. The change began soon after Shipley returned from the national franchise convention in New York, where he had spoken about marketing Reading Dynamics to small towns. Doug had suggested Shipley as a speaker to Charles Durakis, the new president of DEAR. Webster was gone, leaving Durakis, an FAS International officer, in charge.

"I'm sure all our franchisees can profit from this presentation," Durakis wrote Doug from FAS International headquarters in Westport, Connecticut, where hundreds of not-so-famous writers and artists had been fired. The company had been operating under bankruptcy reorganization since February. Instead of three-year courses, the Famous Schools division sold one lesson at a time—for cash. Its few remaining instructors worked from home.

Durakis wrote that he hoped to stop by the franchise convention to see Doug and Shipley. He sounded tentative, as if this one-hour trip might not be worth the effort. FAS International had already shed two ill-considered acquisitions, Welcome Wagon and the mail-order accounting school, for a total of $12 million. DEAR and its only active division, Evelyn Wood Reading Dynamics, were almost certainly on the block.

Still, there could have been little doubt that someone would buy it. It had already changed hands twice, with no stunting of growth. Its very enormity drew criticism: Kump wrote that Carver was "attempting to build a career, or at least a reputation, through attacking Goliath."

So what could explain Shipley's loss of interest, which ended in his departure from the company? Marlene Bennett, the Woods' family friend and part-time instructor, remembered what happened next. Evelyn and Doug "realized that right here in Utah there was someone teaching their method."

That someone was, of course, Dick Shipley. Recruiting some of the Woods' instructors and promising students, he'd incorporated a competing business, calling it Reading Development Institute. Taking a cue from Ron Carver on how to play David against Goliath, Shipley described his own system as "not skimming" and—in a fresh challenge to Reading Dynamics—not "light novel reading." In ads placed in the *Daily Universe*, Brigham Young University's student newspaper, Shipley's system promised to focus on textbook reading. Then came the main selling point: a Reading Development Institute course was "a fraction of the cost of any of the expensive reading programs," the ads declared. The Woods' ex-employee knew that price was their weak spot.

The ads didn't give an address, just a phone number, but it didn't take the Woods long to piece things together. They were outraged that

Shipley had taken some of their ex-students with him. "He had complete access to the files. He stole some of the registrations," recalled Nielsen, referring to the enrollment forms.

They were also hurt. The attack had come from an active member of their own church, and among his conspirators, as Evelyn and Doug saw them, were devout Mormons. One of Shipley's new partners was Kenneth Orme, a former missionary and church counselor who taught high school in Garland, Utah. That was not far from Logan, where someone had been handing out leaflets advertising Shipley's new enterprise.

"We all felt that we had been let down by him. We all had a relationship with him, we really liked him," said Bennett. Nielsen said she'd been impressed, too, but there was "one thing about Richard that bugged me to death. I always, always called her Mrs. Wood, he called her Evelyn. There was a big difference in their ages."

Communication from that point on was on a strictly formal basis, through their lawyers. The Woods quickly sued Richard L. Shipley et al., basing their claim on the nondisclosure agreements that Shipley and the others had signed as instructors or students. The suit charged that even while still employed by their company, Shipley had actively solicited their workers and enrollees to join his competing business. The instructors had "acquired special, secret, and confidential skills and information," said the claim. It added that, as promotional director, Shipley had "had access to all the privileged and confidential materials and information belonging to plaintiff," which he'd used in violation of the agreement.

The suit also charged Shipley with slandering the good name and reputation of Reading Dynamics. He and his associates were said to have misrepresented the cost and effectiveness of the Evelyn Wood course, as well as the time required by it. The new competitor was also accused of having "seriously undercut plaintiff's prices"—although this point seemed to confirm Shipley's representations.

The suit requested an injunction to stop Shipley from running his company while damages were calculated.

Not content to leave matters to the court, the Woods, through intermediaries, contacted someone at Brigham Young University about putting a stop to Shipley's ads in the student newspaper. For years, Evelyn's name had been splashed over the advertising sections of the *Daily Universe*. Undoubtedly afraid of losing a major advertiser, the university accepted the Woods' argument that Shipley's company was illegitimate. The *Universe* decided not to honor the remainder of his advertising contract.

Intimidation had often worked for the Woods and the company they'd founded. They hadn't always stopped their competitors and detractors, but resisters didn't escape unscathed. Ehrlich, so outspoken in his *Saturday Evening Post* article, had pulled his punch in his debate with Evelyn in the *NEA Journal*. Spache had taken pains to avoid the appearance of defamation after his bold anti-Evelyn pronouncements drew a letter from a lawyer. Babbel refused to sign the employment agreement but lost his new house.

With Shipley, however, the Woods met their Waterloo. His answer was a countersuit for court costs plus $115,000—$50,000 in damages to himself, $50,000 for damages to his company, and $15,000 in punitive damages.

The Woods' so-called agreement was void, Shipley claimed, because he'd been hired on false premises. He said the Woods had "induced" him to accept their offer by promising he'd eventually earn $20,000 a year and share in the profits. Neither of those outcomes had happened, he said, even as he proved an exemplary employee and helped grow the company. For that reason, he sought damages for himself. The company had been harmed, he said, when the Woods meddled with his advertising contract "with no legal right whatever."

Denying allegations made by the Woods' suit, Shipley's response raised broader questions about the entire Reading Dynamics universe. He contended that the student agreements were void because no compensation was paid for signing them, and because some of the students who'd signed were legal minors. His countersuit also characterized the instructor's and student's agreements as unreasonable restraint of trade.

Back in the Ironrite age, Doug had used the restraint-of-trade argument to force a reluctant distributor to send him pressing machines. Now the same argument worked against him.

The trip to the New York convention may have inspired Shipley's final defense. The Woods' company "and its licensor, DEAR, have attempted to monopolize the field of reading improvement . . . on a nationwide basis," the suit charged. Somehow Shipley had picked up the national perspective, possibly meeting others who were contemplating their own breakouts.

According to Nielsen, Doug Wood decided not to fight it. "He was like a little mouse," she recalled. There was a settlement that amounted to a win for Shipley. The Woods paid him a substantial amount in damages, and he continued to compete with them head-on in several markets, including Salt Lake City. Shipley ads asked U students, "What's the most popular speed-reading program in Utah? . . . No, it's not Evelyn Wood," and asserted that "hundreds of students in Utah" were enrolling in Reading Development Institute courses "at a fraction of the cost of Reading Dynamics."

Shipley had launched his attack at a time when the Woods could ill afford to lose any students. In January 1972, their Utah-Idaho franchise enrolled a total of 56 new students and 123 the following month. An attempt to branch into Montana proved too costly to be worthwhile. By late 1973, Evelyn and Doug had reached another settlement—this time to accept office furniture in lieu of rent owed to them by their own corporation, EWRD of Utah-Idaho. Such agreements typically indicate financial distress. Doug's executive chair was valued at $84 and Evelyn's at $72.

There were other changes afoot. Once considered ironclad, the employment agreements were raising questions about monopolization. As for the *Psychology Today* piece, as Kump told the franchisees: "An article such as this one can be brushed off; it probably will not cause you a large amount of trouble, or a loss in sales. But it is very indicative of a new trend. It is certainly to be expected that at some point someone will start attacking us from a 'consumerism' vantage point. And if our house is not in order we could be very vulnerable."

That attack was already underway in Seattle, where another young man named Richard was organizing a group called Students Against Evelyn Wood.

11

White Knight

Richard J. Hernandez had wanted to marry his high school sweetheart, but his parents insisted on college. So, in the fall of 1971, he drove from his Los Angeles home to Seattle to begin his first year at the University of Washington. He made the trip in his 1969 Chevrolet Impala lowrider, polished to a high shine. "I was into cars," he recalled.

Hernandez's parents paid his tuition, but all other expenses, including housing, were up to him. With work and studies consuming virtually all his time, Hernandez was a prime target for the speed-reading siren song. Inevitably, he saw an ad for Evelyn Wood Reading Dynamics in the student-run *Daily of the University of Washington.* "Hey freshman," many of these ads began, "Welcome to a first-quarter workload you aren't going to believe."

The ad seemed to read Hernandez's mind. "The amount of reading I had to do in college compared to high school was substantial," he remembered. The ads, as he remembered, "showed a guy playing tennis," presumably after quickly dispensing with schoolwork.

Evelyn Wood demonstrations were a frequent occurrence at the University Tower Hotel. Hernandez attended one. "I was blown away," he recalled. Desperate for some spare time, he signed up, even though the $175 fee seemed steep to him. He was working in a hospital laundry and at fast-food restaurants to pay for his dorm room and incidentals, even collecting bottles to redeem them for gas money. Evelyn in her prime didn't surpass Hernandez for industriousness.

But then, "I took the course and the only thing I could speed-read was the page numbers," said Hernandez. "I felt like I'd been cheated." He said he'd been told that, with practice, he could slide his hand over pages and "miraculously" see and retain every word. If that were true, he said, "There must be something wrong with my eyes or my brain" because it didn't happen.

He submitted a request for a refund in writing but was refused on the grounds that his reading index had tripled. Like other Evelyn Wood skeptics, Hernandez considered this measurement farcical. He also began to sense that other Evelyn Wood grads felt as he did. Still, he might have left things there if not for an incident involving his beloved customized car.

The rainy Pacific Northwest was no place for a lowrider, Hernandez quickly discovered. Despite all his constant polishing, his Impala was rusting out. After saving enough to restore it with what he called a "one-of-a-kind paint job," he couldn't wait to show it to coworkers at the University of Washington laundry. But moments after he parked, a delivery truck collided with it. "Minutes out of the body shop, it got rammed and dented," he said.

Hernandez called the company that employed the driver and threatened to sue. That was all it took to get a settlement. He remembered this as a watershed moment. It galvanized his decision to expose the Evelyn Wood scam.

Working through a list of attorneys in the phone book, he found one willing to take the case on a contingency basis, not charging legal fees unless it was won. This was David DeLaittre, an unusual lawyer for a matter involving a reading system: he was totally blind. Now a judge, DeLaittre recalled that the Evelyn Wood claims seemed questionable from his own experiences with reading. Whether having law books read to him, as he did in that era, or using today's high-speed digital audio, "When it comes to the more technical work, you can't read it that fast," DeLaittre said. He said he might spend a week on a book about law or foreign policy without making much progress. But when it comes to Louis L'Amour's Western novels, of which he's a fan, "I can read one a day."

Then a young lawyer only recently admitted to the Washington state bar, DeLaittre took Hernandez's case. Hernandez was pleased to have found a lawyer who "was gung-ho about it," as he recalled. They decided to file a class action suit applicable to all UW students who'd taken the course. Although only one plaintiff is required for such an action, Hernandez was confident that he could get others to sign on.

Small signs sprang up on walls all over the Seattle campus, reading, "If you think you were taken by Evelyn Wood call 543-0577 immediately." Before long, thirty-one former Wood students had signed on as coplaintiffs. The suit, filed against Evelyn Wood Reading Dynamics and DEAR, charged that the company had violated the state's Consumer Protection Act by failing to fulfill its money-back guarantee and giving unfair tests. It sought refunds for all plaintiffs and double that total in punitive damages.

Identified in the University of Washington's student newspaper and in radio interviews as president of Students Against Evelyn Wood, Hernandez had become Peter Kump's nightmare: a consumer activist who fit the profile of the company's prime customer, the male college student.

A few years earlier, Ira West had noted in the *Wall Street Journal* that businesses were souring on speed-reading. This became evident as the company collected data on its own customers. Dozens of corporations still offered Reading Dynamics to its employees, but colleges and high schools were its meat and potatoes. In late 1969, 100 percent of the nation's new enrollees were students, and 72 percent were male.

The University of Washington case advanced as the suit was certified as a class action. The *Daily of the University of Washington*, covered the controversy in the spring of 1973, reporting that seventy-nine students had joined the suit. In the piece, headed "Reading Dynamics Is a Rip-off, Say Students," Hernandez described the method as a wildly overpriced skimming course and pointed to the same failings of the reading index that Carver and West had criticized.

An official for the Washington State franchisee told the paper, "We offered him the course again with extra attention, anything he wanted, because we don't like seeing unsatisfied graduates." But, because Hernandez had dropped out after five lessons—increasing his reading index more than threefold nevertheless—he would "never receive a refund," the official told the paper, adding, "He kept finding fault with things."

In fact, Hernandez remembered, the local Reading Dynamics director called him to a meeting and offered to settle with him alone, asking in return that Hernandez turn over contact information for all the other discontented students. "I said no," Hernandez recalled, and, "I was infuriated." Instead, he deployed a new weapon: disrupting Evelyn Wood demonstrations.

Organizing had introduced Hernandez to many new friends. Accompanied by some of these, he returned to the hotel where an Evelyn Wood demonstration had seduced him into registering for the course. Now it all seemed like fakery. "There'd be a ringer in the audience," he said, referring to people who asked questions after the reading performance. He and his pals interrupted, shouting out that the method didn't work.

The heckling produced results. Eventually, fewer people attended the demonstrations, and the company notified Hernandez and his lawyer that they planned to countersue for defamation. "I got carried away," Hernandez said, acknowledging that the media attention had gone to his head. He said his lawyer warned him to tone things down or at least delegate another person to speak up at the hotel meetings. However, no one stepped up to take Hernandez's place. "I was the leader of the pack," he said.

In DeLaittre's recollection, the company's lawyer deposed Hernandez and "took him apart." His grade point average had risen since taking the Evelyn Wood course, which could be used as evidence of its benefits. Acting on his attorney's advice, Hernandez dropped the suit. He'd learned that it was easier to prove defamation than to show that speed-reading didn't work. After all, Evelyn Wood Reading Dynamics provided students with a teacher, a classroom, and texts. "They did have a structured business model. It wasn't like they just had a post office box," DeLaittre said.

In the end, Hernandez got nothing. Evelyn Wood ads continued to run in the *Daily of the University of Washington*, striving for a hip, with-it tone. Ironically, the ads featured a cartoon drawing of student activists carrying protest signs inscribed, "Reading Lib Now!" "We Want Evvy, Baby!" and "Wood Is Good, Man!" A long-haired, bearded man lies on his stomach in the foreground. Apparently naked, with flowers concealing his groin, this reclined figure also holds a sign, which lists the schedule of upcoming speed-reading demonstrations.

If anything, the ad underscored how out-of-touch the company had become. Seattle wasn't the only place where demonstrators were encountering hecklers. When the Woods lent a speed-reader named Alan to another franchise, he bombed in California. An official at the Evelyn Wood institute in Burbank wrote to the Woods that Southern Californians tended to be "highly skeptical, perhaps even jaded, as regards any kind of a sales promotion. Their reaction was almost one of 'they must be doing it with mirrors.'"

Evelyn's once-celebrated demonstrators now seemed as dated as vaudeville. Abandoning live presenters altogether, the California franchisee said he'd revert to giving mini lessons and showing films. He concluded his letter to Evelyn and Doug by asking about updated television spots.

At the once-thriving Evelyn Wood institute in midtown Manhattan, tumbleweeds danced down the hallways. The institute's franchisee, the Lyceum, once so close to selling out for $1 million, had gone broke. Kramer, the franchisee who'd defended the method in the University of Pennsylvania student paper, laid off the entire staff in the summer of 1973. The parent company, FAS, rehired a few instructors to keep the office open, but the state labor board and consumer help lines were busy handling complaints.

The kinescope of the 1961 ABC segment on the senators by now was a relic. All four senators who'd graduated from that early Reading Dynamics class still held office. But in newspaper ads for Evelyn Wood courses, Proxmire was the last man standing. A New Jersey consumer appealed to him; the man was owed money due to the Lyceum fiasco and apparently believed the senator could do something about it. Proxmire passed the consumer's letter on to the New York institute, where a rehired employee took the trouble to answer it four months later.

Proxmire's decade-old endorsement brought in customers, but the text around it had changed over time. Once said to devour tens of thousands of words per minute, Proxmire was now described to read at a speed that "even on the toughest material seldom dips below 1,000 words per minute." Also new was the assertion, "You can't believe that he's actually reading. He must be skimming. But he's not."

The public was growing curious about Proxmire's relationship with Evelyn Wood Reading Dynamics. "I must protest this use of your name and office to support a solely private, profit-making organization," one man wrote the senator. In the early 1970s, a teacher, a college student, a magazine columnist, and the Council of Better Business Bureaus asked him to verify his endorsement. He did, often noting that "the harder you worked on the course and I did work very hard, the more you learned," and that maintaining the skill "requires constant use." He said he could still read a three-hundred-page novel in forty minutes.

One correspondent got the senator's special attention: Arthur R. Woods, assistant to the director of the Federal Trade Commission's Bureau of Consumer Protection. Clipped to his letter was an ad with Proxmire's photo, looking as he had in 1961, and his assertion that an Evelyn Wood course outranked Harvard and Yale. Woods asked Proxmire to comment on "the accuracy of the representations made in the advertisement" and to state whether his name was used with permission "before deciding on what action, if any, should be taken by the Commission."

Proxmire replied to the FTC as he did to all other such inquiries. "I have not lent my name or photograph to the course. I took the course several years ago and it was at this time that I made the statement attributed to me," he wrote, adding, "Absolutely no money is received for the advertisement."

It might be argued that the senator benefited from years of free nationwide publicity. Certainly, he'd done nothing to stop the company from using his name or photograph. The FTC seems to have let the matter drop. Soon after, Proxmire published a book, *You Can Do It! Senator Proxmire's Exercise, Diet, and Relaxation Plan.* Like Evelyn, he was a firm believer in self-improvement.

So was Maurice C. Thompson Jr., an advertising executive turned entrepreneur who saw a ripening market for self-improvement products. As a turnaround artist, "Tommy" Thompson, as he was known, belonged in the Louvre. He'd salvaged a company that marketed self-improvement audiocassettes, and now his eye was on speed-reading. FAS International, just emerging from Chapter 11 bankruptcy, could finally get Evelyn Wood off its hands.

With backing from two prominent venture capitalists, Dan W. Lufkin and Louis Marx Jr., Thompson paid a small amount of cash, $425,000, for $1.3 million in notes received by banks as a consequence of the bankruptcy. The banks eagerly accepted this small sum in exchange for notes of questionable value. FAS International swapped Evelyn Wood—or, more precisely, DEAR—for the notes, thus wiping out more than $1 million in liabilities. Thompson, an art collector then in his midthirties, also acquired some works from Famous Artists' heyday.

Thompson then set out to clean up the mess that Evelyn Wood Reading Dynamics had become under FAS International. Most of the company-owned franchises were losing money, and many of the licensed ones were, as Thompson told *Forbes*, "semi-dormant." Under FAS International's loose reins, even the profitable ones weren't necessarily paying what they owed in royalties. Thompson's mission was to bring them all under corporate control, offering deals to renegotiate contracts. For some of the lucrative franchises, like California, Thompson paid about $3 million, recalled his wife, Patricia. But not every franchisee got an attractive offer. There were some holdouts, lawsuits, and closures.

The Woods were immune to these disturbances. Their lifetime licensing agreement protected their franchise from sale or transfer. Even if it hadn't, Tommy Thompson wouldn't have dreamed of antagonizing Evelyn, his wife said. He had tremendous respect for brands and their creators. "He was the original Mad Man," Patricia said, referring to a popular television program about midcentury Madison Avenue. "He put her on a pedestal," said Patricia. "He believed she should be honored, and that this was her accomplishment, but the business side should be left to other people."

The balance sheet of the Utah-Idaho franchise supported that theory. Following the Shipley debacle, the Woods' franchise was moribund. For the year ended January 31, 1974, it reported a loss of nearly $28,000. The ad budget had been decimated from its previous level. Tuition revenues, less than robust for some time, had dipped to $136,000 from $263,000 the year before. Since 1970, franchises had been encouraged to raise the price of an Evelyn Wood course, to $250 and beyond. In some areas of the country, consumers barely blinked, but Utahans were balking. With Shipley's new company drawing the Woods into a price war, they were giving discounts, offering a shorter and cheaper "accelerated" course, and generally flailing.

Nonetheless, Tommy approached Evelyn like a courtier, albeit one from a different planet. Partly this was for business reasons, Patricia said, because "the last thing you want is to have the person who developed the product bad-mouthing the company." Tommy visited the Woods in Utah, accidentally leaving his expensive fur-lined leather jacket on a Salt Lake City street and marveling that no one stole it. An entirely social animal, he invited Doug and Evelyn to a gathering of franchisees in Westport, Connecticut, still the headquarters of DEAR. To Tommy, Evelyn was the woman with the golden name. As he told *Forbes*, as of the time he made the deal, $15 million had been spent to promote her brand, but "you can't just sit and expect the name to do all the work."

Evelyn was a fish out of water in this social setting. "I think she might have been a little uncomfortable," recalled Patricia, who was then in her twenties. "Most of the people were really young, very hard-charging, they partied a lot, and if you're a Mormon, that's probably not your social circle." She met the Woods on two occasions and remembered Evelyn as "very quiet," dressed in "pearls and a cardigan."

As for Doug, Patricia remembered, "He kind of walked behind her, like a queen. There are husbands and wives who take the credit for their spouse's accomplishments, and he was the absolute antithesis of that."

Patricia said her husband was a great believer in bringing together the "people who really believed in the product" and those purely interested in profit. Skepticism and consumer activism hadn't rattled the faith of Peter Kump, whom Patricia described as "an enthusiast," one of

the "dedicated Evelyn Wood lifers." She said her husband set up events
with the hope that enthusiasts would "inspire" the more money-driven
types. (Tommy never took the course himself, she said—something she
often ribbed him about.)

Among the profit-oriented types was one of Tommy's favorite
franchisees, Bernard Kelly, who with his partner, Max Cohen, owned
institutes in Washington, DC, and Florida. When FAS International
was in control, Kelly had tried to organize a franchisee rebellion—an
echo of the failed Sponsor's Council uprising against George Webster
of the 1960s. Thompson's new broom cheered Kelly, who'd described
the former DEAR management as unsupportive and "inept." Patricia
remembered him as a "character," who'd considered marketing a
weight-reduction soap said to wash fat away. "He said people would
buy so much of it before they realized it didn't work," she recalled
with amusement.

But did Reading Dynamics wash? Patricia once sold it. A "natural
speed reader," by her own description, she met her husband through
the company: she was previously married to a Texas franchisee. Asked
to comment on current scientific evidence that contradicts claims made
for the course, she said, "It was an outstanding product at the time."
Using today's phraseology, she added, "Everybody learns differently, but
with the blanket guarantee, that was tricky."

From a business perspective, she said, "People liked the product. In
those days, people really wanted to improve themselves." However, "it
wasn't going to last forever. It wasn't Palmolive or Dove. You needed
imagination to sell it."

Approaching the task with Madison Avenue savvy, Thompson
replaced the quietly persuasive ads with hard-sell messages and pop-
cultural punch. "It Sounds Incredible," read the headline of one, "But
Evelyn Wood Graduates Can Read *The Godfather* in 64 Minutes." A
cartoon of a cigar-chomping wise guy illustrated the ad. In another,
a shark bared its teeth next to a message promising that *Jaws* could
be devoured in forty-one minutes. Reading Dynamics was riding the
wave of the era's blockbuster movies. Lest anyone scoff at the light-
weight material, the ad also stated that Evelyn Wood grads "can devour

a textbook like Hofstadter's *American Political Tradition* and wrap up each chapter in eleven minutes."

Gone were the live demonstrators, replaced by "mini-lessons." The firm had instituted a new guarantee: the sample lesson alone was promised to double each attendee's reading efficiency—which, the ad explained, "combines" speed and comprehension. A bold dare replaced the old skimming defenses: "If you think this is another advertising con job, take a free mini-lesson and settle it once and for all."

Even after the introduction of movie themes, Evelyn Wood ads continued to tout the alleged John F. Kennedy connection. But as the Watergate hearings transfixed the nation, all references to Nixon were out. One of Kump's speed-reading students, Dwight Chapin, was sent to jail for lying to a grand jury. Another, Rose Mary Woods, became a laughingstock for testifying that she'd accidentally erased eighteen and a half minutes of a taped Nixon conversation by acrobatically reaching for a ringing phone. A third, Ron Ziegler, stood by the president as Nixon sank into the inferno.

One advertising element hadn't changed. The company continued to boast of its number of graduates, presenting popularity as proof of effectiveness. "Find out if we've pulled the wool over 500,000 graduates' eyes," the new ads taunted.

The number had been ticking up since the advent of Tommy and the infusion of cash from his investor group. In addition to the slick ads, the company put substantial money into an aggressive public relations campaign devised by the New York firm Robert Marston and Associates. Patricia recalled that Bob Marston was friendly with one of Tommy's backers. The investors had given Tommy a 40 percent stake in the equity in the form of a non-interest-bearing note, with the condition that he use half of this amount to motivate management. A large part of the motivational portion went to Marston's public relations program, which was intended to revitalize sales efforts. Initially, Patricia said, Tommy wasn't sure that the PR firm would merit its hefty fee.

Marston immediately took Evelyn out of mothballs, putting her back on the TV and radio talk show circuit. She'd been out of the public eye for so long that some newspaper articles addressed the question of her existence along the lines of, *Yes, Virginia, there really is an Evelyn Wood.* For Evelyn, this was a second chance to shine in the spotlight. It was also a chance to earn some additional income. At the close of 1973, as the Woods were visiting Carol and her family in Tucson, Evelyn's consulting contract had been transferred from FAS International to DEAR in anticipation of the ownership change. The other terms had been left intact. Over a period that saw the cost of an Evelyn Wood course double in some places, Evelyn hadn't seen a raise in the $20,000 annual consulting fee guaranteed to her by Famous Artists. A letter sent to her by Durakis wished her happy holidays but indicated no change in the contract beyond a brief amendment about the corporate name. Six years into a fifteen-year agreement losing value to inflation, she and Doug apparently made no attempt to renegotiate terms.

The company treated its founder not all that much better than its customers. Under FAS International, she'd developed two new products aimed at the promising juvenile market—Junior Reading Dynamics and Operation: R.E.A.D.—that a number of franchises were promoting aggressively. Yet Evelyn wasn't owed a dime for them. Her contract stated that any reading products she created belonged to the company.

The terms still offered her extra consulting fees, plus expenses, for travel outside Utah. After years of Famous Artists neglect, Evelyn seized Thompson's offer to hit the airwaves again. It relieved a blue period that followed the Shipley mutiny. Doug had fallen from a ladder, injuring his back and breaking his leg in several places. Evelyn had banged up her four-year-old Buick Riviera by crawling on the highway during a snowstorm and getting rear-ended. Now she could forget all that. Bob Marston had her booked for the new hit TV show *Good Morning America* on the same day as Sammy Davis Jr.

The PR agency also sent her on a whirlwind tour of local media in Detroit and Chicago. In some of the interviews, Evelyn focused on her latest project, a remedial-reading program she was piloting on Native American children in conjunction with Brigham Young University. Although unwilling to finance this plan through his investor group,

Thompson was helping her apply for foundation or government fund-
ing. Amid all the consumer accusations, it didn't hurt to connect the
Evelyn Wood brand with public service.

Not surprisingly, Evelyn claimed she'd again worked miracles,
advancing struggling Indian kids by several grade levels in a matter of
weeks. That was one topic covered in one fruit of Marston's efforts, a
King Features Syndicate feature that ran nationwide. Evelyn hadn't mel-
lowed with age. Invariably described as soft-spoken a decade before, she
had now become a "snappy sexagenarian," in the words of columnist
Phyllis Battelle. Speaking of the Nixon staffers, she said, "I was sorry
we ever taught them to read."

The syndicated piece ended by noting that Senator Herman Talmadge had never realized his dream of seeing the Wood method used
in every American school. As Evelyn told the reporter, school districts
had consistently turned it down.

Reporting on Evelyn's Midwest broadcast blitz, the Marston agency
gave her high marks. She'd dominated a panel discussing public education on a Chicago radio station and steered a Detroit TV news program
away from a general discussion of reading instruction and back to Reading Dynamics. In a business interview on a local TV show, she'd managed to mention the address and phone number of the Chicago institute.
No such wiles were needed on the morning television show *A.M. Detroit*.
There, host and Evelyn Wood grad Dennis Wholey introduced her as
"the most famous reading teacher in the world" and bestowed his ringing endorsement on the course.

But the crowning achievement of the public relations campaign
didn't feature Evelyn. The hugely popular television personality Johnny
Carson invited a Junior Reading Dynamics graduate to pit her reading skills against his in a mock battle staged on his top-rated *Tonight
Show*. Given one minute to read sixteen pages of a book on biofeedback,
thirteen-year-old Beth Jaffe of Skokie, Illinois, breezed through, quickly
scrubbing each page with a side-to-side movement as if she were erasing it. Finishing with time to spare, she went back to reread two pages.
Carson, meanwhile, perused his own copy of the book with clownishly
raised eyebrows and exaggerated slowness, evoking howls of laughter as

he licked a finger before page-turning, then abandoning the effort and miming Jaffe's scrubbing movement.

The two were then quizzed by Carson's television sidekick, Ed McMahon, who had a list of questions. This was a departure from the recall format, which, as pointed out by Evelyn's critics, allowed skilled demonstrators to weave authentic-sounding fabrications. Jaffe gave accurate answers to five questions, several of them difficult. (Carson joked his way through them.) The book was a challenging one, *New Mind, New Body: Biofeedback, New Directions for the Mind* by Barbara Brown. It's conceivable that two of the questions could have been answered by the reader's prior knowledge, but others were specific to the book and seemed to require the comprehension of long narrative passages.

There were some strange elements in this televised stunt. For one thing, four pages of the section assigned to Carson and Jaffe contain large graphs, printed sideways on the page. Jaffe didn't appear to turn the book sideways while reading, although she was not always visible during the reading "contest"—the camera frequently cut away to Carson, who, more entertaining to watch, was often shown in close-up. McMahon's questions didn't ask about the information in the graphs. Also, Jaffe, seated at a small desk between the two men, left her book open during the quiz. Flailing at the answers and evoking laughs, Carson pulled her book toward him. Presumably, he was checking to see whether they'd read the same book, but he carefully left it open while sliding it back to her. A skeptic might wonder if she was referring to notes—perhaps taken by her in the controversial "preview" stage of prior demonstrations. TV game shows had been tightly monitored since the scandals of the 1950s, but this was not a game, and there was no prize.

There were huge rewards, though. The Johnny Carson segment sold Reading Dynamics all over again. It was introduced to a new generation that bore little resemblance to Bob Darling in his jacket and tie, Louise Mahru in her fitted dress, or the other demonstrators of the early 1960s. Now teenagers looked like Beth Jaffe as she'd dressed for the show, in jeans and a long-sleeved T-shirt, with her glass curtain of hair parted in the middle. Above all, America's favorite late-night host had essentially endorsed the method.

As the show went on the air, the company expected to post $10.5 million in revenues for 1975—more than nine times the revenue from three years before—and net about $2.6 million. The Carson boost made the outlook even rosier. In the following year, even with the price of a course creeping up past $395, between 30 and 40 percent of attendees at the free mini lessons signed up for the full course, and some institutes were running those free sessions, which were essentially sales pitches, five days a week.

To be sure, there were still some naysayers. In 1976, the Pennsylvania Bureau of Consumer Protection received complaints accusing a local Evelyn Wood institute of misleading claims and unreasonable refund policies. The bureau opened an investigation of the Eastern Pennsylvania franchise, still operated by the Lyceum—the company that had closed abruptly in New York, leaving employees and consumers in the lurch.

The consumer protection agency, directed by Pennsylvania's attorney general, obtained a court order to force the firm to turn over documents. But the franchisee refused to comply with subpoenas, claiming that moving files would disrupt business. The consumer protection bureau apparently settled or dropped the case. There was no further news about it, and records from that time have not been preserved.

Having done her bit, Evelyn returned to Utah. She was expecting to devote much of her time to the remedial project she'd been piloting with Native Americans in coordination with the Institute for Computer Uses in Education at Brigham Young. Evelyn was optimistic that they'd meet or approach her goal for them: reading twenty books in seven weeks.

Despite all her other involvements, the founder still spent time at Evelyn Wood Reading Dynamics of Utah and Idaho. As a newspaper reporter had noted earlier in her career, "'Dynamic' must be her middle name." Marlene Bennett was still on staff. Her husband, Mike, also worked in the office, helping to set up mini lessons. Mike had also worked in the LDS Hospital as a medical technician. Knowing that, Evelyn called Mike over one day when they were both at the office.

"She said, 'The whole side of my body is tingling,'" Marlene recalled, "and Mike said, 'Get her to the hospital.'"

Evelyn had suffered a devastating stroke. For the next two years, she would not be able to walk or read.

12

Rehab

EVELYN'S BELIEF THAT PEOPLE can do anything they set their minds to would be put to the test. The stroke left her, quite literally, unable to lift a finger. "It was frustrating. Utterly frustrating," she reflected much later, "and I couldn't imagine it was happening to me."

The stroke plunged the "snappy sexagenarian" of the newspaper feature into helpless old age. Evelyn was about to begin a long course of rehabilitation, though she would never recover her previous levels of mobility and vitality. Although still owners of the Utah-Idaho franchise, she and Doug left most matters to their staff and had doubtlessly planned to spend more time at their canyon cabin, enjoying the wildflowers and mountain views. Now, using a wheelchair, Evelyn looked bent and frail.

For two years, she couldn't read. "You can imagine how that hit her," Doug reflected later. The Woods' lives had undergone devastating changes, but one thing remained the same: their eagerness to defend Reading Dynamics, even when a reporter suggested that Evelyn might not have been paid all that was due to her.

That issue was raised by an Orange County, California, paper, the *Daily Pilot*. The reporter who placed the call to Utah, Philip Rosmarin, knew nothing about the stroke. In fact, he was amazed that there really was such a person as Evelyn Wood. Like many others at this time, he thought she might be fictitious, like Betty Crocker or Aunt Jemima.

In a lengthy piece that appeared on the same page as a consumer helpline column, Rosmarin took a critical look at the claims of the local Reading Dynamics institute. His sources included a so-called self-employed economist named John King, who said he'd put himself through graduate school by teaching at Evelyn Wood institutes all over Southern California. King told the reporter that the system was a "ripoff" that used fraudulent tests, that most students made little progress, and that he and other teachers routinely told students to "stick with it" and they'd improve, while knowing that wasn't true. No dates for this former instructor's employment were given, but the article indicated it had been some years before. He was also concerned about Evelyn's treatment during the various purchases of the company. "She didn't get a goddamn dime out of it," he said.

That was true only in a figurative sense, in light of the millions made by others. The *Pilot* mentioned the consulting arrangement, having fact-checked with a call to the Wood home. Doug, now retired, handled the interview, explaining that "an illness" made Evelyn unable to participate. He rushed to defend the current owners, saying they "were doing a marvelous job. They're going great guns again."

But Tommy Thompson was no longer needed to man those guns, as his backers soon made clear. "Nineteen seventy-six was a peculiar year for all of us," Thompson wrote Evelyn and Doug soon after its close. That was certainly true for the Woods, with Evelyn still severely disabled. Tommy had to deal with less critical changes. According to his wife, the venture capitalists eased him out of Reading Dynamics. Wanting an older, more stable hand at the wheel, they approached a retired advertising executive named Alan Sidnam. "He was a lovely, lovely man," said Patricia. She recalled that Sidnam had a younger wife, also from the advertising world, who was a "real go-getter."

Sidnam became chairman and CEO of DEAR, soon announcing the departure of Doug Hall, a former Seattle franchisee who'd created the movie-themed ads for Thompson and had run operations. There were no hard feelings, Patricia said. Proof of that is that Hall, as well as DEAR's president, James A. De Sanctis, would later reunite with Thompson on his next successful project: Smokenders, also founded by a woman, Jacquelyn Rogers. (At least one franchise would run Smok-enders and Evelyn Wood classes at the same site.) Tommy was much more like Jackie than Evelyn, Patricia said. The founder of the popular smoking cessation program—herself a former heavy smoker, begged by her family to stop—didn't mind if Tommy fought with her. Patricia recalled that the two would often vehemently disagree about some point of business, only to quickly make up.

Patricia, who had only known Evelyn when she was well, said Tommy never fought with the Reading Dynamics founder. "I think she had a bit of an ego. She was no shrinking violet. My husband stroked her ego in a way."

Now struggling to relearn the basics of life, Evelyn needed more than ego stroking. She was working hard on physical therapy and improving somewhat. "Her persistence pulled her through," Doug said. While she was still unable to read, the Woods received a heartening letter. A US president had invited an Evelyn Wood instructor to come to the White House (not to the office building that had accommodated Kump). What's more, the nation's chief executive was going to attend the lessons himself.

One month into his presidency, Jimmy Carter had arranged to have the Wood method taught to himself, his aides, and his family. More accurately, he had accepted an offer for a free course. There are conflicting versions of how this came about. When Sidnam passed away years later, a paid death notice placed in the *New York Times* associated him with it. The notice mentioned that it gave a "quick lift" to Evelyn Wood Reading Dynamics. The Carter lessons were listed among Sidnam's other accomplishments, including coining the phrase, "When Tide goes in, dirt comes out." However, Patricia Thompson credits her husband, saying that Tommy worked it through Howard J. Samuels, the creator of Baggie trash bags and a figure in New York Democratic politics, whom she described as one of Carter's closest friends. Nicknamed "Howie the Horse," Samuels had brought off-track betting to New York State.

Defensive about their Georgia origins, Jimmy and Rosalynn Carter were trying to project a cultured image far removed from connections with Tide detergent, Baggies, and OTB parlors. The Carters' avid interest in self-improvement inspired a newspaper feature that chronicled their Spanish studies, literary interests, and appreciation of classical music—all pursued with dogged discipline. The report lumped speed-reading with these other activities. Similarly, a Carter biography by Bruce Mazlish and Edwin Diamond connected Carter's religious beliefs to his zeal for what the biographers called the "mind-cure movement." The idea, they wrote, was, "Success seekers must take a positive hand in the journey to grace." Evelyn and Carter didn't share the same faith, but in this they agreed.

Evelyn's method wasn't the first that the president had tried. Fifteen years earlier, when he was first running for Georgia state senate, Jimmy and Rosalynn Carter had taken a reading-improvement course at the institution now known as Georgia Southwestern State University, where both had once matriculated. Interviewed more than a decade later, their former teacher claimed to remember details of their progress. Both had done well, she said, with the future president reading 2,000 wpm at the end, with 90 percent comprehension. Carter had reportedly vowed to read every bill before signing it as a state senator, and his newfound skills allowed him to keep that promise.

Evidently, he had backslid between that time and his ascension to the presidency. This was something of a surprise, considering the mountains of paperwork he'd encountered as governor of Georgia, seemingly ripe for speed-reading practice. Then again, Evelyn Wood Reading Dynamics was offering the classes not only to him but also to his entire family and White House staffers.

There is no doubt that the Evelyn Wood lessons were *offered* to the Carter administration, not solicited. That raised ethical questions, discussed in memos exchanged by Carter's legal staff. The question was resolved by having the course taught not by one of the "believers," as Patricia Thompson called the dedicated instructors, but by Bernie Kelly— the Washington franchisee who'd mulled marketing a weight-reduction soap. Because Kelly was a salaried executive who taught nowhere else, he could be viewed as a "volunteer." As explained by deputy White House counsel Margaret McKenna, a present from Evelyn Wood Reading Dynamics to the White House or the president would violate gift guidelines, but Bernie Kelly could donate his time.

Kelly also had to sign a letter promising not to use the White House engagement for any promotional purposes during Carter's administration or after he'd left office. Such assurances were hardly necessary, because Kelly's teaching debut drew widespread national attention that didn't cost a cent. Through either leaks or news releases, the presidential lessons became widely known, and the White House press office eagerly answered reporters' questions. Coyly declining to disclose his students' reading scores, Kelly suggested to the *Atlanta Constitution* that the class star was the president's daughter, Amy, then nine. Aside from her, Kelly named the president as the best of the six thousand students he'd taught—an apparent contradiction of the nonteaching image he'd presented to the White House. Carter said he'd finished the course reading 1,200 wpm, the very same rate attributed to John F. Kennedy.

Evelyn had a long road ahead of her in Salt Lake City; at some point she suffered a second stroke. But as she struggled to regain speech, her name was on everyone's lips again. Scheduled to make one of the self-deprecatory speeches expected of presidents at Washington's Gridiron Club, Carter received a list of possible jokes from his staffers. One suggestion was to say he used the Evelyn Wood method to read *Playboy* magazine, which had run a famously controversial interview with him.

Meanwhile, the company made sure no one forgot about Beth Jaffe and the Johnny Carson show. The young prodigy's name and face appeared in Evelyn Wood ads, and the *Tonight Show* segment was regularly screened at sales sessions masquerading as free introductory lessons. But Jaffe said she hadn't consented to the use of her name and image in the company's promotions. A lawyer representing her filed a lawsuit in Cook County Circuit Court seeking $6.5 million in damages.

Skepticism still bubbled under the surface. But just as Evelyn had excelled in rebuttal during her days of college-debating glory, her company moved quickly to quash dissent. When the University of North Carolina's campus newspaper unfavorably compared the Evelyn Wood course to the school's equivalent (tuition: ten dollars), the director of the Evelyn Wood institute in Atlanta responded with a letter to the editor, charging the student reporter with sloppiness. With no fact-checking or comment by the editors—and with Evelyn Wood Reading Dynamics breaking into Chapel Hill with ad buys—the institute director had the last word. Among his objections was the report's frequent citations of Carver's article in *Psychology Today*. "I wonder how much of that article is misquoted or taken out of context," the company official insinuated.

In fact, the student newspaper had accurately reported on Carver's findings, which had since been confirmed by a second *Psychology Today* article. Addressing the howls of protest evoked by the Carver article, the magazine published the results of a speed-reading experiment conducted by Richard G. Graf. Unlike Carver, Graf could not be accused of bias against speed-reading. Indeed, a company that competed with Reading Dynamics in Southern California, Educational and Industrial Research, had invited Graf to run the experiment, obviously hoping to undermine Carver.

Graf found that graduates of a speed-reading course nearly tripled their reading rates of both light and heavy material, but, at the same time, their comprehension plummeted. Graf noted that a small number of experimental subjects managed to increase their comprehension scores while upping their speed. These overall improvers also tended to have high grade-point averages, he noted. "Perhaps there is a correlation between the efficacy of speed-reading programs and general intellectual ability, so that the brighter the student the more she or he should understand while rocketing through the literature," Graf wrote, adding that these cases were too small in number to analyze statistically.

Carver would have described these outliers as skillful skimmers, noting that "Kennedy Skims at 1,200 Word Per Minute" might have been a lousy headline but an accurate statement. (During his presidency, one White House correspondent described what he was doing as "mountain-goat reading," by which "one leaps from point to point, grasping ideas as one skips along.")

Peter Kump was no longer available to issue point-by-point refutations of debunking stories in the company bulletin. Patricia Thompson had used the term "lifer" to describe Kump and other devotees of the Evelyn Wood way, but few things last a lifetime. No longer with the company, he was competing with it on price. Kump placed a small ad in the *New York Amsterdam News*, a newspaper owned by and written

for African Americans. Identifying himself as the former national educational director of Evelyn Wood Reading Dynamics, Kump, who was
white, offered his own personal teaching services at "one-third the cost
of a comparable course." The small ad was headed, "Read *Roots* in
Four Hours. All 688 pages." Blatantly hijacking the Reading Dynamics
advertising theme, although tailoring it to a black audience, Kump also
seemed to be violating the nondisclosure and noncompete restrictions
of the firm's employee agreement.

Kump wasn't the only Evelyn Wood employee to go rogue. Calling themselves Dynamic Reading, a group of Wood-trained instructors
had rented space on campuses in Ohio, Michigan, and Indiana to teach
speed-reading courses. They brought the tricks of the trade with them.
A Notre Dame senior who'd taken their courses sued for fraud, saying
they'd inflated reading-speed scores. But, like the Evelyn Wood course,
this breakaway firm came armed with a refund policy and testimonials.
"If you can get your money back, I don't see how people can be hurt,"
one satisfied student told the Notre Dame student newspaper, unboth-
ered by charges that exit tests involved false timings and exaggerated
word counts.

Meanwhile, the company became fodder for satire on the hit TV
show *Saturday Night Live*, then in its third season. Dan Aykroyd, Jane
Curtin, and Bill Murray created a mock commercial for the "Evelyn
Woodski Slow Reading Course," about the joys of reading at normal
speeds. One actor spoke of discovering that Mark Twain's writing was
humorous. Another played a surgeon who'd stopped botching operations
since giving up speed-reading. In a surprise cameo, blind entertainer
Ray Charles said his hands, blistered by rapid braille reading, had finally
healed.

But Tommy Thompson and his investor partners had the last laugh.
In October 1977, they sold Evelyn Wood Reading Dynamics to URS
Corporation of San Mateo, California, for $7 million. Tommy's mind
was on other things—in fact, he'd started a new company called Mind
Inc., which would eventually turn Smokenders around. But, still owning
a 20 percent stake in Evelyn Wood, he "made some good dough," said
his wife. Johnny Carson and Jimmy Carter had clinched the sale. The

balance sheet was another attraction. Annual enrollment had soared to thirty-two thousand, and the company was earning $2 million in pretax profits on sales of $11 million.

Evelyn Wood and URS made an odd couple. The California-based firm offered architectural and engineering services. It had had a hand in building New York City's Shea Stadium. But, owned publicly and headed by a former brokerage executive, URS sought less dependence on government contracts and stronger profits. Speed-reading looked more in line with these goals than the engineering firm's usual business, which included cleanup of toxic waste sites. For the same reason, URS also bought Advanced Systems, a provider of video-based training programs.

In fact, although Reading Dynamics was scarcely dependent on the US government for revenues, the company had at least one military contract. Records indicate that, in its last year of ownership by Thompson and his partners, Evelyn Wood Reading Dynamics had a military contract valued between $10,000 and $25,000. Despite the US Air Force's disappointments with the Evelyn Wood method, reported years earlier by the *Wall Street Journal*, the army had contracted the company's services, apparently supplied by an institute in Michigan.

By the time URS acquired Reading Dynamics, Thompson had bought up virtually all the franchises. Only 4 percent remained outside corporate ownership. One of those, Evelyn Wood Reading Dynamics of Utah, lay mostly dormant. With Thompson gone and Evelyn struggling to regain basic functions, the Woods apparently knew nothing of the Carter lessons. Months after the fact, headquarters shared the news with her, along with some White House photos. Carter had scrawled a message of thanks to Evelyn over a photograph of himself reading—using a pen, not fingers, as a pacer. The autographed picture was framed and placed over the Woods' fireplace mantel.

Warnings issued to Salt Lakers about their last chance for a free introductory lesson were not empty threats. Once unavoidable in campus newspapers, the ads went on hiatus for most of 1977, resuming in October, around the time that URS made its acquisition. At year's end, despite the lifetime licensing arrangement, the state of Utah involuntarily dissolved the Woods' corporation.

Thompson's venture capitalist partners made a fortune with the URS deal. Evelyn did not. The new owners picked up her consulting contract, amending it to a base compensation of $22,000 per year. Adjusted for inflation, that was close to what George Webster had offered in 1963. In the past, she'd earned more than the base through additional promotional work, but she was no longer capable of much. It's possible that her last whirlwind tour, much as she welcomed it, had precipitated the stroke. Evelyn had a history of neglecting her health when busy, as evidenced fifteen years before by the neglect of her thyroid malignancy. Now all she could do to earn the consulting fee was wish her owners well, or at least appear to.

Evelyn still used a wheelchair much of the time. However, she'd regained her ability to speak, frame thoughts, follow arguments, and even dissemble. That was evident as she and Doug sat for a ninety-minute conversation about the 1939 evacuation of the European missions. The session at was one of several interviews with former mission presidents conducted by LDS Church historian Richard O. Cowan and his research assistant David F. Boone. The coordinator of the oral history project, Gordon Irving, who described the Woods as "charming people," later selected their interview for inclusion in an oral history of the church and gave them a transcript of the tape he'd recorded for editing and approval.

Boone, then a graduate student in BYU's history department, had read Doug's 1940 conference paper about the evacuation of the West German mission. Fascinated by this and similar accounts of war-related evacuations around the globe, Boone decided to write his master's thesis on the topic. His enthusiasm had spread to Cowan, a scholar of the church in the twentieth century. As their audiotape rolled at the Woods' home, Doug had a chance to relive the high point of his service to his church, and perhaps his life.

Doug did most of the talking. After all, the interview was about his mission presidency. However, Evelyn also participated, briefly elaborating on Doug's remarks or even correcting him. The historians told the couple they hadn't expected that Sister Wood of the Frankfurt mission would be *the* Evelyn Wood. Either due to her celebrity or at Doug's insistence, her name is in the title of the oral history, and her photo is next to his. Other interviews in the series didn't include spouses.

Doug gave essentially the same account of the faith-promoting evacuation as in his long-ago conference paper. Receiving orders to get the missionaries out while he was away from his office, he reserved a flight to Frankfurt on a packed plane, not through luck but by a miracle. Ordering missionaries to neutral territory in the Netherlands, but then finding that border restricted, he sent an emissary to search train stations for these lost sheep. Equipped with tickets, currency, and a whistled code, the emissary located them and sent them on to Denmark. As before, Doug's telling conveyed a strong sense of divine intervention. Once again, he portrayed the evacuation as a close escape from the Nazis by cleverly resistant Mormons.

In the introduction to his master's thesis, Boone said the interviews had opened his eyes to the accommodations that Mormons had made with the Nazis. Some disturbing information had emerged from an interview with an Idaho man who'd served a mission under Albert C. Rees, Doug's Berlin-based counterpart, president of the East German mission. The Idahoan said he'd been ordered to contact church members with Jewish ancestry and tell them they could no longer come to church. The former missionary said he'd "felt pretty small" about that, "but he was doing as he was directed." Boone said he'd also learned that Rees had a "fascination with some of the doctrines of the Nazi party" and "some kind of working relationship or understanding" with Nazi officials that had allowed American Mormons to stay in Germany for years, doing church work.

Boone pinned the blame on Rees, long deceased, for "tolerating the mistreatment of the Jewish people, even if one disagreed with what was happening . . . in an obvious attempt to stay inconspicuous." But Doug, despite the hand-wringing in his letters home, had done the same. He'd abandoned a church member who'd converted from Judaism, refusing to help him emigrate to America. Doug had also made anti-Semitic remarks to a German occupant of his train compartment, feeling embarrassed only because the man turned out to be Jewish.

The subject came up only at the end of the historians' lengthy conversation with the Woods. An hour into the interview, the tape recorder switched off before coming on again, with Doug apparently answering an unheard question about Nazi persecution of the Jews. He answered by giving the date of Kristallnacht and describing it as "the first reprisal against the Jews." His next words indicated his own reliance on stereotypes. "There were 25,000 Jews in Frankfurt alone, and of course they controlled a lot of the businesses," he continued.

Rejecting the Nazi explanation that these orchestrated acts of terrorism were spontaneous, Doug called them "terrible." He seemed uncomfortable talking about the events, confusing the term "spontaneous" with "spontaneous combustion." Similarly, he described stores that had been "plundered," then said he thought the Nazis hadn't stolen anything. That last comment evoked a correction from Evelyn, who said she'd seen furniture thrown from windows.

The Woods' interviewers soon changed the subject, asking them about their feelings on leaving Frankfurt. To conclude, Doug shared a comment he attributed to a Gestapo member and which he took as compliment. "They said, 'We've never seen anybody that could evade the law and get by with it like you Americans, you Mormons especially.'" Minor infractions of the law by Doug's young missionaries had, in fact, been ignored, undoubtedly due to the special understanding between the LDS Church and the National Socialists. As usual, Doug singled out Evelyn as the heroine of this tale, saying, "My wife was a jump ahead of the Nazis most of the time."

The Woods became known to a wider audience as two new books came on the market. *Breakthrough Rapid Reading* by Peter Kump was published in 1979. Either released from, or in flagrant violation of, Evelyn Wood Reading Dynamics' standard employee agreement, Kump identified himself as its former national director, now turned independent reading consultant. He wrote that his book was "an entirely new self-teaching format" designed for those who "can't afford the expensive classroom instruction." But, while not calling his method Reading Dynamics, Kump included finger-movement diagrams and page-turning techniques straight out of Evelyn's playbook.

If the Woods didn't profit from this publication, they don't seem to have objected to it either. Evelyn's name crops up in the text more than a dozen times, as Kump recounts her discoveries and praises her teaching. The book is dedicated to Evelyn and Doug, and a practice passage reads, "Doug Wood has one of the sunniest dispositions of anyone I know." The greatest Reading Dynamics teachers, wrote Kump, were those in Salt Lake City, trained by the founder. Immortalizing one in a reading drill, he wrote, "Verla Nielsen is a wonderful teacher. One of her great qualities is patience."

Kump had already started a cooking school in his apartment, and he was being talked about in culinary circles. He made no mention of this in *Breakthrough Rapid Reading*, but he included these sentences for practice: "Simone Beck is an inventive cook. She manages to balance her career and home life and still comes up with great meals. Her husband says she should try catering." Beck, of course, had done more than that. She'd written the bestselling *Mastering the Art of French Cooking* with Julia Child, who later joined Kump in founding the James Beard Foundation.

Reading Dynamics responded two years later with its own book, published by Simon and Schuster. The title, *How to Read Faster and Better*, was printed on the cover beneath a banner reading, "The Evelyn Wood Reading Dynamics Program." Lest that not seem sufficiently official, the author was named as "Franklin J. Agardy, Ph.D., president, Evelyn Wood Reading Dynamics, Inc." Agardy held a doctorate, but not in a field related to reading. He was a URS vice president, and his other published works were journal articles about waste management and water works. Verla Nielsen recalled being visited in Salt Lake City by a different writer, perhaps Agardy's collaborator. The book's acknowledgments include thanks to Nielsen for her "zeal in reconstructing Evelyn Wood's life." Evidently, the founder had not made herself available, an unusual lapse in Evelyn's lifelong quest to control her own publicity.

The Woods had ceded control of their franchise to the parent company. They'd released the rights to use the trademarks "Evelyn Wood" or "Reading Dynamics" in the state of Utah. Agardy and other URS executives were listed in corporate documents as officers of the Salt Lake

City institute, with Nielsen as business agent. The transfer of ownership may not have gone smoothly. Sales of Evelyn Wood courses were in a slump, and several institutes, including the one in Salt Lake City, had been closed temporarily at the start of the year. Some reopened with new managers, or with part-time instructors replacing full-time staff. The Chicago institute, which had closed for a few months in the early 1970s when its franchisees went bust, shut down again.

In an interview with the *Chicago Tribune*, Agardy blamed the weakened economy. Evelyn Wood courses now cost between $425 and $495. "When the economy gets bad, people would prefer to buy a refrigerator than Reading Dynamics or Weight Watchers," he said. Interviewed shortly before his book launched, he said he hoped its appearance would rekindle business.

The company-produced book offered nothing like Kump's step-by-step drills and lessons. A review in *Library Journal* said it "basically seems an inducement to attend an Evelyn Wood course." It's a slim volume with type surrounded by ample white margins. One-tenth of the text is devoted to Evelyn's biography.

The chapter about her life included the evacuation story. In this Hollywood-ready version, the danger obliquely implied by Doug is clearly spelled out. There is no hint of cooperation with Nazis here. According to the author of *How to Read Faster and Better*, Doug phoned all the missionaries and said, "Get out of your homes. The war might break out at any time, and the Gestapo will come for you."

13

Carved in Stone

As URS FIDDLED WITH EVELYN Wood Reading Dynamics, the speed-reading salad days were over. The first year after the acquisition, profits dropped $500,000 on falling revenues. The engineering company tinkered with ad buys, packaged the course on audiocassettes, created Evelyn Wood Corporate Training Programs, and tried reverting to a franchising system. It renamed the stale Reading Dynamics course "RD2," suggesting a connection with the cresting digital age. Nothing worked.

As Agardy said in his *Chicago Tribune* interview, the entire speed-reading industry was suffering, and this was not just due to the economy. The media had soured on Reading Dynamics and its ilk. News organizations that had once ignored skeptics now had them on speed dial. In 1960, the *Washington Post* had helped Evelyn vault to fame. Two decades later, it asked in a headline, "The Speedreading Courses: Are They Just Skimming?" and essentially answered yes. Ample space in the lengthy feature was devoted to Ronald Carver's debunking of the Wood method. Other skeptics were quoted, too, including John Guthrie, research director of the International Reading Association—once headed by Evelyn's champion, Russell Stauffer.

Contacted in Utah, Evelyn and Doug had their say too. Never one for false modesty, Evelyn described her discovery as "the greatest thing since the printing press," something "so new, it frightened me." Adding a scientific gloss to this familiar thread, Agardy told the *Post*, "It's like teaching Darwin against the Bible." But years of complaints by consumers, including several quoted in this article, had taken their toll. Evelyn could no longer play the embattled resistance fighter.

Beth Jaffe, the wunderkind of the Johnny Carson show, was now in college and "not really a speed reader anymore," according to the report, because she found the method useful only for some types of reading. Jaffe was said to have received $25,000 in an out-of-court settlement of the lawsuit regarding the use of her name and image. Concluding with the Woody Allen joke about speed-reading *War and Peace*—now a staple in academic literature about reading—the feature went out on the *Post*'s wire service and ran in other papers.

Another reformed Evelyn booster, the *Baltimore Sun*, ran a similar piece, only slightly less critical. A *Sun* reporter enrolled in the course and disclosed her purpose, as Ira West of the *Wall Street Journal* had done years before. She attended an institute owned by Max Cohen and Bernie Kelly, Carter's teacher. They were running a Smokenders franchise at the same location. More than half the reporter's classmates dropped out before the end of the course.

The Baltimore reporter contacted Carver for comment. The article also quoted an attendee at an introductory lesson who complained, "I can read faster without this finger business," and a course graduate who compared the method to "gulping Dom Perignon," and said, "I wouldn't dream of using it for something I considered worthwhile literature."

The tide had turned. Still operating in twenty-six cities and claiming one million graduates—although that was probably an exaggeration—"Evelyn Wood has become a part of American pop culture," the *Sun* wrote. But the woman herself hadn't been visible for years. Seeking comment from a company spokesperson, the Baltimore paper talked to Cohen, the Washington franchisee, not Evelyn.

A Utah television station brought Evelyn back into the public eye, at least locally. A segment on KUTV's *PM* news-magazine program focused on her latest achievement, recovering from the stroke. Speaking to a reporter at their home and in a rehabilitation facility, the Woods described Evelyn's battle to regain mobility and speech. The production recapped her speed-reading career and included clips from the 1961

ABC show, with appearances by Senator William Proxmire, Bob Darling, and Evelyn.

Introducing Evelyn in the segment, the reporter said, "She has
touched the lives of over one million people either personally or through
her classes around the world, but she has become her own best student
since 1976." That was the date of the stroke. In this show, produced
five years later, Evelyn appeared much older than her seventy-two years.
Doug, six years her senior, seemed alert and well but almost skeletally
thin.

Obviously taking their cues from the Woods, the production drew
comparisons between Evelyn's current challenges and her battles against
narrow-mindedness. The narration began, "Evelyn Wood became used
to adversity early in her career, confronting many disbelievers and critics
who challenged the claims of her reading method." A recap of the career
showed Evelyn and Doug pointing to framed pictures and certificates
hanging over their fireplace. The photo of Jimmy Carter inscribed to
Evelyn appeared in close-up.

But no props accompanied a short discussion of the famed Kennedy connection. "They [the Woods] were part of the New Frontier,"
the reporter said as the camera closed in on a stock photo of JFK. The
soundtrack played a few bars of "Camelot," the song from the Broadway
show of the same name, often associated with Kennedy's brief presidency.
Cut to the Woods' living room, where the reporter prompted, "Tell me
what it was like to work for the John F. Kennedy administration."

Almost twenty years had passed since Kennedy was assassinated.
The reporter in the segment was a young woman, but she might have
remembered that tragic day from her childhood. Memories of the young
president were still vivid in the American imagination. Giving their
answer, the Woods were treading on sacred ground. Evelyn's interviews
and Reading Dynamics ads had offered conflicting accounts of when
and where she taught Kennedy aides, if she ever had. The *PM* television
segment made it worse.

"He was a brilliant guy," Evelyn began, although the reporter had
asked about her experiences with the administration, not the man. The
couple continued:

DOUG: He averaged nine newspapers every morning before breakfast. Ted Kennedy took our course, but Jack was a natural. He couldn't stand to see his slow-reading staff—

EVELYN: (interrupting) Wasn't that fun? That was one of the most exciting things that ever happened to me.

DOUG: —to struggle through what they were doing. So that's why he invited us to come into the White House.

Married for more than a half-century and veterans of countless interviews, the couple often answered reporter's questions in tandem. In this instance, however, Evelyn uncharacteristically cut Doug off to steer the discussion back to the question and to cultivate the Camelot magic. Sensing this, her husband self-corrected.

By then, many Americans, including journalists, believed Evelyn had taught John F. Kennedy himself. At least one ad placed by a franchise said as much. Apparently, Evelyn was in no rush to correct that impression. But if Evelyn, in fact, had taught the joint chiefs of staff or other Kennedy aides, she apparently had no photos or letters as documentation. If she had, the producers of this show undoubtedly would have used them as visuals.

The tone darkened as Evelyn was shown struggling with physical therapy. Even aided by rails, she walked unsteadily. "She achieved a lot," her therapist said, adding, "She's very interested in self-improvement and doing the best she could with the situation she was living in." To the camera, the reporter said, "Her life was suddenly filled with hours of intense joy and frustrating immobilization," while in the background Doug leaned solicitously over Evelyn. Seated in a wheelchair, she dabbed her eyes with a tissue. It was heartbreaking.

But Doug couldn't resist turning this touching moment into a promo. Appropriating her caregivers' encouragement and undoubtedly inventing dialogue, Doug declared, "The nurse and doctors said, 'We never have seen a patient with such persistence. It's no wonder she has led the field in her profession.'" Clearly repeating what the Woods had told her, the reporter declared that Evelyn was still reading "two to three books a day." That would be a remarkable achievement for anyone, the TV journalist noted without stating the obvious: in this case, it was unbelievable.

The segment closed with Evelyn reading in an easy chair. Tracing slow circles over the words, she said, "It's like water rippling over the stones. The words are the stones, and the fingers are the water rippling smoothly over them." Making sense was beside the point. In the words of this report, "Evelyn Wood, like Betty Crocker, has become a permanent part of American culture."

A woman who'd compared herself to Galileo had been reduced to the status of a cake-mix brand. There were some advantages. Like mom and apple pie, she was beyond reproach.

Supporters saw her as separate—purer—than the publicity machine she'd wound up. Around this time, four Wood enthusiasts based at Brigham Young University published a survey of the rapid-reading literature. They'd asked Evelyn, pre-stroke, to teach them her method. The lead investigator, Bruce L. Brown, a psychology professor, described the course as a life-changing experience. Acknowledging her fallen status in the academic community, the researchers placed blame elsewhere. "There is little doubt that the Madison Avenue promoters have overdone it," they wrote.

The die-hard Wood fans attributed growing skepticism about her method to a "Western philosophical tradition that is authoritarian in structure, even in its most liberal forms," with its demands for proof and evidence. Their paper reexamined the work of Evelyn's detractors, reinterpreting graphs, questioning experimental designs, and accusing Carver and Graf of using hype to get published in *Psychology Today*.

The authors were particularly irked by Eugene Ehrlich's long-ago *Saturday Evening Post* anecdote about interspersing sentences from two different articles, giving the mashup to Wood grads, and watching them zip through it several times without detecting the ruse. Ehrlich's experiment had become a favorite topic at late-night conference bull sessions, oft-cited by "otherwise careful researchers" to refute speed-reading claims, wrote the BYU scholars. They said they wished they'd seen his amalgam because, "one can with a little effort interleave two articles in a way that is very subtle." Essentially, they charged Ehrlich with dishonesty.

Their main beef was with science itself. Kim Barrus, one of the authors, had coined a term for his Evelyn defense, one that supporters of President Donald Trump would use decades later. Barrus wrote, "We should not expect that a new discovery will confirm our present assumptions and inferences about the facts. Indeed, it is highly plausible that we will need alternative facts . . . to account for a new discovery."

Agreeing with their opponents that speed-reading had come to mean the ability to read faster than 800 or 900 words per minute without losing comprehension, the BYU researchers found no other common ground. They questioned whether reading meant looking at all the words and cited a scholar who said it was impossible to distinguish reading from "skipping." They praised Peter Kump, fond of comparing reading to looking for a number in a phone book.

That kind of "reading"—now called searching—would soon become so simple that nobody would need a course to learn how to do it. Phone books were on their way out. Computers were cropping up at workplaces and universities if not yet in homes. New ads for Evelyn Wood courses took note. "How to get the most from the computer between your ears," one began, continuing, "Think what you could accomplish if you had your own personal computer." For most, this was still the stuff of science fiction. "Of course, you already have such a device—it's called a brain," the message reassured, while warning that only an Evelyn Wood course could boot it up.

That ad ran soon after URS acquired Evelyn Wood. Things changed fast. In 1982 *Time* magazine replaced its customary Person of the Year cover with a photo of a personal computer, marking the astounding growth in sales. The internet was years away, but searchable files recorded on floppy disks or magnetic tape were becoming familiar. Indeed, URS hoped to embrace this technology by slapping the Evelyn Wood name on multimedia training courses. The company had pulled most of its national advertising, shifting spending to the lower-cost campus market. It seemed eager to pull away from the public altogether, courting businesses and other groups instead.

URS had quickly soured on running schools that sold services directly to the public. The tech-savvy firm may also have sensed that speed-reading would hold less allure in a digitally enhanced future. In 1982 it split into two companies, one to focus exclusively on engineering operations. Evelyn Wood went to the other new enterprise, which would produce and distribute media-based training programs. Explaining the reorganization, URS said it wanted to "simplify" matters for investors who'd had a difficult time "comprehending" a company that cleaned up toxic spills with one hand while teaching speed-reading with the other. In truth, it seemed a first step toward URS's plan to get rid of Evelyn Wood, or, as the company put it, "divest" it.

Evelyn's name remained marketable, or so URS thought. While awaiting a suitor for Reading Dynamics, the California-based firm registered several trademarks to extend her brand. These included Evelyn Wood Corporate Programs and Evelyn Wood Young Adult Programs. Recording the registrations, the US Patent and Trademark Office noted that Evelyn Wood was the name of a living person whose consent to the trademark registration was on file.

No surviving records indicate whether Evelyn requested payment for her consent. Her medical bills must have been staggering. She had kept records showing that she and Doug for years were covered by DEAR's medical insurance plan. Assuming that URS continued the coverage, the nursing required for her home care might well have exceeded insurance limits.

Her name was still worth a million dollars, or $1.1 million, to be precise. In 1986 American Learning Corporation paid that amount for worldwide rights to the service marks Evelyn Wood and Reading Dynamics. Newly acquired by Encyclopaedia Britannica, American Learning was in the supplemental-education business, competing with Sylvan Learning and Huntington Learning Center. The school dismissal bell didn't send kids out to play anymore. Now they were going straight from school to cram sessions in storefronts.

At Reading Game centers located mostly in California and Texas, American Learning offered after-school reading and math. High schoolers could get prepped for the Scholastic Aptitude Test. There was also something for adults, and this is where Evelyn Wood came in. Some American Learning sites also taught speed-reading with machines, both old-school tachistoscopes and a new computer-based pacing program. American Learning's new parent, Encyclopaedia Britannica, had big plans to expand the tutoring centers, and building their speed-reading business would be part of this.

Evelyn's reputation brought free publicity. Shortly after Britannica announced the purchase of her name, the *Los Angeles Times* ran an admiring feature about her career, her struggle with disability, and her plans to stay involved with the new trademark owners. Interviewing Evelyn as she sat in a wheelchair, her voice barely raised above a whisper, the reporter raised no issues about the method's effectiveness. Headlined "A Quick Read Through the Life of Evelyn Wood," it was anything but. Starting below the fold of one broadsheet page and occupying most of a second one, the piece included artistically shot photos of Evelyn and Doug, now in advanced old age. They were accompanied by Carol, who'd divorced and remarried.

The Woods said they'd been traveling through California anyway and decided to drop by the Huntington Beach offices of American Learning. More likely, this in-depth feature in a major newspaper had been arranged by a publicist. Evelyn was earning her keep again. She was now a consultant to American Learning.

The terms of the new consulting agreement were not made public, but the timing might have been fortunate for the Woods. The clock had run out on the consulting arrangement that Famous Artists had signed and then transferred, through DEAR, to Tommy Thompson's investor group. URS referred twice in correspondence to an amendment concerning the base compensation rate, $22,000. The engineering company may or may not also have extended the length of the contract.

Whatever American Learning had offered Evelyn, she was ready to dive in on Day One. Referring to the company as "this new outfit," she told the *LA Times*, "I intend to be actively engaged again," claiming unbelievably to walk a mile a day and use a wheelchair only while traveling. The puff piece presented her to Generation X, likely to have heard of her but not to have seen her. Even the young president of

American Learning, present at the interview, said he'd heard her name in commercials when he was a New York schoolboy.

But Evelyn was no longer the middle-aged teacher of those days, small but authoritative and sturdy. She came across as a wreck in the *LA Times* piece, often giving, as the report said, "only the briefest of answers" and deferring questions to Carol "when her memory failed her—or when apparent modesty intervened." Yet she did display "occasional flashes of a pixieish sense of humor." Asked if her daughter was their only child, Evelyn responded, "The only *and* brightest." Anna's existence had bubbled up from the unconscious and produced a cruel joke.

Printed on the same page with this feature was a small ad for a store selling clothes "for women in business," an indication of the conflicts surrounding the changing roles of women. This was the era of power dressing. Silhouettes of the suits and dresses advertised featured big shoulders and modest skirt lengths. Uncertain about how to dress for the workplace, women sought advice from retailers. Similarly confused about gender, this profile of a company founder began by describing Evelyn as "grandmotherly."

She was, indeed a grandmother, with a unique way of showing her affection for Carol's four children, Stanton Davis recalled: "We'd say, 'I love you, Mimi,' and she'd say, 'You'd better.'" Remembering his grandmother before the stroke, as well as after, Stanton described her as "very outspoken" in contrast to other women at the time. He said she'd inspired his mother to open her own counseling practice. But, not the stereotypical granny, "she was a very intense woman," he said.

Through Anna, she had four more grandchildren, unacknowledged by the Woods as such. One, Scott North, said he'd had "feelings, not strong feelings" upon hearing Evelyn's name mentioned in connection with her business. "I thought, 'Oh yeah, she was my mother's adoptive parent.'" His sister, Barbara North Smith, said she'd met the Woods on only two occasions during her early childhood, after which they stopped acknowledging her mother's existence. "I, along with my three brothers, have never referred to the Woods as our grandparents," she said.

Not long after her retrospective profile appeared, Evelyn got a chance to perform in her new consulting role. The Associated Press asked her to comment on a fresh speed-reading study. Marcel Just, a psychology professor at Carnegie Mellon University, and Patricia A. Carpenter, his research partner and wife, tested recent graduates of a Reading Dynamics class taught at the university. In a new wrinkle, they asked Wood-trained speed-readers and normal readers to read text displayed on a video screen. (A long pointer was provided as a pacer.) A computer recorded what words were being looked at and for how long. The researchers found that the speed-readers looked at only 33 percent of the words, compared with 64 percent for the normal readers, and spent less time gazing at each word.

"You don't want your lawyer speed reading," the lead researcher told an AP reporter. The study found that normal readers performed better than the speedy ones on nearly all comprehension tests.

As usual, Evelyn sowed doubt about these particular Wood grads and the quality of their course. The piece quoted her as saying, "A person who speed reads and does it correctly can read with better comprehension, I'm sure of it." Evelyn had long eschewed the term *speed-reading* as a descriptor of her method, but American Learning embraced it.

A year later, the Associated Press had something else about the Woods to report. M. Douglas Wood died a few days before his eighty-fourth birthday. The wire service noted his passing in a brief item, describing him as a Salt Lake City businessman and a cofounder of Evelyn Wood Reading Dynamics. It had been fifty-eight years since he'd worn out a Victrola record titled "Girl of My Dreams," longing for Evelyn during the separation following their engagement. Evelyn's method had created a long, respectable career for him after the indignities of Ironrite. Ceding the spotlight to her had benefited him. Still, he'd been an unusually supportive husband for the era, always quick to praise her.

With Doug gone, Evelyn left Salt Lake City for Tucson, where she moved in with Carol and her son-in-law, Robert Evans. (According to Stanton, Carol's furniture included pieces from liquidated Evelyn Wood offices.) As Evelyn celebrated a milestone birthday, the *Arizona Daily Star* ran a feature about the state's famous new resident. With skepticism by now pervasive, it began on the defensive: "At age eighty, Evelyn Wood still speed reads. The critics, who over the years have contended that quickness and comprehension are not compatible, could not stop her. A massive stroke could, but only for a couple of years."

Photographed seated in a wheelchair, with a large-print copy of *Reader's Digest* balanced on her lap, Evelyn looked unable to do much at high velocity. She'd colored her hair since the interview in Los Angeles, where a photo showed it as gray and clipped, and her natural curls were back in abundance. But the debilitating effects of the stroke were still evident in her body and facial features. According to the piece, she was still challenging herself, walking laps around the Evanses' pool.

Recapping her career, the Arizona paper cited her endorsement by Senator Proxmire, who'd died a few days before the feature ran. Proxmire, who'd lived to see the Wood method scientifically discredited, never disassociated himself from it, saying only that he was "down to" 1,000 words per minute. He'd gained fame in the second half of his senate career by issuing his Golden Fleece Awards to government-funded projects he considered worthless. Consequently, he obstructed some legitimate scientific projects, later apologizing for doing so.

As always, Evelyn countered her detractors by citing the massive number of Wood graduates. Moreover, the report noted, ten thousand people were still enrolling in Evelyn Wood Reading Dynamics annually. The source for that figure was Dan Warner, director of American Learning's Evelyn Wood division. Warner, who demonstrated his own reading speed on local television, came out of the showman mold that had produced Bob Darling and Evelyn's other top-billed demonstrators. To prove to a class that hand pacing helped them tune out distractions, he'd spin around the classroom with a wastebasket balanced on his head.

Warner's levity was much needed by American Learning Corporation, which was posting losses. Encyclopaedia Britannica had rapidly expanded the tutoring chain beyond California and Texas, where it had long operated after-school centers called the Reading Game. Renamed Britannica Learning Centers and scattered over eleven states, the subsidiary was suffering from high overhead and constant managerial turnover.

Yet, amid this gloom and some consequent site closures, Evelyn's brand cast at least a soft glow. At an annual meeting of the publicly held company in 1990, the president of American Learning leavened some grim news—a loss of $6 million in the past fiscal year and a falling stock price—by predicting that its Evelyn Wood Reading Dynamics division would "continue to increase its revenues."

As promised when it purchased the trademark, American Learning had revamped the brand, paring the traditional course down to five weeks, offering it on corporate sites as a two-day seminar, and selling it as software and on audiocassette. It also produced a book, *Remember Everything You Read: The Evelyn Wood Seven-Day Speed Reading and Learning Program* by Stanley D. Frank. The initials Ed.D. were printed after Frank's name, indicating his doctorate in education. It was released in several editions, some crediting him as the executive vice president of Encyclopaedia Britannica. He was also chairman and chief executive of American Learning, suggesting that this book, like the one attributed to the URS chairman, was mainly the work of a collaborator. An audiocassette version of the work identified Frank as "co-developer of the Evelyn Wood Speed Reading Program."

Mostly old wine in a new bottle, the book conceded some points to science under the guise of clearing up misconceptions. Stating that "some" believe that the Evelyn Wood method can widen peripheral vision beyond human capacity, and others think that successful Wood grads can read any book "at a phenomenal rate, with superior comprehension," the author dismisses these as "partial truths." Of course, these so-called fallacies were promoted by none other than Evelyn and the successive owners of her namesake trademark.

The book also dialed back the Camelot connection, stating that Kennedy brought "teachers from Evelyn Wood," not the founder herself, into the White House to teach staff. Britannica, revered for its authoritative encyclopedias, may have fact-checked the claim. Nevertheless, the book promised that, with its methods, "Your original reading speed should double, triple, quadruple, or soar to even higher rates."

Consumers might gamble the price of a paperback on that, but they were not lining up for the course anymore. By announcing in 1991 that speed-reading was making a "comeback," a Florida newspaper effectively marked its demise. The paper's interview with Warner revealed that his company had essentially stopped advertising the course. It was now sold mainly as a corporate training program.

The report interpreted the step away from advertising as a "reaction to some of the earlier days of the program . . . when a degree of hucksterism was associated with the franchising system then being used." The so-called grandmotherly Evelyn, the greatest huckster of them all, remained immune from these charges. Any sins committed were the work of people around her. Even when younger and able-bodied, she'd effectively pinned the blame for extravagant claims on overly enthusiastic public relations people she allegedly couldn't control.

The Florida article ended with an assertion that speed-reading was as much in demand as ever because "anxious people" are "buried in billions of words they cannot process." That line probably came directly from Warner or one of his press releases. But 1991 was the year the World Wide Web went live. The information explosion had been harmlessly detonated. PCs and productivity tools streamlined routine business tasks, leaving more time to read. Search engines were beginning to curate those billions of words. The anxieties that Evelyn Wood fed on were shifting to other things. In 1993 American Learning shed the Evelyn Wood trademark and exited the speed-reading business.

Evelyn's name had lost its mass-market value. However, it remained a household name, a standard reference on C-SPAN, invoked whenever cumbersome legislation was introduced. "This is Evelyn Wood," read the caption on a political cartoon that pictured a small woman with tightly curled hair flipping madly through papers. "She's going to read the arms pact for us before we sign it." In Wisconsin, a man stopped for drunk driving objected to the manner in which he was informed of his rights, sarcastically asking the arresting officer if he'd taken an Evelyn Wood course. On-air meteorologists pressed for time apologized for giving the "Evelyn Woods [sic] speed-reading forecast."

Evelyn died in Tucson on August 26, 1995, at age eighty-six. Her death, noted around the world, didn't halt the controversy surrounding her method. The New York Times found that out after it memorialized her as a "tiny, soft-spoken woman" who "liberated students, professionals and business people from the habits that shackled them to the average American's reading rate of 250 to 300 words a minute."

This drew a letter to the editor from Phyllis Mindell of Pittsford, New York, who faulted the obituary for failing to mention that the Wood method "has long since been discredited by serious investigators." Identifying herself as an international communications consultant, Mindell said she'd worked with hundreds of people trained in the system or similar ones, and "not one uses the technique anymore. . . . They gain substantially no comprehension in the process." Mindell quoted Carver, along with his favorite Woody Allen joke about speed-reading *War and Peace*. Joke intact, the letter was printed in the *Times* two days after Evelyn's funeral in Salt Lake City.

Local obituaries, apparently placed by the family, stated that she was survived by a daughter, a son-in-law, four grandchildren, and three step-grandchildren. In the latter category were children brought by Bob Evans to his marriage with Carol. There was no mention of an adopted daughter.

Anna learned of both her parents' deaths only through the media. She attended the funeral services for Evelyn, where the rest of the family ignored her. Did they fear she would make a claim on the estate? "That's the sense that my mom got, but since there was no money to inherit, that was moot," said Stanton, recalling Carol's reaction to Anna's presence. The last of his grandmother's Reading Dynamics money was spent on the funeral brunch, he said.

Anna's daughter, Barbara, said money had nothing to with her mother's attendance at her adoptive mother's funeral. As for the brunch, she didn't think Anna was invited. "She never mentioned it," said Smith, noting that, in any case, the invitation might have been declined.

It was a fitting end to an evasive life: the cast-off daughter showing up, refusing to have her existence denied. In the operas Evelyn had enjoyed so much in Frankfurt, an apparition like this would have led to dramatic consequences. In real life, however, those who tried to unmask Evelyn were threatened, ignored, labeled as narrow-minded, relegated to the Letters column, or not invited to brunch.

Epilogue

Evelyn Wood was perhaps the greatest scammer of the twentieth century, never recognized as such outside a small academic community. She suppressed or opposed scientific evidence about her method's negative effects on reading comprehension. Yet she was aware of her system's shortcomings from early in her career—that's evident in her dismissive attitude toward standardized tests and her insistence that meaning resides in the reader, not the author. Further proof is her report on the University of Delaware study conducted by her friend and admirer William Liddle, in which she ignored his troubling findings to give only the good news.

Detractors were invited to demonstrations, as if stagecraft trumped science. In this, Evelyn excelled, casting bright and appealing youngsters, lugging piles of books to the stage for them to choose from, and skillfully moderating Q&A sessions to avoid embarrassment. Like Doug's thrilling tales of fleeing Nazis with whom his church had cozy relations, this was straight out of the faith-promoting mold. Reporters hungry for novelty eagerly ate it up.

The testimonials of senators were proof enough for the media. While taking credit for Capitol Hill classes arranged and taught by others, Evelyn acquired her first coat of Teflon in DuPont-dominated Delaware. Vaulting from sales executive club instructor to assistant professor at a major state university, she attracted followers who swarmed her first challenger. Lawyers and surrogates would help her with future ones.

Although the Woods quickly sold the company, subsequent owners followed her cues for dealing with dissidents, ignoring facts, and crafting lessons out of nonsense.

The press and the public found Evelyn's appearance "reassuringly normal," as one writer phrased it. If their own biases prevented them from recognizing a conservatively dressed white woman as a con artist, that was not Evelyn's fault. But she did portray herself as former mother hen to the "troubled" girls of Jordan High, suggesting that speed-reading helped students who, in truth, it undoubtedly harmed. A company memo stated that the Evelyn Wood method was not remedial.

If two million people had taken the course, as the obituaries claimed, then hundreds of millions of dollars had been wasted. Even Evelyn's harshest critics conceded that the course taught a skimming technique that could be useful to some, but it came wrongly labeled and at an exorbitant price. Nondisclosure agreements had restrained teachers, and even students, from working in the reading field. Reputations of university-based reading educators were threatened, and student protesters were squelched. Worst of all, some Evelyn Wood institutes had failed to counsel struggling readers out of the program.

Through the company's changes of hand, Evelyn could have spoken out about these practices. Instead, she renewed her consulting contract with each successive owner. She and her husband never made a killing from Evelyn Wood Reading Dynamics while others did, but that's not the point. She proudly remained the company's symbol and spokeswoman, unapologetic for the wild claims she'd made for her method, even as the consumer movement forced a retreat from them.

She and the subsequent owners of her trademark turned John F. Kennedy's tragic death to commercial advantage. While he was in office, she was at the height of her career, constantly interviewed. She used every opportunity to mention that senators and congresspeople had taken her course. Yet, during Kennedy's lifetime she never spoke of being summoned to teach his aides at the White House.

Kennedy did recommend speed-reading for others, pressing his brother Ted to apply himself more to an Evelyn Wood Reading Dynamics course. Some Kennedy aides took Evelyn Wood courses through Fred

Babbel's institute. However, White House correspondence indicates that on the subject of which reading course to take, JFK was brand neutral. He wouldn't live to see his name exploited in decades of advertising, or to hear Evelyn's shifting recollections of personally teaching ten aides, twelve advisers, or the joint chiefs of staff in various years of his administration.

Through the years, Evelyn's name became inseparable from Kennedy's. Just a few years after his death, major news organizations falsely said that she'd gone to Washington at his behest. In fact, her move preceded not only his presidency but even his candidacy. She was also assumed to have been personal reading tutor to the much-admired president. While Evelyn never said that, she wove the web that ended in this tangle.

Even the *Life* magazine journalist who'd interviewed Kennedy on his reading habits came to believe the myth. In the year of Evelyn's death, conservative book publisher Regnery Publishing released Kennedy's 1945 European diary with an introduction by Hugh Sidey. Early in his long Time-Life career, Sidey had written the *Life* piece. In the introduction, Sidey wrote that he'd collaborated with Kennedy on estimating the presidential reading speed without actually measuring it. He added that he checked the estimate with Evelyn Wood because "when Evelyn Wood devised her speed-reading course Kennedy, along with other members of his family, signed up. He took a few sessions but, according to Ms. Wood later, dropped out when it was apparent he was beyond the instruction."

This is obviously a confusion with the Foundation for Better Reading course that Kennedy took in Baltimore while serving in Congress. Millions of dollars spent to link Evelyn's name to Kennedy's had given her an unearned place in the JFK legacy. Legend eroded reality, even in the mind of a journalist who'd been on the scene.

Evelyn's brand retained value despite decades of scientific opposition and consumer complaints. Her endorsement by senators and her support, real or exaggerated, by three US presidents kept her reputation untarnished. It also may have shielded her method from regulatory action.

Three years after her death, the US Federal Trade Commission moved swiftly to stop another speed-reading marketer, Howard S. Berg, from making phenomenal claims for his Mega Speed Reading system. In TV infomercials, Berg had taken the incautious step of saying he could boost reading rates and comprehension for all adults and children, including those with severe brain damage. The FTC compelled him to stop claiming that his system could help anyone read above 800 words per minute while substantially comprehending and retaining the material.

By contrast, the FTC had dropped its 1972 exchange of letters with Senator Proxmire, apparently content with finding that his endorsement—including his claims of reading tens of thousands of words per minute—was unpaid. In response to a Freedom of Information Act request, the commission said it had no records of investigations of Evelyn Wood Reading Dynamics. A major franchisee, the Lyceum, failed to pay its New York employees and ignored a subpoena from the Pennsylvania attorney general, apparently with impunity. Only the Federal Communications Commission seems to have applied restraints, demanding that a program-length Evelyn Wood commercial be labeled as advertising.

Speed-reading has recently experienced a revival through the marketing of text-presentation apps for smartphones and other digital devices. A technology called rapid visual serial presentation presents one word at a time on a screen, claiming that reading can be accelerated by eliminating the need for eye movement. Another technology changes text colors to guide the eyes from the end of one line to the beginning of the next. In 2017, researchers at the University of California, San Diego, and other institutions reviewed the few studies on these text-presentations apps, finding no indication they could significantly accelerate reading while maintaining comprehension. "Language skill is at the heart of reading speed," the researchers concluded. Their paper brought Evelyn in for a thorough drubbing, pointing out that regression and phonological responses to text—what Evelyn called subvocalization—have been found to help reading, not hurt it, as she maintained.

Ironically, other technologies have slaked the thirst for speed-reading. Evelyn Wood Reading Dynamics debuted in a world of typewriters, carbon paper, and hand-drawn graphs. Just obtaining reading material consumed enormous chunks of time. Students haunted college libraries and, before copiers were widely available, took elaborate notes from noncirculating books. Executives shared one copy of a magazine, crossing out names on a list as it passed from one desk to another. Now that technology has expedited so many tasks, there's not as much widespread panic about reading slowly.

But marketers are trying to start it all up again. As noted by neuroscientist Mark Seidenberg in his recent book on reading, *Language at the Speed of Sight*, a new industry of Reading Dynamics clones litters the internet. Social media spins fresh myths about the reading rates of successful people, plugging worthless remedies for an imaginary deficiency. "Although we now know the claims are false, they are as difficult to eliminate as bedbugs," wrote Seidenberg, adding, "I think Evelyn Wood has a lot to answer for, or would if she weren't dead."

As it happens, in death she gives her answer. She and Doug are buried under a stone engraved with their names and "Evelyn Wood Reading Dynamics."

Acknowledgments

I WISH TO THANK THE STAFF members of the Research Center of the Utah State Archives and Utah State History for their invaluable assistance. I'm also grateful to Karen Adler Abramson, director of archives at the John F. Kennedy Presidential Library and Museum, for her help in releasing the transcript of a telephone conversation between JFK and his brother Ted. Special thanks to my editor, Yuval Taylor, and my agent, James Fitzgerald, for believing in this project, and to Ellen Hornor for her critical eye.

Notes

Abbreviations

EW	Evelyn Nielsen Wood
MDW	Myron Douglas "Doug" Wood
EW Papers	Evelyn Nielsen Wood Papers, ca. 1925–1979, Utah State Historical Society, Salt Lake City, Utah
EWRD	Evelyn Wood Reading Dynamics
JFK Papers	Papers of John F. Kennedy, Presidential Papers, John F. Kennedy Presidential Library and Museum, Boston, Massachusetts

Prologue

"concepts and thoughts": Associated Press, "One Hundred Twenty Pages in Three Minutes," Kansas City (MO) Times, July 3, 1961.

"Tell him how many" . . . "revolutionary reading method": Chicago News World Service, "New Reading Method Gives Lad 7,000 Books in Year," Lincoln (NE) Star, July 2, 1961.

"high spot": "CTA Gives Challenge to Northern Schools Following State Convention," Eureka (CA) Humboldt Standard, July 17, 1961.

"the 'dynamic' reading method" . . . "reading wizard": George Gerbner, "The Press and the Dialogue in Education: The Case Study of a National Educational Convention and Its Depiction in America's Daily Newspapers," Journalism Monographs no. 5 (September 1967): 22–23.

"Slim, earnest": "Read Faster and Better," *Time*, August 22, 1960, 41.

"Everything she said" . . . *"Mount Holyoke or Wellesley lady"*: Robert Darling, interview by author, June 25, 2017.

"One thing I was paid for": Robert Darling, telephone conversation with author, July 6, 2017.

"like soap, cigarettes, and toothpaste": Associated Press, "Educator Charges Academic Lockstep," *Washington Post, Times Herald*, June 27, 1961.

"quasi-commercial": Gerbner, "Press and the Dialogue," 22.

"shadows on the silver screen": Terry Ferrer, "Teachers Hear TV Classes Assailed as Schizophrenia," *New York Herald-Tribune*, June 27, 1961.

"When you see this": Stephen Breen to Emmett O'Grady, December 19, 1960, EW Papers, Box 14, Folder 1.

Chapter 1: Charm School

"religious": Verla Nielsen, interview by author, December 6, 2017.

"residence contract": Residence contract, "Mimi and Grandpa" and Doug Davis, n.d., EW Papers.

"I think it was": EW to parents, January 21, 1939, EW Papers, Box 30, Folder 1. Note: all EW and MDW letters to parents are in various folders of Box 30 and will hereafter be cited by date alone.

"aquamarine" . . . *"sparkling with warmth and intelligence"*: Franklin J. Agardy, *How to Read Faster and Better: How to Get Everything You Want from Anything You Read as Fast as You Can Think; the Evelyn Wood Reading Dynamics Program*, Fireside Edition (New York: Simon and Schuster, 1981), 35.

"Girl of My Dreams": MDW to Evelyn Nielsen, July 7, 1928, EW Papers, Box 30, Folder 1.

"We were told once": MDW to Evelyn Nielsen, July 21, 1928, EW Papers, Box 30, Folder 1.

"certainly a dandy" . . . *"head full of curls"*: MDW to Evelyn Nielsen, August 8, 1928, EW Papers, Box 30, Folder 1.

"I don't know whether" . . . *"I don't like to go"*: MDW to Evelyn Nielsen, June 30, 1928, EW Papers, Box 30, Folder 1.

"prominent in debate work": "Weddings and Engagements," *Salt Lake Tribune*, May 19, 1929.

"his apartment houses": MDW to his brother Alan, October 13, 1938.

"He did not marry": Katie C. Jensen, "The Challenge of Charm: The Art of Being a Woman," *Improvement Era*, July 1935, 435.

Chapter 2: Third-Reich Interlude

"real joy" . . . *"everything we have done for her"*: EW to parents, October 2, 1938.

"Anna Marie Wood shall henceforth": Decree of Adoption, Anna Marie Pearson, Third Judicial District, Salt Lake County, UT.

"tense": Scott North, interview by author, May 30, 2017.

"anti-Semitic drive" . . . *"in many ways more ruthless"*: "Anti-Semitism Spreads in Balkan Nations," *Salt Lake Tribune*, April 18, 1937.

"to build a superior race" . . . *"the German woman's* Führer": Elizabeth H. Welker, "The German Girl of Today," *Improvement Era*, May 1937, 294–95.

"his wife and daughter": "New West German Mission Head Appointed," *Improvement Era*, May 1938.

"were accompanied by their": "Woods Embark June 15 for Nazi Mission," *Ogden (UT) Standard-Examiner*, June 12, 1938.

"basking in the moonlight" . . . *"I'm afraid she's going"*: MDW to parents, June 16, 1938.

"three-year vacation": MWD to his brother Alan Wood, October 13, 1938.

"the people were absolutely thrilled" . . . *"[I] said my own"*: EW to parents, July 6, 1938.

"short" . . . *"an unlimited knowledge"*: George R. Blake, 1938 diary, Church of Jesus Christ of Latter-Day Saints, Church History Library, 148–49.

"a very sweet black haired" . . . *"helped"*: EW to parents, July 6, 1938.

"bestest [sic] cook": Blake, 1939 diary, 207.

"the national salute": EW to parents, July 6, 1938.

"Don't ever use the name" . . . *"the Jewish situation"*: MDW to parents, July 21, 1938.

"She wrote the priesthood": Richard O. Cowan and David F. Boone, MDW and EW interview, February 3, 1978, James Moyle Oral History Program, Church of Jesus Christ of Latter-Day Saints Historical Department, 11.

"that any subject even remotely": David Conley Nelson, *Moroni and the Swastika: Mormons in Nazi Germany* (Norman: University of Oklahoma Press, 2015), loc. 1850.

"This is the life": EW to parents, December 26, 1938.

"you can see the whole": EW to parents, July 6, 1938.

"mission sweetheart" . . . *"mission mother"*: Terry Bohle Montague, *"Mine Angels Round About": Mormon Missionary Evacuation from West Germany, 1939* (Orem, UT: Granite, 1989), 2.

"So far as the Jew" . . . *"It is the fartherest"*: MDW to parents, July 21, 1938.

"a continuous line of soldiers" . . . *"Keep your chin up"*: EW to parents and MDW to parents, September 16, 1938. The letter was written by EW for her family. MDW sent a carbon copy to his parents with a handwritten note indicating that it was a copy.

"a fire drill": MDW to parents, August 25, 1939.

"Hitler . . . thought it wise" . . . *"It seems that these people"*: EW to parents, October 2, 1938.

"I enjoy talking with them": EW to parents, February 25, 1939.

"inhumane" . . . *"I had a strange feeling"*: Frederick William Babbel, journal, First Mission 1936–1939, collection of Bonnie Babbel Lewis.

"Really Hitler has done" . . . *"I wouldn't be surprised"*: EW to parents, December 10, 1938.

"She takes care of Carol": EW to parents, October 2, 1938.

"Dear Grandma and Grandpa": Signed "Anna" to "Grandpa and Grandma," October 22, 1938.

"It is really a queer" . . . *"That is why we lay"*: EW to parents, dated only "18th." The contents of the letter indicate it was around February 1939.

"I surely get a thump": EW to parents, December 26, 1938.

"a real artist" . . . *"for the whole conference"*: MDW to parents, May 26, 1939.

felt sorry for Anna: Interview with Terry Bohle Montague, October 7, 2017.

"Anna usually wants to": Blake diary, 1939, 208.

"great faults" . . . *"Sometimes she acts"*: Blake diary, 1938, 319–20. Emphasis in original.

"veritable golden age": Roger P. Minert, *Under the Gun: West German and Austrian Latter-Day Saints in World War II* (Provo, UT: Brigham Young University Religious Study Center, and Salt Lake City: Deseret Book, 2011), 27.

"politically, things look" . . . *"We had such a good"*: MDW to parents, August 7, 1939.

"it might be best": Minert, *Under the Gun*, 28.

"I have to be a different self": EW to parents, dated only "18th."

Chapter 3: Habits of Highly Effective Readers

"She is her man's helper": Blake, 1938 diary, 149.

"We were brokenhearted": Cowan and Boone, 20.

"in glory" . . . "all this ended": Blake, 1939 diary, 222.

"The German press" . . . "only the German side": "Nazi Press Policy Told," *Salt Lake Telegram*, October 23, 1939.

"the most progressive": "Missionary Declares Germans Unified," *Salt Lake Tribune*, October 28, 1939.

"We are choosing sides" . . . "pro-British propagandists": Blake, 1939 diary, 284.

"I never could find it": "B.P.W. Meeting Hears War Talk," *Salt Lake Tribune*, October 18, 1940.

"We had seen the treatment": Latter-Day Saints' Church, *One Hundred Tenth Annual Conference of the Church of Jesus Christ of Latter-Day Saints* (Salt Lake City, 1940), 79.

"The missionaries were in a hurry": Minert, *Under the Gun*, 40.

"faith-stirring story": Latter-Day Saints' Church, *One Hundred Tenth Annual*, 81.

"superb scenery": "Throng Sees Pageant of LDS Beliefs," *Salt Lake Tribune*, October 2, 1941.

"never warm and fuzzy": North interview.

"The first woman ever": Beth Keele, "Busy Mother Finds Time to Work for MA Degree," *Salt Lake Telegram*, May 18, 1943.

"at arm's length": North interview.

"boring" . . . "have felt the need": Evelyn N. Wood, "A Centennial Radio Project for Elementary Schools," unpublished master's thesis, University of Utah, 1947, EW Papers, Box 35, Folders 4–7.

"I turned in my thesis": Advertisement for Evelyn Wood Reading Dynamics, *Austin (TX) Statesman*, September 14, 1966. Versions of this paragraph appeared in ads for many years.

"diffident" . . . "thought it was lightning": "Sixty Indians Visit S.L. from Uintah," *Salt Lake Telegram*, March 14, 1947.

"Lowell Lees was a strange man": Ralph E. Margetts, interview by Everett L. Cooley, Cooley Oral History Project, J. Willard Marriott Library, University of Utah, Salt Lake City.

"*Statistics prove that over seventy*": "Prof Explains Lack of Speech Classes," *Daily Utah Chronicle* (University of Utah, Salt Lake City), September 28, 1957.

"*with Lees*": EW résumé, 1974, EW Papers, Box 7, Folder 3.

"*the faster a person*": "Class Scheduled in Oral Reading, *Ogden (UT) Standard-Examiner*, October 10, 1951.

"*more time for thought*": Elden A. Bond, "The Yale-Harvard Freshmen Speed-Reading Experiment," *School and Society* 54, no. 1390 (August 16, 1941): 107–11.

"*The slow reader*" . . . "*could result in a revolutionary*": Jack Cooper, "New Teaching Mode Doubles Reading Speed," *Chicago Daily Tribune*, March 25, 1951.

In a résumé written years later: EW résumé, 1974.

"*slick chicks*": "Fashion Forum Tells Teens How to Be 'Slick Chicks,'" *Salt Lake Tribune*, October 25, 1950.

"*troubled girls*": Agardy, *Read Faster and Better*, 23.

"*below-level readers*": Display ad, *English Journal* 48, no. 3 (March 1958): unnumbered page.

"*who urged the writing*": Evelyn Nielsen Wood and Marjorie Wescott Barrows, *Reading Skills* (New York: Holt, Rinehart and Winston, 1958), vi.

"*correct faulty eye movements,*" "*enlarge eye span,*" *and see words* "*as meaning groups*": Wood and Barrows, *Reading Skills*, iv.

"*Swish-back, swish-back*": Wood and Barrows, 24.

"*requires no special equipment*": Display ad, *English Journal* 47, no. 3 (March 1958).

"*We have them around*" . . . "*No one yet understands*": David O. Ives, "More Companies Teach Employees How to Read—and Absorb—Faster," *Wall Street Journal*, January 9, 1957.

"*Anna is a very pretty girl*" . . . "*maybe her parents would stop*": Wood and Barrows, *Reading Skills*, 10.

"*I'm sure it was a stab*": Barbara North Smith, electronic chat with author, October 12, 2018.

"*snobby*" . . . "*I'm better than you*": North interview.

"*We are very much at risk*": Mabel S. Noall, "The Philosophy Behind the Machine Approach to Reading," in Clay A. Ketcham, ed., *Proceedings of the College Reading Association* 3 (Summer 1962): 60.

Chapter 4: We Have Liftoff

Or so said a reporter: Phil Hanna, "Teaching Little Johnnie to Read," *Ontario-Upland (CA) Daily Report*, November 19, 1972.

"Mrs. M. George Wood's" . . . *"several methods for developing speed"*: "Read This Story . . . Time's Up!" *Salt Lake Tribune*, October 12, 1958.

"they are too slow" . . . *"Comprehension is stressed"*: "Read This Story," *Salt Lake Tribune*.

the Bennett boys' glowing reviews: Ruth Montgomery, "Senators Try Rapid Reading Course," *Albany (NY) Times-Union*, July 31, 1961.

"I sure liked him a lot" . . . *"If brother Babbel comes"*: EW to parents, April 6, 1939.

"It was certainly a thrill": MDW to parents, May 26, 1939.

"The average person reads" . . . *"Now over eight hundred"*: Display ad, *Salt Lake Tribune*, September 4, 1959.

"Gordon wants to sell" . . . *"a feeling of insecurity"*: MDW, n.d., EW Papers, Box 29, Folder 1.

"I fear no character assassin": Gordon (no surname), Deseret Ironrite Corp., to MDW, n.d., EW Papers, Box 29, Folder 1.

"It will be almost impossible": MDW, n.d., EW Papers, Box 29, Folder 1.

"much more doing": EW to parents, April 6, 1939.

"If Dad did the ironing": Display ad, *Ogden (UT) Standard-Examiner*, December 6, 1963.

"Rapid Reading for executives, businessmen": Display ad, *Salt Lake Tribune*, September 4, 1959.

"privilege" . . . *"My speed improved"*: Fred S. Thomas to EW, August 11, 1959, EW Papers, Box 14, Folder 1.

"It is most impressive": Wallace L. Chambers, MD, to EW, August 7, 1959, EW Papers, Box 14, Folder 1.

"I was chided for a little habit": Frederick W. Babbel, journal, December 3, 1938, 160.

"Sister Wood took a short walk": Babbel journal, December 5, 1938, 161.

"lowly" job: MDW to parents, August 2, 1938.

"ear to the sky" . . . *"D.C. may have School"*: *Little Listening Post* (Washington, DC), October–November 1959.

"before you and your wife": Howard T. Mather to MDW, September 1, 1960, EW Papers, Box 14, Folder 1.

"I was super-drilled": Bonnie Babbel Lewis, interview by author, November 9, 2017.

"I was afraid that people": Lewis interview.

"far out front" . . . *"throw slippers and toothbrushes"*: *Little Listening Post* (Washington, DC), January–February 1963.

"top business executives": "Rapid Reading to Be Shown in Monday Demonstrations," *Wilmington (DE) News-Journal*, December 12, 1959.

"It is one of the most outstanding": "Executives Re-learn the First R,'" *Salesweek*, March 21, 1960, 31.

"Claims of fantastic achievements": George W. Gibson, letter to editor, *Salesweek*, July 25, 1960, 23.

"in effect, questioned the integrity" . . . *"'run-of-the-mill' speed reading courses"*: L.L. Stirland, letter to editor, *Salesweek*, August 22, 1960, 30.

"in the accuracy of the claims" . . . *"I trust you would not mind"*: Gibson, letter to editor, *Salesweek*, August 22, 1960, 30.

"one intrepid individual" . . . *"Can he read at 4,000 wpm?"*: R. H. Darling, letter to editor, *Salesweek*, September 5, 1960.

"We've been deluged": Letters and comments, *Salesweek*, October 17, 1960.

"We don't feel we have": "'Unshackled' Readers Gain Speed," *Washington Post*, August 7, 1960.

"A Woodman can mop up Dr. Zhivago*"* . . . *"Washington has seen nothing"*: "Read Faster and Better," *Time*, August 22, 1960, 41.

Chapter 5: The Kid Farm

"at least" . . . *"mere skimming"*: Hugh Sidey, "The President's Voracious Reading Habits," *Life*, March 17, 1961, 55–60.

"picked up": An account of how JFK came to accompany his friend to the lessons is in David Pitts, *Jack and Lem* (New York: Da Capo, 2008), 128. Letters from the White House named the Foundation for Better Reading as the course provider. Also Ralph A. Dungan, special assistant to the president, to Sandra McGibbon, July 25, 1961, Papers of John F. Kennedy, Presidential Papers 15-5.

"If you don't read" . . . *a milkman*: Leslie and Elizabeth Carpenter, "One-City, Three-Year Test Is Planned for Pay Teevee," *Abilene (TX) Reporter News*, March 5, 1961.

"amusing": Fred Remington, "An Engrossing TV Documentary," *Pittsburgh Press*, June 28, 1961.

"trim, tanned physical culturist" . . . *"slowed down"*: Gwen Gibson, "D.C. Wash," *New York Daily News*, April 15, 1961.

"I must say that this": William Proxmire, "Speed Reading and Responsible Citizenship," *Proceedings of the 44th Annual Education Conference* (Newark: University of Delaware, 1962), 68. The statement made at the conference appeared for decades in Evelyn Wood Reading Dynamics ads.

"guarantee phenomenal increases" . . . *"check with your nearest"*: George W. Gibson, "Some Ideas on Reading Courses," *Harvard Business School Bulletin* 37, no. 2 (April 1961): 24.

"breakthrough": Curtis Mitchell, "She Can Teach You to Read 2,500 Words a Minute," *Family Weekly*, February 5, 1961, 13.

"All at once, I was living": Mitchell, "She Can Teach," 14.

"One student, speed-reading": Jean Sharley, "Is a Revolution in Reading Coming?" *Detroit Free Press*, February 12, 1961.

"Inasmuch as our students" . . . *"cast an aura of erudition"*: George W. Gibson to George M. Ferris Jr., April 27, 1961, EW Papers, Box 14, Folder 2.

"She gave me pistachio": Lewis interview.

"way over market price" . . . *"fierce mustache"*: Darling interview, June 25, 2017.

"We didn't need the money" . . . *"I liked being applauded"*: Darling interview, June 25, 2017.

"a 16-year-old all-American boy": Ben David, "Boy Reads 15,000 Words a Minute Using New Technique, *Auckland (NZ) Sun*, March 1, 1961.

"It was fantastic" . . . *"You'll have a great life"*: Darling interview, June 25, 2017.

"We were just talking about this" . . . *"Louise, I tell you"*: *I've Got a Secret*, week 472, aired June 28, 1961, on CBS.

"Dear Mr. Kennedy": Sandra McGibbon to JFK, June 2, 1961 [Note: This date, handwritten by letter writer is probably incorrect, as the television show had not yet aired. A notation near the date indicates it was received on July 5.], JFK Papers, 15-5.

"In reply to your query": Dungan to McGibbon, JFK Papers.

"They were gone": Thora Qaddumi, "Woman's Reading Methods Now Used Internationally," *Schenectady (NY) Gazette*, July 17, 1967. Qaddumi's byline

included the name of a Eugene, Oregon, paper, the *Register-Guard*, indicating
that the article was distributed by a news service.

"solons" had been sent back to school: Associated Press, "Solons Speed Up the
'Hardy Boys,'" *Wausau (WI) Daily Herald*, June 10, 1961.

"Evelyn N. Wood, executive" . . . *"Use the fingers to guide"*: EW, "Study-reading *All*
Your Daily Mail," *American Salesman*, September 1961, 61.

"Your mind doesn't register": EW, Student Manual, 1962, EW Papers, Box 3,
Folder 2.

"In the course at Reading Dynamics Institute": EW, "Study-reading," 61.

"See you in Washington": EW to Dr. John Ise Jr., March 31, 1961, EW Papers, Box
14, Folder 2.

"pocket institute" . . . *"I believe that Boeing"*: Fred Chouinard to MDW, September 24, 1961, EW Papers, Box 14, Folder 2.

"wonderful friends" . . . *"You should see the Danish"*: EW to Darling, n.d., private
collection.

"some other revolutionary ideas" . . . *"I feel very strongly"*: Frances Lide, "Rapid
Reading Program Grows," *Washington (DC) Sunday Star*, January 28, 1962.

74 percent of course enrollees were men: Statistical report, October 1969, EW Papers,
Box 17, Folder 7.

"the flavor of what the man's writing": Display ad, *State News* (Michigan State
University, East Lansing), June 28, 1971. The ad included the transcript of the
Linkletter show, aired ten years before.

"Mrs. Wood claims" . . . *"I hope to be able"*: Fred Schneider, "Reading Dynamics
Hit by Dr. Spache," *Daily Alligator* (University of Florida, Gainesville), n.d.,
ca. September 1961, EW Papers, Box 14, Folder 2.

"reports which have reached" . . . *"impugn the reputation"*: Ronald E. Madsen to
George D. Spache, September 26, 1961, EW Papers, Box 14, Folder 2. The letter is signed with the name of a law firm, Douglas, Obear, and Campbell, and
the initials R.E.M., indicating it was written by Madsen.

Chapter 6: Bunk and Debunkers

"The confusion on her face" . . . *"snide remarks"*: William Liddle to Russell Stauffer,
February 2, 1962, EW Papers, Box 14, Folder 3. The letter is signed only "Bill,"
but the contents indicate it was written by Liddle.

"beverages of choice": Norman A. Stahl and M. Trika Smith-Burke, "The National Reading Conference: The College and Adult Reading Years," *Journal of Literacy Research* 3, no. 1 (1999): 57.

"Is This a Breakthrough in Reading?": George D. Spache, *Reading Teacher* 15, no. 4 (January 1962): 258–63.

"then practically all present methods": Spache, "Breakthrough in Reading?" 259.

He cited findings . . . "processing": Spache, 260.

"hinges on the definition" . . . "reading most words": Spache, 259.

"facile oral reports" . . . "on the information gained": Spache, 262.

"versatility". . . look at pictures or captions: Liddle to Stauffer, February 2, 1962.

"Meaning is Inside People": Evelyn N. Wood, "A New Approach to Reading," *Proceedings of the 44th Annual Education Conference* (Newark: University of Delaware, 1962), 60.

"There is no meaning": Typescript of Instructor's Manual, Lesson One, n.d., EW Papers, Box 18, Folder 19.

"overly enthusiastic" . . . "My mind is open": Liddle to Stauffer, February 2, 1962.

"Mrs. Wood has frequently stated": Stanford E. Taylor, "An Evaluation of Forty-One Trainees Who Had Recently Completed the 'Reading Dynamics' Program," *College and Adult Reading 1* (North Central Reading Association, St. Paul), May 1962, 65.

"The presentation of this data": Taylor, "Evaluation," 71.

"This article is not written": Spache, "Breakthrough in Reading?" 262.

"2,000 W.P.M.—But Is It Reading?": Lawrence Galton, *New York Times*, August 27, 1961.

"evidence" . . . "at least one member": Galton, "2,000 W.P.M."

"You have nothing to lose": Display ad, *Barnard Bulletin*, March 26, 1962.

"Speed Reading Is the Bunk" . . . "as revolutionary as hers": Eugene Ehrlich, *Saturday Evening Post*, June 9, 1962, 15.

"had borrowed from the summary" . . . "Obviously these men honestly believed": Ehrlich, "Speed Reading Is the Bunk," 16.

"I left Mr. Ehrlich's classroom": DeWitt E. Carroll to Robert Sherrod (ed., *Saturday Evening Post*), June 14, 1962, EW Papers, Box 14, Folder 4.

"People ask: 'Is Russia ahead?'": Associated Press, "Reading School Business Booming," *Oil City (PA) Derrick*, June 1, 1962.

"The eye simply cannot": Galton, "2,000 W.P.M."

"This investigator is admittedly not an authority": William Liddle, "Results of Experimentation on the Wood Reading Technique," *Proceedings of the College Reading Association*, Summer 1962, 14.

"Opinions Differ on Speed Reading": Eugene Ehrlich and EW, *NEA Journal* (April 1963): 44–46.

"our founder" . . . *"The next move is up to you"*: "Evelyn Goes West," *Evelyn Wood Reading Dynamiker*, August 15, 1962, 1.

"We have a tremendous man": EW to Bob Darling, January 15, 1963, private collection.

"After seeing what he could do" . . . *"but we accomplished many things"*: EW to Bob Darling, January 15, 1963.

Chapter 7: Civil War

"We are very happy to inform you": EWRD bulletin no. 12-63, July 5, 1963, EW Papers, Box 18, Folder 1.

"to stop the bleeding": Stanton Davis, interview by author, September 11, 2017.

Senators Talmadge and Bennett had previously failed: Wallace F. Bennett and Herman E. Talmadge to US Senate colleagues, March 7, 1962, EW Papers, Box 14, Folder 3.

"confound the opposition" . . . *"Not one of my students"*: Robert Crater, "Secret Weapons," *Pittsburgh Press*, February 23, 1963.

"We can't quarrel": "Teddy, Veddy Ready," *Newport News (VA) Daily Press*, February 12, 1963.

"How's your reading going ahead?" . . . *"and just keeping your mind on it"*: "EMK's Speed Reading Course; Prospective Visit; President Kennedy Speech at Boston College for April 19, 1963," March 7, 1963, JFK Papers, President's Office Files, Presidential Recordings.

"steal": Martha J. Maxwell, "Ethics Revisited: The Current Dilemma Facing the College-Adult Reading Specialist," *Multidisciplinary Aspects of College-Adult Reading: Seventeenth Yearbook of the National Reading Conference* (Milwaukee), 1968, 104.

"supersonic reading": Cecil Holland, "Speedy Readers Make Weighty Words Light," *Washington (DC) Evening Star*, April 19, 1963.

"quite finished" . . . *"the beauty of the English language"*: Holland, "Speedy Readers."

"shop talk": Cecil Holland, UPI, "JFK Reported Ready to Give Views on Steel Hikes," *Harrisburg (IL) Daily Register*, April 19, 1963.

"pupil": "Reading System Originator Due," *Honolulu Advertiser*, August 14, 1963.

"having been telling some pretty wild stories" . . . *"Even [if] we terminate"*: Madsen to MDW, September 17, 1963, EW Papers, Box 14, Folder 5.

"with the help of a friend's": Mitchell, "She Can Teach," 14.

"who cheated" . . . *"When you speed-read"*: Lewis interview.

"Read now, laugh later": Katherine Evans, "They're Speed-Reading," *New York Herald Tribune*, June 1, 1961.

"They got scared": Lewis interview.

"information," "assistance," and "advice": Franchise Contract, EWRD, Conference Board, 63.

his father was left in debt: David F. Babbel, interview by author, November 7, 2017.

Chapter 8: Consulting the Oracle

"busy, busy businesswoman": Davis interview.

"patchworked by various people" . . . *"if pushed"*: EWRD Institute Convention (Washington, DC), June 12, 1965, EW Papers, Box 18, Folder 23.

"Young lady, if there is any doubt": Jeffrey C. Alexander, "Most Just Waste the Money," *Crimson* (Harvard University, Cambridge, MA), May 3, 1967.

"You must have a desire": EWRD student manual, 1962, EW Papers, unpaginated, Box 3, Folder 2.

"research and development" . . . *"for the inspiration"*: Recommendations of Sponsors Council to Executive Committee of DEAR, March 13, 1967, 4, EW Papers, Box 14, Folder 7.

War and Peace *in eighteen minutes*: EWRD full-page ad, *Austin (TX) Statesman*, April 19, 1966.

"Has the New Man" . . . *"your promotion potential"*: EWRD display ad, *San Rafael (CA) Daily Independent Journal*, July 12, 1967.

"unbelievable" . . . *"previews"*: Lawrence R. James, "Study Examines Evelyn Wood Claims," *Daily Utah Chronicle* (Salt Lake City), January 16, 1967.

"Charges Untrue, Says Evelyn Wood" . . . *"humble beginnings"*: EW letter to editor, *Daily Utah Chronicle*, January 20, 1967.

"I've been called a charlatan" . . . *"I spent twenty minutes"*: "But Can the Publishers Keep Up with Her?" *Newsday*, February 10, 1967.

"certain movie star": Qaddumi, "Woman's Reading Methods."

"Most Just Waste the Money" . . . *"people who are conscientious enough"*: Alexander, "Waste the Money."

"motherly smile" . . . *"My vision blurred"*: Alexander, "Waste the Money."

"They are everywhere": Jeffrey C. Alexander, "The Evolution of an Idea," *Crimson* (Harvard University, Cambridge, MA), April 27, 1967.

Quoting the reporter's words: John Kilgo, letter to editor, *Crimson* (Harvard University, Cambridge, MA), May 26, 1967.

"Don Golembia of Detroit": Full-page ad, Famous Artists Schools, *Marion (OH) Star*, February 29, 1964.

"It is contemplated that the Employee": Agreement FAS and EW, August 25, 1967, EW Papers, Box 22, Folder 1.

Chapter 9: Times Are A-Changin'

"I loved pontificating" . . . *"telling you to tell yourself to read faster"*: Ira West, interview by author, June 13, 2018.

"He always would have wanted" . . . *"I can't see him"*: John Stutesman, interview by author, April 5, 2018.

"fifteen-million-dollar-plus": Classified ad for financial officer, *Wall Street Journal*, November 15, 1967.

"Famous Artists Schools Inc. has acquired": Display ad, *Wall Street Journal*, December 1, 1967.

"really good at cooking German food": Nielsen interview.

"They bought the most expensive steaks": Marlene Bennett, interview by author, November 15, 2017.

"Meet Ralph Frey, Jr.": Display ad, *Salt Lake Tribune*, January 9, 1967.

"I went to work rich": Howard J. Ruff, *How to Prosper in the Age of Obamanomics* (Saratoga Springs, NY: Saratoga Publishing, 2009), xx.

"The parent company": Susan Lyman-Whitney, "Failure Is Key to Success," *Deseret News* (Salt Lake City, UT), April 6, 1990.

"inconsistent with the public interest": In re: complaint concerning Multimedia Inc., Knoxville, TN, re: commercial status of station WBIR-TV program, *Federal Communication Commission Reports*, March 11, 1970.

"I was Evelyn's right hand" . . . "We had a parking lot": Nielsen interview.

"My friends were getting cars" . . . "My kids didn't even know": Bennett interview.

Observing religious tithing: 1969 federal tax return, EW Papers, Box 27, Folder 10.

"they treated us like royalty": Davis interview.

Its ostensible purpose . . . "S.I. Hayakawa can zip through": Steven Reiner, Newsweek Feature Service, "Speed Reading Doesn't Require Superhuman Mental Prowess," San Bernardino (CA) County Sun, July 11, 1969.

Teachers who quit: Maxwell, "Ethics Revisited," 104.

"Would they qualify": Preston, letter to editor, Daily Pennsylvanian (University of Pennsylvania, Philadelphia), October 27, 1969.

"What the eyes do": Kramer, letter to editor, Daily Pennsylvanian, March 11, 1970.

"extravagant claims": Preston, letter to editor, Daily Pennsylvanian, March 31, 1970.

"[That] is where I really learned": Howard Ruffner, email to author, September 14, 2018.

"We hit a rather bad problem": Greg McGarry, "Teaches Reading to Nixon Staff," Schenectady (NY) Gazette, September 29, 1970.

"Invited Mrs. Wood to teach" . . . "Reading Dynamics Held Here": Display ad, EWRD, Kokomo (IN) Tribune, June 29, 1970.

She settled temporarily in a mobile home: Sandal English, "Everybody Cooks: with Herbs," Arizona Daily Star, June 10, 1970.

Chapter 10: Snake in the Grass

"Evelyn Wood, a name you can trust" . . . "much more than just a speed-reading program": Full-page ad, Salt Lake Tribune, June 6, 1971.

framed portraits of a gray-haired Evelyn: Grace Lichtenstein, "The Moving Finger Reads," New York Magazine, June 23, 1969, 62.

"She was disorganized" . . . "Is my wig straight?": Nieslen interview.

"Mr. Wood could sell you his false teeth" . . . "I wish we could have taught": Nielsen interview.

"no longer a fad" . . . "While there have been some claims": William K. Stevens, "Speed Reading Has Become a Permanent Fixture in Education in America," New York Times, September 19, 1971.

"psychedelic": Ronald Paul Carver, Sense and Nonsense in Speed Reading (Silver Spring, MD: Revrac, 1971), 8.

"What happened to the breakthrough": Carver, *Sense and Nonsense*, 108.

"Anyone who is moving his eyes": Carver, 106.

"During this class it occurred to me": Carver, 31.

"Eye movements are not the cause": Carver, 19.

"Someone who covers reading material": Carver, 20–21.

"disturbed": Carver, 79.

"clairvoyant reading": Carver, 80.

"of little consequence" . . . *"practice running your hand"*: Carver, 113.

"Regardless of what your results": Carver, 101.

"I took a speed-reading course" . . . *"Evelyn Wood Moves Her Lips"*: Ronald P. Carver, "Speed Readers Don't Read; They Skim," *Psychology Today*, August 1972.

"Some of the theories and techniques" . . . *"Evelyn Wood's latest lesson manual"*: Peter Kump, EWRD Bulletin, August 1972.

"I'm sure all our franchisees": Durakis to MDW, April 11, 1972, EW Papers, Box 16, Folder 4.

"attempting to build a career": Kump, EWRD Bulletin, August 7, 1972.

"realized that right here in Utah": Bennett interview.

"not skimming" . . . *"a fraction of the cost"*: *Daily Universe*, September 13, 1973.

"He had complete access": Nielsen interview.

"We all felt that we had": Bennett interview.

"one thing about Richard": Nielsen interview.

"acquired special, secret, and confidential" . . . *"seriously undercut plaintiff's prices"*: EWRD Institute v. Richard Shipley, et al. Civil No. 207680, District Court Salt Lake County, EW Papers, Box 22, Folder 7.

"induced" . . . *"and its licensor, DEAR"*: Answer and counterclaim re: EWRD Institute v. Richard Shipley et al., received September 28, 1977, District Court Salt Lake County, EW Papers, EWRD Institute v. Richard Shipley, et al., Box 22, Folder 7.

"He was like a little mouse": Nielsen interview.

"What's the most popular" . . . *"at a fraction of the cost"*: Display ad, RDI, *Daily Utah Chronicle*, October 2, 1974

In January 1972: Ellen Gunderson, office employee, EWRD Utah, to DEAR, January 27, 1972, EW Papers, Box 17, Folder 2.

By late 1973 . . . Doug's executive chair: Assignment and Settlement of Claim, November 19, 1973, EW Papers

"An article such as this one": Kump, Bulletin.

Chapter 11: White Knight

"I was into cars": Richard J. Hernandez, interview by author, June 19, 2017.

"Hey freshman": *Daily of the University of Washington* (Seattle), October 3, 1972.

"The amount of reading I had" . . . "Minutes out of the body shop": Hernandez interview.

"When it comes to the more technical work" . . . "I can read one a day": David DeLaittre, interview by author, May 20, 2017.

"was gung-ho about it": Hernandez interview.

"If you think you were taken" . . . "He kept finding fault with things": Peter Rinearson, "Reading Dynamics Is a Rip-off, Say Students," *Daily of the University of Washington* (Seattle), May 24, 1973.

"I said no" . . . "I was the leader of the pack": Hernandez interview.

"took him apart" . . . "They did have a structured": DeLaittre interview.

"Reading Lib Now!" et al.: *Daily of the University of Washington* (Seattle), October 3, 1972.

"highly skeptical, perhaps even jaded": Richard W. Summers to EW and MDW, August 10, 1972, EW Papers.

"even on the toughest material" . . . "You can't believe that he's": Display ad, Lyceum, *New York Times*, February 1, 1972.

"I must protest this use of your name": John Sherman to Proxmire, September 26, 1973, Proxmire Papers, Box 205, Folder 15. All letters cited from Proxmire Papers come from the same box and folder.

"the harder you worked on the course" . . . "requires constant use": Proxmire to David Kubal, January 15, 1973, Proxmire Papers.

"the accuracy of the representations made" . . . "before deciding on what action": Arthur R. Woods to Proxmire, March 27, 1972, Proxmire Papers.

"I have not lent my name": Proxmire to Arthur Woods, FTC, March 30, 1972, Proxmire Papers.

"semi-dormant": "Corporate Repair Work," *Forbes*, November 15, 1975, 29–30.

about $3 million: Patricia Thompson, interview by author, June 28, 2018. For reasons related to health, Maurice "Tommy" Thompson Jr. asked his wife, Patricia, to handle the interview. She was closely involved in his business matters.

"He was the original Mad Man" . . . *"He believed she should be honored"*: Thompson interview.

"the last thing you want": Thompson interview.

"you can't just sit": "Corporate Repair Work," 30.

"I think she might have been a little uncomfortable" . . . *"inspire"*: Thompson interview.

"inept": Kelly to other sponsors, March 18, 1971, EW Papers, Box 17, Folder 3.

"character" . . . *"it wasn't going to last forever"*: Thompson interview.

"It Sounds Incredible" . . . *"Find out if we've pulled the wool"*: Display ad, EWRD, *Bridgeport (CT) Post*, June 10, 1973.

"snappy sexagenarian" . . . *"I was sorry we ever taught them to read"*: Phyllis Battelle, "Read Fast—Learn More," *McAllen (TX) Monitor*, December 19, 1975.

"the most famous reading teacher in the world": Robert Marston & Associates, Work Status Report, October 1975, EW Papers, Box 19, Folder 29.

television personality Johnny Carson: Clip from *The Tonight Show*, November 12, 1975, posted to YouTube as "Speed reading demonstration" by "Dynamic Speed Reading," August 4, 2013, https://youtu.be/oLgBDHhV-xM.

$10.5 million in revenue for 1975: "Corporate Repair Work," 29.

The consumer protection agency, directed by: "Suburbs," *Philadelphia Inquirer*, March 2, 1978.

"'Dynamic' must be her middle name": Polly Nash, "Reading Dynamics Class 'Zooms' Through Books," *St. Louise Globe-Democrat*, March 16–17, 1963.

"She said, 'The whole side of my body'": Bennett interview.

Chapter 12: Rehab

"It was frustrating" . . . *"You can imagine"*: PM television program segment, "Evelyn Wood Reading Dynamics," Aloysius S. Church restaurant review video collection, DVD2, Special Collections and Archives, J. Willard Marriott Library, University of Utah, Salt Lake City.

"ripoff" . . . *"were doing a marvelous job"*: Philip Rosmarin, "Speed Reading: Is 5,000 wpm Out of Sight?" *Daily Pilot* (Orange County, CA), July 11, 1976.

"Nineteen seventy-six was a peculiar": Thompson to EW and MDW, January 4, 1977, EW Papers, Box 17, Folder 1.

"He was a lovely, lovely man" . . . *"I think she had a bit of an ego"*: Thompson interview.

"Her persistence pulled her through": PM television program segment.

"quick lift" . . . *"When Tide goes in"*: Paid notice, Alan Northcote Sidnam, *New York Times*, August 28, 2008.

"mind-cure movement" . . . *"Success seekers must take"*: Bruce Mazlish and Edwin Diamond, *Jimmy Carter: A Character Portrait* (New York: Simon and Schuster, 1979), 160.

Interviewed more than a decade later: Joy Billington, "School Is Never Out in the Carter White House," *Chicago Tribune*, July 2, 1977.

As explained by deputy White House counsel: Margaret McKenna to Bob Lipshutz, February 28, 1977, and Bernard W. Kelly to Bob Lipshutz, February 21, 1977, Jimmy Carter Presidential Library and Museum, Atlanta, Presidential Files, Records of the White House Office of Counsel to the President, Container 137, Folder 2/77–3/77.

Coyly declining to disclose: UPI, "Carter Tops Pupils, Reading Teacher Says," *Atlanta Constitution*, June 20, 1977.

Carter received a list: Suggested remarks to the Gridiron Club, Jimmy Carter Presidential Files, Container 12, Folder 3/21/77.

But Jaffe said she hadn't consented: "Suit Charges Deceptive Ads," *Des Plaines (IL) Herald*, February 18, 1977.

"I wonder how much of that article": Merton Vance, "National Speed-Reading Course Has University Counterpart," *Daily Tar Heel* (University of North Carolina, Chapel Hill), February 2, 1977, and EWRD Institute, Atlanta (no name), letter to editor, February 9, 1977.

"Perhaps there is a correlation": Richard G. Graf, "Remember the Tortoise," *Psychology Today*, December 1973, 112–13.

"Kennedy Skims at 1,200 Words Per Minute": Carver, *Sense and Nonsense*, 1.

"mountain-goat reading" . . . *"one leaps from point"*: Esther Wohl, "Here's Johnny Who CAN Read," *Binghamton (NY) Press and Sun-Bulletin*, May 21, 1961.

"one-third the cost of a comparable course" . . . *"Read Roots in Four Hours"*: Small display ad, *New York Amsterdam News*, March 26, 1977.

"If you can get your money back": Bob Varettoni, "Speed Reading Instructor Denies Fraud Charge," *Observer* (University of Notre Dame, IN), February 17, 1978.

"Evelyn Woodski Slow Reading Course": *Saturday Night Live*, November 12, 1977, accessed March 6, 2019, www.nbc.com/saturday-night-live/video /evelyn-woodski-slow-reading-course/3007522.

"made some good dough": Thompson interview.

The balance sheet: "URS Agrees to Acquire Evelyn Wood Reading for Cash and Notes," *Wall Street Journal*, October 3, 1977.

had a military contract: Defense Contract Action Data System, Fiscal Year 1977, US National Archives and Records Administration.

The new owners picked up: Dominick Masella, EWRD controller, to EW, June 9, 1978, EW Papers, Box 17, Folder 3.

"charming people": Gordon Irving, preface to Cowan and Boone.

"felt pretty small" . . . *"tolerating the mistreatment"*: David F. Boone Sr., "The Worldwide Evacuation of Latter-Day Saint Missionaries at the Beginning of World War II" (master's thesis, Brigham Young University, 1981), All theses and dissertations, 4542, 9–10.

"the first reprisal against the Jews" . . . *said she'd seen furniture thrown*: Cowan and Boone, 20.

"They said, 'We've never seen anybody'": Cowan and Boone, 21.

Minor infractions . . . *had, in fact, been ignored*: George Blake, the young Utah diarist who'd served under Doug in Frankfurt, wrote in his 1938 diary of having his camera confiscated by a lower police functionary for taking pictures of the Kristallnacht damage. Blake was not arrested, but he was taken briefly to a police station and told that his camera, but not his film, would be returned to him the next day. Upon his return, a higher official politely gave him back both camera and film, all but apologizing for the subordinate's actions. See Blake, 1938 diary, 280–83.

"My wife was a jump ahead": Cowan and Boone, 20–21.

"an entirely new self-teaching format" . . . *"can't afford"*: Peter Kump, *Breakthrough Rapid Reading*, (West Nyack, NY: Parker, 1979), 9.

"Doug Wood has one of the sunniest" . . . *"Simone Beck is an inventive"*: Kump, *Breakthrough Rapid Reading*, 106.

"zeal in reconstructing Evelyn Wood's life": Agardy, acknowledgments for *Read Faster and Better*, 5.

"When the economy gets bad": Mark Potts, "Evelyn Wood Closes Here, in Other Cities," *Chicago Tribune*, January 10, 1981.

"basically seems an inducement": Carol Eckbert, *Library Journal*, September 15, 1981, 1728.

"Get out of your homes": Agardy, *Read Faster and Better*, 33.

Chapter 13: Carved in Stone

profits dropped . . . ad buys: "Engineering Services to Speed Reading," *Barron's*, December 11, 1978.

"the greatest thing since the printing press" . . . "not really a speed reader anymore": Alexandra D. Korry, "The Speedreading Courses: Are They Just Skimming?" *Washington Post*, August 25, 1980.

"I can read faster" . . . "Evelyn Wood has become": Randi Henderson, "Sp'd Read'ng or Skimm'ng?" *Baltimore Sun*, January 19, 1982.

"She has touched the lives" . . . "Evelyn Wood, like Betty Crocker": *PM* television program segment.

"There is little doubt" . . . "one can with a little effort": Bruce L. Brown, Dillon K. Inouye, Kim Barrus, and Dorothy M. Hansen, "An Analysis of the Rapid Reading Controversy," in *The Social Psychology of Reading* 1, John R. Edwards, ed. (Silver Spring, MD: Institute of Modern Languages, 1981), 29–40.

"We should not expect": Kim B. Barrus, "Rapid Reading Reconsidered," (doctoral dissertation, Brigham Young University, August 1978), 5.

"How to get the most" . . . "Of course, you already have such a device": Display ad, *Daily Utah Chronicle*, October 18, 1978.

"simplify" . . . "divest": URS Corp, company history, n.d, accessed October 30, 2018, www.referenceforbusiness.com/history2/95/URS-Corporation.html.

Recording the registrations: US Patent and Trademark Office, *Official Gazette*, February 11, 1984.

American Learning Corporation paid: P. J. Bednarski, "Encyclopaedia Britannica's American Learning Unit Going Public," *Chicago Sun-Times*, June 12, 1986.

She was now a consultant: P. J. Bednarski, "Britannica Unit Buys Speed-Reading Rights," *Chicago Sun-Times*, May 22, 1986.

an amendment concerning the base compensation rate, $22,000: Masella to EW, June 9, 1978. Also, R. Stephen Heinrichs, URS treasurer, to EW, May 15, 1979, EW Papers.

"this new outfit" . . . "The only and brightest": Dennis McLellan, "A Quick Read Through the Life of Evelyn Wood," *Los Angeles Times*, August 14, 1986.

"grandmotherly": McLellan, "Quick Read."

"We'd say, 'I love you, Mimi'" . . . *"she was a very intense woman"*: Davis interview.

"feelings, not strong feelings" . . . *"I thought, 'Oh yeah'"*: North interview.

"I, along with my three brothers": Smith electronic chat.

"You don't want your lawyer" . . . *"A person who speed reads"*: Marcia Dunn (AP), "Researchers Take Closer Look at Speed Reading," *Richmond County Daily Journal* (Rockingham, NC), March 22, 1987.

"At age eighty, Evelyn Wood": Jim Radcliffe, "Speed Is Still the Essence and Legacy of Evelyn Wood," *Arizona Daily Star*, January 10, 1989.

"down to" 1,000 words per minute: Korry, "Speedreading Courses."

"continue to increase its revenues": Julie Bennett, "American Learning Gets Low Marks, *Crain's Chicago Business*, March 5, 1990.

"some" . . . *"Your original reading speed"*: Stanley D. Frank, *Remember Everything You Read: The Evelyn Wood Seven-Day Speed Reading and Learning Program* (New York: Fall River, 1994), 7.

"comeback" . . . *"buried in billions of words"*: John Cunniff, "Speed Reading Making a Comeback—Rapidly," *St. Petersburg (FL) Times*, August 19, 1991.

"This is Evelyn Wood": Jim Borgman (Cincinnati Enquirer), *Wisconsin Rapids Daily Tribune*, November 27, 1987.

On-air meteorologists: News captions, *KPIX 5 News at 11 PM*, December 2, 2017.

"tiny, soft-spoken woman": Lawrence Van Gelder, "Evelyn Wood, Who Promoted Speed Reading, Is Dead at 86," *New York Times*, August 30, 1995.

"has long since" . . . *"not one uses the technique"*: Phyllis Mindell, letter to editor, *New York Times*, September 3, 1995.

"That's the sense my mom got": Davis interview.

"She never mentioned it": Smith electronic chat.

Epilogue

"reassuringly normal": Robert L. Hampel, *Fast and Curious: A History of Shortcuts in American Education* (Lanham, MD: Rowman and Littlefield, 2017), 143.

the Evelyn Wood method was not remedial: EWRD bulletin, n.d., EW Papers, Box 18, Folder 4. This bulletin was probably issued around 1969 as it refers to a 1968 study and claims "400,000 successful" course graduates.

"When Evelyn Wood devised": Hugh Sidey, introduction to *Prelude to Leadership: The European Diary of John F. Kennedy, Summer 1945* (New York: Regnery, 1995), xxxv–xxxvi.

the US Federal Trade Commission . . . compelled him to stop claiming that his system: US Federal Trade Commission, "In the Matter of Howard S. Berg," Docket No. C-3812, June 8, 1998.

"Language skill is at the heart": Keith Rayner et al., "So Much to Read, So Little Time: How Do We Read, and Can Speed-Reading Help?" *Psychological Science in the Public Interest* 17, no. 1 (January 14, 2016): 4–34.

"Although we now know the claims are false": Mark Seidenberg, *Language at the Speed of Sight: How We Read, Why So Many Can't, and What Can Be Done About It* (New York: Basic Books, 2017), 77.

Selected Bibliography

Books

Agardy, Franklin J. *How to Read Faster and Better: How to Get Everything You Want from Anything You Read as Fast as You Can Think; the Evelyn Wood Reading Dynamics Program*. Fireside Edition. New York: Simon and Schuster, 1981.

Carver, Ronald Paul. *Sense and Nonsense in Speed Reading*. Silver Spring, MD: Revrac, 1971.

Frank, Stanley D. *Remember Everything You Read: The Evelyn Wood Seven-Day Speed Reading and Learning Program*. New York: Fall River, 1994.

Kump, Peter. *Breakthrough Rapid Reading*. West Nyack, NY: Parker, 1979.

Minert, Roger P. *Under the Gun: West German and Austrian Saints in World War II*. Salt Lake City, UT: Deseret Book, 2011.

Montague, Terry Bohle. *"Mine Angels Round About": Mormon Missionary Evacuation from Western Germany, 1939*. Orem, UT: Granite, 1989.

Nelson, David Conley. *Moroni and the Swastika: Mormons in Nazi Germany*. Norman: University of Oklahoma Press, 2015.

Seidenberg, Mark. *Language at the Speed of Sight: How We Read, Why So Many Can't, and What Can Be Done about It*. New York: Basic Books, 2018.

Wood, Evelyn Nielsen, and Marjorie Wescott Barrows. *Reading Skills*.
New York: Holt, Rinehart and Winston, 1958.

Documents and Collections

Blake, George R. "Journals, 1938 and 1939." Ms.17781. Church History
Library, Church of Jesus Christ of Latter-Day Saints.

Kennedy, John F. Papers. Presidential Papers and Presidential Recordings. John F. Kennedy Presidential Library and Museum. Boston,
Massachusetts.

Liddle, William. "An Initial Investigation of the Wood Reading Dynamics Method." Dissertation, University of Delaware, 1965.

Proxmire, William. Papers. 1938–2004. Mss 738. Wisconsin Historical
Society. Madison, Wisconsin.

Wood, Evelyn Nielsen. Papers. Ca. 1925–1979. Mss B272. Utah State
Historical Society. Salt Lake City, Utah.

Index

Aaronic Priesthood, 40
Advanced Systems, 184
Agardy, Franklin J., 188–189, 191
Agony and the Ecstasy (Stone), 83, 151
Alexander, Jeffrey C., 124
Allen, Woody, 155, 192
A.M. Detroit, 172
American Junior Red Cross, 41–43
American Learning Corporation, 197–203
American Salesman, 80–81
American Society of Newspaper Editors, 106
Andersen, Rollo, 57
Andrew, June, 55
Anschluss, 25
anti-Semitism, 24–25, 186–187
Arlington, VA, 70, 73, 101
Art Linkletter's House Party, 83, 120, 151
Atlanta, GA, 133
Atlantic City, NJ, ix
Austria, 19, 25, 29–30

Babbel, Bonnie, 61–62, 74, 108–109, 112–113
Babbel, David F., 111
Babbel, Frederick "Fred"
  Bonnie and, 113
  Evelyn and, 59–61
  in Germany, 29
  nondisclosure agreement and, 159
  Washington institute and, 80, 93
  Webster and, 102–112
  Wood family and, 54–55
Babbel, June, 109
Baltimore Sun, 192
Barlow, Milton, 103
Barnard College, 93
Barrows, Marjorie Wescott, 47–48
Barrus, Kim, 196
Battelle, Phyllis, 172
Bay of Pigs, 78
Bayh, Birch, 103
Bear, Stanley H., 143
Beck, Simone, 188
Bendix, 120

Benjamin Franklin University, 60
Bennett, Marlene, 137, 148, 157–158,
  174–175
Bennett, Mike, 174–175
Bennett, Wallace F., 54, 71, 103
Benson, Ezra Taft, 55, 103
Berg, Howard S., 208
Berlin, Germany, 16, 21
Better Business Bureaus, 118
Blake, George R., 22, 29, 33, 35–37, 39
Bloom, Floyd E., 106
Boeing, 81, 120
Boles, Robert, 119
Book of Mormon, xii, 6
Boone, David F., 185–187
Breakthrough Rapid Reading (Kump),
  187–189
Breen, Stephen, xiii–xiv
Brigham Young University, 12, 39,
  113, 121, 157–159, 171, 174,
  195–196
Brilliant, Ashleigh, 129
Brinkley, David, 71
Brothers, Joyce, 140
Brown, Bruce L., 195–196
Buchanan, Patrick, 143
Bundy, McGeorge, 79
Bureau of Consumer Protection, 166, 174

Carlson, Elsie, 103–105, 107, 111
Carnegie Mellon University, 200
Carpenter, Patricia A., 200
Carson, Johnny, 172–174, 181, 183
Carter, Amy, 181
Carter, Jimmy, 179–181, 183–184,
  193
Carter, Rosalynn, 179

Carver, Ronald P., 151–157, 182,
  191–192, 195
Catholic Church, 30
Central Junior High School, 1–3
Chamberlain, Neville, 28
Chambers, Wallace L., 58–59
Chapin, Dwight, 143, 170
charm school, 15
Chicago Tribune, 189
Child, Julia, 188
Church of Jesus Christ of Latter-Day
  Saints
  Babbel and, 102–103
  Doug and, 14
  gender roles and, 137
  in Germany, 21, 23–33, 36–39,
    185–187
  missionary work and, 9–10
  Nielsen family and, 7–8
  in Ogden, 1–3
  religious instruction and, 5–6
  settlement of Utah and, 41–42
  Wood and, xii
  Wood family and, 17
Clark, J. Reuben, Jr., 21, 24–26
Clifton, Chester V., 79
Cohen, Max, 169, 192
Cold War, 96
College Reading Association, xiv,
  94, 96
Colson, Jackie Horner, 116
Columbia University, 47, 50, 91, 94
comprehension
  Reading Dynamics and, 54,
    63–66, 81
  skimming and, x, 153–155
  Spache and, 83–84

speed reading and, 88–90, 182, 208
tests for, 96–97, 116, 124, 130
concentration camps, 28
Conceptual-Visual Method, 111
Conference Board, 110, 149
Conscience of a Conservative, The
    (Goldwater), 129
Consumer Protection Act, 163
Cooper, Jack, 46
Copenhagen, Denmark, 36, 82
corporations, 81, 120, 163
correspondence schools, 126,
    142–143, 149
Cowan, Richard O., 185
Czechoslovakia, 26–27, 37–38

Daily Alligator, 83
Daily of the University of
    Washington, 161–165
Daily Pennsylvanian, 141
Daily Pilot, 177–178
Daily Universe, 157–159
Daily Utah Chronicle, 121–123
Dale Carnegie Service, 59
Darling, Robert, Sr., 66, 75
Darling, Robert "Bob"
    demonstrations and, 106, 149, 151
    Linkletter and, 82–83
    NEA convention and, x–xiv
    Salesweek and, 66
    Spache and, 87
    Western tour and, 98
    Woods and, 74–76
Davis, Ray Jay, 50, 114
Davis, Stanton, 101, 114, 123,
    137–138, 199, 200, 204
De Sanctis, James A., 178

DeLaittre, David, 162–164
Denmark, 34, 38
des Islets, John C. M., 79, 131
Deseret Ironrite, 57
Deseret News, 24, 39
Detroit Free Press, 72
Dew, Evelyn, 117–119
Dew, Walter, 118
Diamond, Edwin, 180
Diversified Education and Research
    Corp. (DEAR)
    Famous Artists and, 131–132
    FAS International and, 145, 171
    franchising and, 109–110, 149
    Reading Dynamics and, 113–119,
        123–125, 156–157
    Sidnam and, 178
    Thompson and, 167–168
Dixon, Byron, 60
Dorne, Albert, 131–132
Dow Chemicals, 131
Dungan, Ralph A., 78
DuPont, 62–63, 66, 118
Durakis, Charles, 156–157, 171
dynamic reading, 93, 117–118, 156.
    See also speed reading
Dynamic Reading group, 183

East German mission, 16, 26, 186.
    See also Germany; missionary
    work; West German mission
East High School, 36, 40
Eastern Europe, 33
Educational and Industrial
    Research, 182
Ehrlich, Eugene, 94–97, 130, 153,
    159, 195–196

Eisenhower, Dwight D., 55
Eisenhower Executive Office
    Building, 144
Encyclopaedia Britannica, 197–198,
    201–202
Equal Rights Amendment, 137
Evans, Robert, 200, 204
Evelyn Wood Reading Dynamics
    advertising and, 134–135
    American Learning and, 198–203
    Babbel and, 105–111
    book publishing and, 188
    Carter and, 180
    challenges to, 87–91, 94–97, 121–
        125, 130–131, 141, 154–160,
        205–208
    competitors and, 183
    conference and, 115–118
    Darling and, xii–xiv
    DEAR and, 113–114
    demonstrations and, 165
    Evelyn and, 58–67
    expansion of, 81–84, 138–140,
        147
    Famous Artists and, 126–127, 132
    finances and, 101–102, 149–150
    founding of, 55
    franchises and, 92–93, 136–137
    government officials and, 78–80
    Hernandez and, 161–164
    Lees and, 41
    Nixon White House and, 143–144
    public relations and, 171–172
    publicity and, 70–72
    skimming and, 151–153
    subsidiaries and, 73–74
    Thompson and, 167–170

URS and, 184, 191, 196–197
US senators and, 103–104
Evelyn Wood Reading Dynamiker
    (newsletter), 97
Evening Star, 106

Family Night, 6
Family Weekly, 72, 125
Famous Artists Schools, 125–127,
    131–136, 138–139. See also
    FAS International
FAS International, 138, 142–145,
    149, 156–157, 165–167, 171.
    See also Famous Artists
    Schools
Federal Communications
    Commission (FCC), 135, 208
Federal Trade Commission (FTC),
    166, 208
Ferris, George M., Jr., 73, 124
Forbes, 167–168
Foundation for Better Reading, 46,
    69, 78, 207
franchises
    DEAR and, 113–114, 149
    Evelyn and, 105–110, 119–122
    Famous Artists and, 126
    Kump and, 156
    Reading Dynamics and, 92, 97
    Thompson and, 167–169
    Webster and, 102, 134–138
Frank, Stanley D., 202
Frankfurt, Germany, 17, 20–24,
    26–33, 185–187
Frankfurt Opera, 31–32
Frederick W. Babbel & Associates,
    93, 105, 108, 110–111

Gagarin, Yuri, 96
Gainesville, FL, 83–84
Gardner, Hy, 101
Gariepy, Armand J. "Gary," 63
Garment, Leonard, 143
gender roles, 82–83, 133, 137, 199
General Electric, 81, 120
General Motors, 46
Gerbner, George, xi
Germany, 16, 17–34, 36–39
Gibson, George W., 64–66, 72–74,
    124, 153
Glenn, John, 96
Golden Fleece Awards, 201
Goldwater, Barry, 129
Good Morning America, 171
Graf, Richard A., 182, 195
Granet, Gilbert K., 132, 135, 138, 149
Grant, Heber J., 6, 16
Great Britain, 138
Great Depression, 12–13, 58
Gunderson, Ellen, 148
Gussman, Mary, 136–137, 144–145
Guthrie, John, 191

Hailey, Arthur, 135
Hall, Doug, 178
Hammond, West C., 58
Harvard Crimson, 124–126, 130
Harvard University, 45–46, 50,
    64–66, 72–73, 124–125
Hawaii, 106–107
Hayakawa, S. I., 139–141
HBS Bulletin, 72–73
Hernandez, Richard J., 161–164
Hildebrandt, Arnold, 32–33
Hill Air Force Base, 40

Hitler, Adolf, 18–19, 23, 25–30, 37
Holt, Rinehart and Winston, 48
*How to Correct People's Mistakes
    Without Making Them Sore*
    (Carnegie), 59
How to Read Faster and Better
    (Agardy), 188–189
*How to Sell on Purpose Instead of by
    Accident* (Gariepy), 63
Huntley, Chet, 71

IBM, 120
Idaho, 138
Idaho Postman, 102
Improvement Era, 3, 15, 18–19
Ingrid, Queen of Denmark, 139
Inouye, Daniel K., 106
International Accountants Society,
    135–136
International Paper, 120
International Reading Association,
    83, 191
I've Got a Secret, 76, 120

Jaffe, Beth, 172–174, 181, 192
James Beard Foundation, 143, 188
Jehovah's Witnesses, 23
Jensen, Katie C., 14–15
Jesus of Nazareth, 31–33
Jews, mistreatment of, 23–25, 29, 39,
    186–187
Jordan High School, 46–47, 50, 206
Joyce Brothers Reading Development
    Center, 140
Junior Rapid Reading, 147
Junior Reading Dynamics, 171–172
Just, Marcel, 200

Kaplan, Stanley H., 115
Kelly, Bernard, 169, 180–181, 192
Kelly, Philemon M., 21
Kennedy, Edward M. "Ted," 103–105, 107, 206
Kennedy, John F.
  advertising and, 170
  Evelyn and, 114, 139, 144, 193–194
  Life magazine and, 69–70
  NEA convention and, ix
  speed reading and, 77–79, 206–207
  Ted Kennedy and, 104–106
Kent State, 142
Kilgo, John, 124–125
kinescopes, 71, 95
King, John, 178
Kingman, Dong, 135
Klein, Robert, 58
Kramer, Arthur C., 119, 141–142, 165
Kramer, Ilse, 22, 33
Kristallnacht, 29, 187
Kump, Peter
  Breakthrough Rapid Reading and, 187–189
  BYU researchers and, 196
  Carver and, 156–157, 160
  as educational director, 148–149
  Hernandez and, 163
  Nixon White House and, 143–144
  Reading Dynamics and, 168–170, 182–183

La Bohème, 55
LA Times, 198–199
Laggin' Dragon, 61
Lancaster, Burt, 123
Language at the Speed of Sight (Seidenberg), 209

LDS Church. *See* Church of Jesus Christ of Latter-Day Saints
Lees, C. Lowell, 41–44, 48
lesson plans, 115–117
Liddle, William "Bill," 87–90, 96–97, 117, 154, 205
Life magazine, 69, 207
Lincoln, Evelyn, 78
Linguaphone Institute, 135
Linkletter, Art, 83
Lion House, 14–15
Lion's Club, 37
Little Listening Post (newsletter), 59–60, 62
Logan, UT, 7, 158
Loovis, David, 77
Los Angeles, CA, 114
Ludekens, Fred, 132
Lufkin, Dan W., 167
Lyceum, 142, 165, 174, 208

Madsen, Ronald E., 107–108, 110
Mahal Pacer, xiii
Mahood, William, 64
Mahru, Louise, xi, 76–77
Marriott, J. Willard, 55
Marston, Robert "Bob," 170–172
Marx, Louis, Jr., 167
Mastering the Art of French Cooking (Child and Beck), 188
Maw, Herbert M., 43
Mazlish, Bruce, 180
McCullough's, 35. *See also* William Wood & Sons
McEacher, Carleton C. "Mac," 60–61, 107
McGovern, George, 103

McHugh, Godfrey, 79
McKenna, Margaret, 180
McLuhan, Marshall, 141
McMahon, Ed, 173
media, xi, 70–73, 135, 191–193, 205, 209
Mega Speed Reading system, 208
Mind Inc., 183
Mindell, Phyllis, 204
Minert, Roger P., 39
missionary work, 6, 8–9, 16, 20–24, 26–33, 37–38, 54–55, 185–186
Mitchell, N. Lorenzo, 39
Mitford, Jessica, 142–143, 149–150
Moore, Garry, 76–77
Mormon Culture Region, 5
Mormonism. *See* Church of Jesus Christ of Latter-Day Saints
motivational speaking, 63
Munich Agreement, 27–28
Music Man, The, 118
Mutual Improvement Association (MIA), 3, 40

Nagasaki, Japan, 61
National Conference on Higher Education, 75
National Education Association (NEA), ix–xiii, 97
National Reading Conference, 87–90
National Recovery Administration (NRA), 12–13
Native Americans, 171–172, 174
Nazi Women's League, 19
Nazis, 18–19, 23, 26–29, 38, 186–187
NEA Journal, 97
Nelson-Denny Reading Test, 155

Netherlands, 23–24, 27, 33–34
New York Amsterdam News, 182–183
New York Times, 150–152
New York University Reading Clinic, 96
Newsday, 123
Newsweek, 139–140
Nielsen, Ariel, 3, 7, 41, 57–58
Nielsen, Elias, 2, 6–7, 13, 20, 36–37, 41
Nielsen, Rosina "Rose" Stirland, 2, 6–7, 12–13, 20, 36–37, 57–58, 61, 136
Nielsen, Verla, 5, 133, 136, 148–150, 158–160, 188–189
Nixon, Richard, 70, 142–144, 170, 172
Noall, Mabel S., 50
noncompete agreements, 57, 92, 102, 105, 183
nondisclosure agreements, 92, 123, 140, 158, 183, 187, 206
North, Montgomery "Monte," 41, 50
North, Scott, 41, 50, 199
Notre Dame, 183
Nugent, Maurice, 70
Nürnberg, Germany, 26

O. C. Tanner Jewelry Company, 39–40
Occidental College, 129
Ogden, UT, 1–9, 12–13, 36
Ogden High School, 3
Ogden Knitting Mills, 13
Ogden Tabernacle Choir, 2
Operation: R.E.A.D., 147–148, 171
Oral Reading course, 45
Orme, Kenneth, 158

Pearson, Anna Marie
    Babbel and, 55
    Evelyn and, 40–41, 49–50, 199
    in Germany, 20–22, 30–33
    Great Depression and, 58
    Wood family and, 17–18, 121, 204
Pentecost, 31–32
P.E.O. sisterhood, 75
Perkins, John A., 118
Pfingsten (Pentecost) conference,
    31–32
Phoenix, AZ, 57
PM (news show), 192–195
Poland, 34
popular culture, 2, 91, 120–121,
    192, 203
Porter, Maude Dee, 13
"Prepare Ye the Way," 39–40
Preston, Ralph C., 141
Protocols of the Elders of Zion, 25
Provo, UT, 120–121
Proxmire, William, 70–72, 114, 122,
    165–166, 193, 201, 208
Psychology Today, 155, 160, 182, 195
public speaking, 4–7, 37–39, 61–62

Rate-O-Meter, xiii
Read-Ability system, 140
reading. *See* comprehension;
    skimming; speed reading
Reading Development Institute,
    157–160
Reading Dynamics. *See* Evelyn Wood
    Reading Dynamics
Reading Eye Camera, 87, 89, 90, 153
Reading Game centers, 197, 201
Reading Inc., 110–111

Reading Skills (Wood and Barrows),
    47–49
Reading Teacher (journal), 83, 88
Rees, Albert C., 186
Relief Society, 15, 23
Remember Everything You Read
    (Frank), 202
Ribicoff, Abraham, 103
Robert Marston and Associates,
    170–172
Rockwell, Norman, 126–127, 131
Rogers, Jacquelyn, 179
Roosevelt, Franklin D., 12
Rosmarin, Philip, 177–178
Roundup USA, 70–72
Rubenstein, Wilma, 5
Ruff, Howard, 116, 118–120, 124,
    130, 133–135
Ruffner, Howard, 142

Sales Executive Club, 63–66
sales techniques, 62–63, 74, 80–81
Salesweek, 63–66, 72–73
Salk, Jonas, ix
Salt Lake City, UT, 7–14, 36, 43–45,
    55–59, 120–121, 144–145, 160,
    188–189
Salt Lake Regional Welfare Center, 37
Salt Lake Telegram, 36, 40
Salt Lake Tribune, 18, 38, 39–40,
    43, 53
Samuels, Howard J., 179
San Francisco, CA, 129, 134
San Francisco Examiner, 134–135
Sandy, UT, 46
Saturday Evening Post, 94–95
Saturday Night Live, 183

Scholtz-Klink, Gertrud, 19
Seattle, Washington, 161
Securities and Exchange Commission
    (SEC), 149
Seidenberg, Mark, 209
senators, xi, 70–72, 95, 103, 114,
    165–166, 205
*Sense and Nonsense in Speed
    Reading*, 152–154
Shadel, Bill, 70
Shadowscope, xiii
Sheraton Building, 62
Shipley, Richard "Dick," 138, 145,
    148, 156–160, 168
Sidey, Hugh, 69, 207
Sidnam, Alan, 178–179
Silent Reading for Speed and
    Comprehension (Speech 21),
    44–46, 50–51, 53–54
skimming
    Carver and, 152–155
    comprehension and, x, 182, 196
    des Islets and, 131
    Evelyn and, 43
    JKF and, 69
    reading and, 88–90
    Reading Dynamics and, 163
    Spache and, 83
    speed reading and, 141, 206
Smith, Barbara North, 50, 199, 204
Smith, Emma, 33
Smith, Nila Banton, 96
Smokenders, 178–179, 183
Spache, George D., 83–85, 87–91, 95,
    107, 130, 153, 159
speed reading
    Bonnie Babbel and, 108–109

Carter and, 180
    challenges to, 97, 124–125, 141–142
    comprehension and, 63–66, 88–90,
        182, 196, 208
    in DC, 103–105
    decline of, 191–192, 203
    digital apps and, 208–209
    Evelyn and, 41–46
    in *HBS Bulletin*, 72
    normal reading and, 200
    in popular culture, 76–78, 126,
        150–154, 169
    popularity of, 91–95
    Reading Dynamics and, 60, 80
    skimming and, x–xiii, 83–84
    Speech 21 and, 50–51
    Thompson and, 167
    See also dynamic reading
SS Manhattan, 20
Stauffer, Russell G., 83, 89, 117–118,
    151, 191
Stewart, Donnell, 4
Stirland, Leo LeGrande "L.L.," 61–66
Stirland, Thomas, 7
Stone, Irving, 83
Stuart, Constance, 143
Students Against Evelyn Wood,
    160, 163
Stutesman, John, 132
Sunray Heating, 40
Symington, Stuart, 70–71

tachistoscopes, 46, 60, 88, 198
Takeyama, Hilda, 106
Talmadge, Herman. E., 67, 71, 103,
    114, 172
Taylor, Stanford E., 90–91, 95, 153

teenagers, 61, 74, 120–121
testing, x, 96–97, 116, 124, 155
Texas Christian University, 87
Theodocion, Dan, 115–117, 143
Thomas, Wayne B., 9
Thompson, Maurice C. "Tommy,"
    Jr., 167–172, 178–179, 183–
    185, 198
Thompson, Patricia, 167–169,
    178–180
threading, 153
Time magazine, 66–67, 196
Tonight Show, 172–174, 181
Toronto, Martha, 37–38
Truman, Harry S., 70
Tucson, AZ, 144–145, 200
Twin Falls, ID, 102

Uintah Indian School, 43
Union Knitting Mills, 7
University of Alabama, 61
University of Arizona, 57
University of Delaware, ix–x, xiii, 70,
    83, 89, 96, 117–119
University of Florida, 83
University of Pennsylvania, xi,
    141
University of Southern California,
    50–51, 117
University of Utah
    Daily Utah Chronicle and, 121–123
    Evelyn and, 7–8, 40–41
    Lees and, 44, 48
    Shipley and, 160
    Speech 21 and, 50–51
    Stirland and, 65
University of Washington, 161–164

URS Corporation, 183–185, 188–189,
    191, 196–198
US Air Force Academy, 131
US Patent and Trademark Office, 197
Utah, 37, 41

Vicore (visual-conceptual reading),
    111
Vietnam War, 142

Wall Street Journal, 129–132
Warner, Dan, 201–203
Washington, DC, 54–55, 58–62, 101
Washington Post, 66, 111, 191–192
Watergate, 170
Weber College, 4–8, 45
Webster, George C.
    DEAR and, 109–110, 113–115,
        124, 149
    Famous Artists and, 126
    franchises and, 135, 139
    franchising and, 101–107
    sponsor's council and, 119–120, 169
    West and, 130
Welcome Wagon, 136, 157
Welker, Elizabeth H., 19
Welker, Roy A., 24
West, Ira, 129–132, 150, 163
West German mission, 16, 20–21,
        26, 29–33, 35–36, 39, 185–186.
        See also East German mission;
        Germany; missionary work
Westport, CT, 126, 132
Whiterocks, UT, 43
Wholey, Dennis, 172
Why I Am a Mormon (Bennett), 54
Wilkinson, Ernest L., 107

Willard, Henry K., II, 124
William Wood & Sons, 10, 12. *See also* McCullough's
Wilmington, DE, 61–63
Wood, Alan, 10, 19
Wood, Anna Marie. *See* Pearson, Anna Marie
Wood, Carolyn "Carol"
  in Arizona, 57, 114, 136, 171
  birth of, 13–14
  death of grandfather and, 41
  in Germany, 16, 20–22, 26–28, 30–32
  parents and, 198–200
  Pearson and, 17–18, 50, 204
Wood, Evelyn N.
  appearance of, 148
  Babbel and, 109–112
  branding and, 114–115, 197–198
  challenges to, 87–91, 94–97, 122–125, 152–155, 200–201
  as con artist, 205–209
  Darling and, xii–xiv, 75–76
  death of, 203–204
  death of mother and, 136
  Famous Artists and, 126–127
  finances and, 93, 101–102, 149
  franchises and, 92, 119–121
  gender roles and, 137
  in Germany, 19–34, 186–187
  government officials and, 77–80
  graduate studies and, 40–43
  as grandmother, 199
  health issues and, 98–99, 185
  Jensen and, 15
  Kump and, 188
  lecture tour and, 37–38
  marriage to Doug and, 11–13

Mormonism and, 14
  NEA convention and, ix–xi
  Pearson and, 17–18, 50
  public relations and, 170–172
  publicity and, 70–73
  Reading Dynamics and, 55, 58–67, 81–85, 106–107
  reading instruction and, 46–49
  recipes and, 133
  rehabilitation and, 181, 192–195
  religious pageant and, 39–40
  return to US of, 35–36
  Shipley and, 157–160
  Speech 21 and, 44–45, 53–54
  stroke and, 175, 177–179
  subsidiaries and, 74
  testing and, 116–118
  Thompson and, 167–168
  youth of, 1–10
Wood, Myron Douglas "Doug"
  Babbel and, 54–55, 109–110
  business and, 56–57
  death of, 200
  Evelyn and, 168, 193–194
  Famous Artists and, 136, 143, 156
  finances and, 93, 149–150
  franchises and, 120–121, 177–178
  in Germany, 19–34, 185–187
  LDS Church and, 14–16
  lecture tour and, 37–39
  marriage to Evelyn and, 12–13
  Pearson and, 17–18, 50
  Reading Dynamics and, 59–61, 70, 74–75, 92, 107, 114–115
  return to US of, 35–36
  Shipley and, 157–160
  World War II and, 40
  youth of, 9–11

Wood Ironrite, 56–58
Woods, Arthur R., 166
Woods, Rose Mary, 143,
  170
World War II, 26–27, 34, 36,
  185–186

Yale University, 45, 124–125
You Can Do It! (Proxmire), 166
Young Ladies' Mutual Improvement
  Association (MIA), 3, 40

Ziegler, Ron, 143–144, 170